To Jane & George —
War Eagle and best wishes,
Mickey Logue & Jack Simms

AUBURN

A Pictorial History of the Loveliest Village

REVISED

Hurricane Opal roared through Auburn the night of October 4, 1995, on its way north, destroying thousands of trees, and leaving the community in darkness. Downed power lines and fallen trees blocked scores of streets, making movement hazardous where not impossible. Several tornadoes contributed to the total damage. The storm took out many old trees on campus, including most of the remaining evergreens in Samford Park, as witnessed by this picture. On Sunday afternoon, three and one-half days after the storm hit, eight-thousand Auburn residences were still without power. No storm-attributed deaths occurred in Auburn.

—*Photo: Celine Bufkin;*
Opelika-Auburn News

A watermelon cutting in sight of Samford Hall, extreme left, circa 1900. Veterinarian Charles A. Cary is framed between the wagon wheels.
—Photo: Lee County Historical Society

BY MICKEY LOGUE AND JACK SIMMS

Library of Congress Cataloging in Publication Data

Logue, H E Jr.
Auburn Pictorial History, Revised

    1. Auburn, Ala. — Description — Views.
2. Auburn, Ala. — History — Pictorial works.
I. Simms, John D., joint author. II. Title.
F334.A83L63   976.1'55   80-20868

ISBN #1-885860-08-0

The Auburn Knights Orchestra was organized on a permanent basis in 1930. Within a few years it was playing at campuses throughout Alabama, Georgia, and Mississippi. Jazz clarinetist Gerald Yelverton, standing fourth from left in front of bus, played with the Glenn Miller Band after graduation in 1938. Others were from left, same row, Joe Mitchell, Herc Barnard, Julian Van Hodges, and Toby Griffith; on bus, Robin Russell, Chick Hatcher, Hilding Holmberg, Ed Wadsworth, Frank Speight, John Ivey, and Mike Ellis.

—Photo: Auburn Knights Collection; AU Archives

Two draymen with white horse-drawn wagons paused in the middle of East Magnolia Avenue during a day's work of delivering groceries for nearby Hudson's store. The Methodist Church is in the right background. On the left is the sign of the Wright Brothers Bookstore.
—*Photo: George Alfonso Wright*

PREFACE

In producing this picture history, we have many to thank for providing pictures, coming up with identifications, supplying pieces of Auburn history, or just urging us on. We start by offering sincere appreciation to Beveley S. Powers, who shared with us her knowledge of the AU Archives holdings, spent countless hours digging out photo and data files she thought we should see, and, tirelessly and always in good humor, guided us on our treasure hunt. She, herself, is a treasure.

We are grateful to Allen W. Jones, AU professor emeritus of history, who put down his fishing pole to write the foreword for this revised edition. AU archivist fifteen years ago, Jones read a draft, marked errors, and wrote the foreword for the 1981 edition. It also was the second time around for David Rosenblatt of Archives, who supplied valuable help on both editions. Guidance from Bill Summers in 1980-81 shows up on many pages. Archives Head Dwayne Cox and others in the department helped and were supportive, as were Boyd Childress and the always-pleasant Joyce Hicks of Draughon Library. Wendy Hassett, administrative assistant to City Manager Doug Watson, and Watson provided all sorts of data and answers to questions about the community.

Lori Leath-Smith, AU '84, a mother of three children, took a box of pictures and a disk with words on it into her home in Birmingham, and, on her computer in a matter of weeks, she transformed the material into the pages for this book. Michelle Garland-Segrest, AU '89, with EBSCO Media, Birmingham, coordinated the project from start to finish. Both Lori and Michelle had classes at Auburn taught by the authors.

Thanks also goes to Dewey Bedell, Celine Bufkin, Neil O. Davis, Susie Giddens, Meredith Jenkins, Ann B. Pearson, Ernestine Robinson, Glenn L. Rounds, Stan Voit, William White, J. C. Woodall, The *Auburn Bulletin/Eagle*; and the *Opelika-Auburn News*.

Contributing many photos in 1981 that also appeared in this revised edition were 1919 API graduate George Alfonso Wright; Dr. H. C. Morgan, Jr., made available the photo collection of his father-in-law, Leonard W. Thomas, a 1931 Auburn graduate; and Emily Hixon Gunter shared the collection of her father, API Professor Charles R. Hixon. Others making exceptional contributions include Carrie Samford Giles, daughter of the man for whom Samford Hall is named; Ernestine Walker Sherman, granddaughter of the first director of the Auburn Agricultural Experiment Station; and Annie Noll Ellis.

James Stanfield, Les King, Paul Kennedy, Sr., and Charles Jernigan gave valuable advice on photographs, and Stanfield, Jernigan, and Willie Robinson ably enhanced several damaged pictures, as did Diane Shanks. We thank John Logue for proposing that we do this book, and for important professional advice.

Finally, we thank our wives, Glenda Logue and Lassie Jo Simms. They offered countless suggestions and proofread the book; Glenda served as a researcher; Lassie Jo built the index. Neither pointed out it was time to mow the lawn or trim the shrubs. We dedicate this book to them, each a life's companion, best friend and sweetheart to one of us.

Mickey Logue
Jack Simms

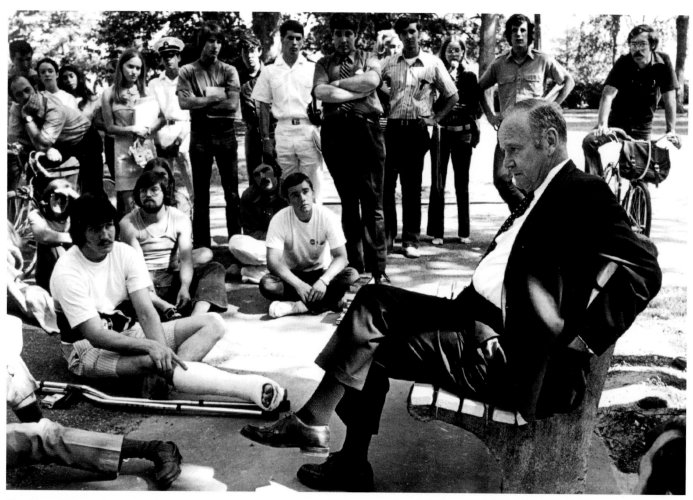

President Harry M. Philpott probably enjoyed Auburn students more than any other of Auburn's first fifteen presidents—at least it seemed that way. He was involved, as were other presidents, with scores of structured functions each year during which he met with student leaders and student groups, but Philpott also found time for countless informal rap sessions, many outdoors under the trees as was this one, with any who wished to show up. He appeared throughout his fifteen years of leadership to be genuinely interested in what the students had to say, and in providing answers to their questions.

—Photo: AU Photographic Services

FOREWORD

Fifteen years have gone by since the first edition of *Auburn: A Pictorial History of the Loveliest Village* appeared in 1981. This revised edition includes new photographs and a new chapter that focuses on people, events, and changes in the University and the City of Auburn during the 1980s and 1990s. The authors sorted through more than fifteen-thousand new pictures to select the almost two hundred that were added. And now the history of Auburn is ready for the twenty-first century.

Founded on the former hunting grounds of the Creek Indians in east Alabama, "Sweet Auburn, loveliest village of the plain," became an educational and religious center in the nineteenth century and was in 1996 the location of Alabama's largest university. The authors, retired professors of journalism and long-time residents of Auburn, capture a rich and unique history through photographs and a narrative of this small, rural town from its settlement in 1836 to the roar of 85,000 football fans in Jordan-Hare Stadium on a mid-1990s Saturday afternoon. It is not intended to be a scholarly book, but one which vividly illuminates the people, places, and events that are a cherished part of Auburn's past.

The plantations and the slaves which characterized Auburn's beginning were altered by the Civil War and the establishment of a Methodist male college. That denominational college became the state's Agricultural and Mechanical College shortly after the war, and the cultural and social climate in the small town changed. Domination of the community by planter and merchant families gave way to the influence of college teachers and administrators. By 1900, the foundation of Auburn's economy was firmly laid as a college town, and the history of the town and the college became inseparable. The interests of the town and college were mutual and have remained so until today.

When the material growth of Auburn and the college increased after the turn of the century, the "Auburn Spirit" reached its maturity and became a marked attribute of the character and life of the community and the University. Auburn has loved its traditions, whether based on fact or myth, and these traditions have helped to create the spirit that has been such a powerful influence in creating the Auburn of the 1990s. Auburn is more than a college or town; it is a way of life. What you will see and read in this book constitutes a benchmark by which the changes during each decade can be measured and perhaps understood.

Many have shared with the authors their photographs and memories. Such cooperation only reflects the spirit of friendliness that prevails in this beautiful east Alabama community. This book is certainly dedicated to the Spirit of Auburn, and all who read it will enjoy traveling through Auburn's past and cherishing memories of bygone days in "the loveliest village."

Allen W. Jones

Professor Emeritus
Auburn University

▲ *Tranquility pervaded the Auburn of about 1910, but at the same time the Village seemed busy. Wagons rolled on a dirt road past hitching posts and shade trees while Alabama Polytechnic Institute cadets relaxed on a convenient bench. The camera recorded at least eighteen people walking, talking, riding, and sitting—and one even running. The water tank and Burton's Bookstore have come and gone, but Toomer Drugstore remains a familiar landmark.*

—Photo: AU Archives

Chapter 1

CREEKS, METHODISTS, AND YANKEES

*A*uburn University and the community of Auburn have been as inseparable as College Street and Magnolia Avenue. They have been as close as the Main Gate and Toomer's Corner during a victory celebration. They have been as necessary to each other as a town barber's clippers to an ROTC cadet's head. They have been as cooperative as students, professors, and merchants passing water buckets to help put out fires before Auburn had a fire department. They at times have been as divided as students and landlords over whether a damage deposit should be returned on an apartment. Before the end of the twentieth century, they had been linked by more than 175,000 Auburn graduates, most of whom found the Loveliest Village the source of both a good education and the Auburn Spirit.

▼ *A horticulture class pruned peach trees in the late 1890s or early 1900s south of the main building, later named Samford Hall. Faculty homes lined what later became West Thach Avenue, in the heart of the campus.*
—Photo: AU Archives

▶ *Auburn owes a debt to Oliver Goldsmith and to a teen-age girl who was reading one of his poems, "The Deserted Village," in the mid-1830s. The girl, Elizabeth "Lizzie" Taylor of Jones County, Georgia, was asked by a visitor to her home to suggest a name for a new settlement in east Alabama. Someone already had suggested "Geneva." She replied to Thomas Harper, son of the settlement's founder and her future husband, "Name it . . . 'Sweet Auburn, loveliest village of the plain.'" The name stuck, identifying the town and the college (since 1960 the university) virtually from their beginnings.*

—Photo: Dorm I

This pairing of town and gown began with the founding of the University as the East Alabama Male College in 1856 in the already twenty-year-old community. Even then they shared a past; both had been hunting grounds for Creek Indians on the trail of turkey and deer. Long before "War Eagle" became Auburn's football cry, an Indian named Sundilla was allotted the right to farm or sell land that now includes Toomer's Corner. A Creek named Lostiyoholo was assigned acreage that includes the Samford Hall site. Such property rights proved of little value, though, to thousands of Indians allotted homesteads under a treaty signed between the United States and the Creek Nation in 1832. The treaty provided for the Creeks to move west, but with the understanding that their families could remain in east Alabama if they chose to live on land assigned to chiefs and heads of families. But land-grabbers routinely cheated naive Creeks out of their property rights and, one historian said, "burned their houses, stole their livestock, and destroyed their crops." Some of the Indians who received fair payment for their holdings "enriched saloonkeepers" rather than buying food. Treaty violations by whites and stealing by hungry Creeks led to war in 1836, causing the forced removal of the Indians to Oklahoma. Whether Sundilla and Lostiyoholo ever occupied Auburn land and whether anyone ever traded directly with them for their patents to the property has not been established. But the original Macon County Tractbook at Tuskegee (Macon included Auburn until 1866) listed the property in the names of two white brothers who speculated in land. In 1839, Nathaniel Macon

▲ These were Alabama A&M cadets, or were they Alabama Polytechnic Institute cadets? Depends on whether the picture was taken before the name changed to API in 1899, and who knows? At any rate, the cadets appeared on good behavior standing with two bearded men at the Auburn depot. A seasoned conductor on the Atlanta & West Point line might have doubted this picture. "I believe they is wuss than Injuns!" such a conductor told Professor James P. C. Southall, who was taking his first ride to Auburn and a teaching job there in 1901. "They don't mean no harm, they's jes' full of life an' up to all kinds of devilment from mornin' to night, and at night too. They never wait for the train to stop, but climbs on board and jumps off again . . . Folks say Auburn's the bes' all-roun' school in these parts, not excep'in' the University at Tuscaloosa or even Georgia Tech in Atlanta . . ." (Quotation reprinted from Southall's Memoirs of The Abbots of Old Bellevue with the permission of the University Press of Virginia.)

—Photo: AU Archives

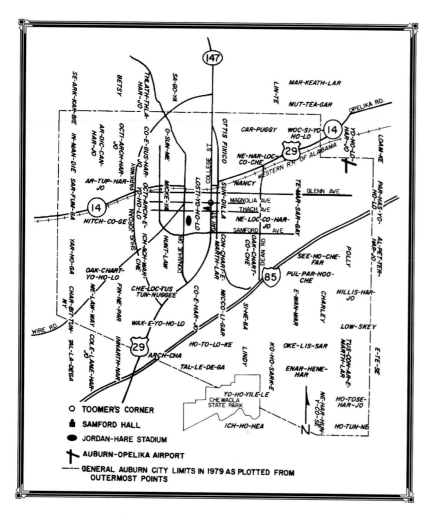

o TOOMER'S CORNER
SAMFORD HALL
JORDAN-HARE STADIUM
AUBURN-OPELIKA AIRPORT
----- GENERAL AUBURN CITY LIMITS IN 1979 AS PLOTTED FROM OUTERMOST POINTS

◀ *Creek Indians were once allotted the land where students and townspeople live today. The names of the Indians are placed on this 1979 outline of the City of Auburn's boundaries near the property they were assigned in 1832 under a treaty with the United States. The placement of the names is based on the original Macon County Tractbook at Tuskegee and on the reconstructed map of Lee County by H. Ray Black and David M. Hall as it would have existed in 1832 if Lee had been a separate county. Lee County was formed in 1866 out of Chambers, Macon, Russell, and Tallapoosa counties. It was named for Robert E. Lee, commanding general of the Confederate Army and later president of Washington and Lee University. The treaty called for the Creek Nation to surrender more than five million acres of land to the U.S. Government. Nearly 2.2 million acres were to be reallocated to the Indians in separate locations in east Alabama. The treaty allotted 640 acres each to ninety Creek chiefs and the tribe's interpreter, 320 acres each to 6,557 heads of families and to each orphan child, and 16,000 acres for the chiefs to sell for the "benefit of the tribe as a whole." But by late 1836, most Creeks had been moved west.*
—The copyrighted 1976 Black-Hall map is used as a source with permission.
Art work: Dianne Rush

Thornton apparently owned acreage that now includes Toomer's Corner, and by 1840, his brother Dozier Thornton had acquired land that today encompasses Samford Park.

White settlers had been attracted to Lee County earlier by the first Methodist missionary to the area's Indians. Although he had nearly lost his life to hostile Creeks, the Reverend Morgan Turrentine liked the fever-free climate, the abundant clear water, and the fertile cotton land so well that he urged his planter friends in Harris County, Georgia, to go there.

Judge John Jackson Harper with eight sons and three daughters, and other settlers with their children—along with slaves and livestock—moved to this promising wilderness, probably in the winter of 1836. Harper's son William had received the deed to a parcel of land there from the U.S. Government in 1835-36. Harper himself traded fairly with friendly Creeks, who "immediately gave him possession and moved toward Loachapoka, Notasulga, and Tuskegee," Mrs. W. B. Frazer wrote in her brief *Early History of Auburn*. But there also were hostile Indians who attacked both whites and friendly Creeks. Soon after the settlers arrived, a hostile band massacred a Jones family, hung their bodies in the trees, and burned their log cabin, which stood "in the rear of the cemetery" (probably what is now the Pine Hill Cemetery on Armstrong Street), according to Mary E.

Reese, who wrote of Auburn's pioneer days. A 1,500-man military company finally put down the uprisings in east Alabama.

By the end of 1836, most east Alabama Creeks had been forced westward before they could gather their crops. The once-prospering Indians were "wretchedly and depravedly poor," many of them naked, said a U.S. Army officer who helped move them. They left behind buried pottery, axes, and arrowheads, which generations of whites have claimed as souvenirs. "Until a few years ago," Alexander Nunn wrote in *Yesterdays in Loachapoka and Communities Nearby*, "there still remained clear markings of a ceremonial ground south of Auburn." Today, Auburn is reminded of its Creek past by such names as Chewacla, Nelocco, and Saugahatchee.

Judge Harper's colony went to work in 1836 building Auburn, about seventeen years after Alabama became a state in 1819 and fifty-five years after Cornwallis surrendered at Yorktown in 1781. In 1839 the Legislature approved incorporating Auburn, a town of 1,280 acres.

Harper built the first house in this settlement, a double log cabin, south of where Samford Avenue and Moore's Mill Road meet today. His son Thomas and the young man's teen-age bride, Elizabeth, called "Lizzie," lived in the first frame house in Auburn on a lot just north of today's old

▼ *Amid the hope, sweat, and doubt of Auburn's beginning in 1836, its founder, John J. Harper, did not forget the certainty of death. Early on, he gave wooded land for a cemetery in the southeast part of town. Sadly, one of the first to be buried there was his son, William, age twenty-five, who died of consumption in 1838. Two brothers soon followed William to Pine Hill, and their father, dead at fifty-seven, joined them there in 1847. "Some of Auburn's finest citizens lie in Pine Hill, the town's oldest cemetery, located on the quiet byway of Armstrong Street . . . ," local historian Ann Pearson wrote in 1979.*

—Photo: Paul Kennedy Sr.

counties. One of his successors accepted a special challenge from Thomas Harper.

Harper persuaded a prominent Georgia schoolmaster, C. C. Flanagan, "an Irish gentleman educated for the Catholic priesthood . . . to come and build up a male academy to prepare boys for Emory [at Oxford, Georgia] and the University of Georgia," Charles W. Edwards wrote in *Auburn Starts a Second Century*. Flanagan, a respected teacher, taught in Auburn for more than twenty years. After meeting the black-haired, gray-eyed, quite charming Mrs. Harper, Flanagan said she was the most beautiful woman he had ever seen. "He little dreamed that she would one day become his wife," Mary Reese wrote. Yet, a few years later, after consumption had shortened Tom Harper's life, as it did the lives of other Harper men, his widow married Flanagan.

By 1856, Auburn had two excellent boarding schools in the same block as the old Yancey schoolhouse. W. F. Slaton's Male Academy stood near where Gay Street meets Tichenor Avenue today. The Auburn Masonic Female College, with the largest auditorium in east Alabama, occu-

Tiger Theatre site. Tom Harper and his brother John ran the town's first store, a grocery, at the theatre location. Tom's wife had the town's first piano and its first cooking stove. She also is credited with naming Auburn.

Auburn citizens believed in churches. The Methodists built a log church in about 1837 on land Judge Harper provided near today's Methodist corner at Gay Street and Magnolia Avenue. The persuasive Reverend Turrentine was the first preacher. The Baptists formed a congregation in about 1838 and built their first church in about 1843 on Harper-provided land. The Presbyterians built in 1850-51, and the Episcopalians in the early 1850s. On July 4, 1850, the Methodists laid the cornerstone for a new church that included balconies for slaves to attend services.

"Book learning" was cherished from the town's earliest days, writer Ann Pearson said. Simeon Yancey taught the first classes, in the log church, and in 1838 he opened a new school, built by Methodists and Baptists. It was located across what is now Magnolia Avenue from the Methodist Church. Yancey's school for boys and girls attracted many boarding pupils from neighboring

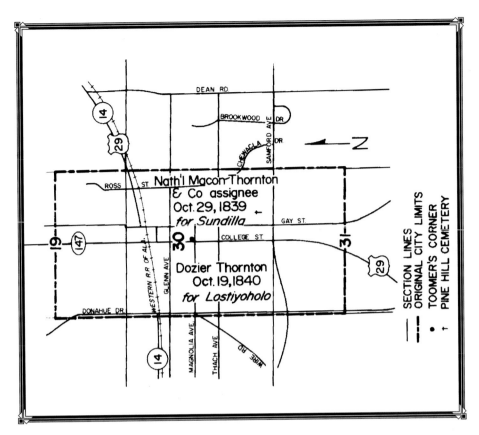

DEAN RD.
BROOKWOOD DR.
Nath'l Macon Thornton & Co assignee Oct. 29, 1839 for Sundilla
ROSS ST.
GAY ST.
COLLEGE ST.
Dozier Thornton Oct. 19, 1840 for Lostiyoholo
DONAHUE DR.
MAGNOLIA AVE.
THACH AVE.
WIRE RD.
WESTERN R.R. OF ALA.
GLENN AVE.
SAMFORD AVE.
CHEWACLA DR.
SECTION LINES
ORIGINAL CITY LIMITS
TOOMER'S CORNER
PINE HILL CEMETERY

◀ The heavy broken line marks Auburn's original boundaries as set by the Legislature in 1839. The present streets and railroad help show the size of the town at that time. Under the Creek Treaty of 1832, two Indians were allocated the land that became the center of town. In 1839, Auburn contained section 30, the north half of section 31, and the south half of section 19 in township 19, range 26. In 1839, Auburn comprised two square miles; in 1996, thirty-eight square miles.

—Art work: Dianne Rush

▼ When Auburn Presbyterians put up their first church building in 1850-51 at what is now College Street and Thach Avenue, they included a front porch and two front doors. In those days, the men entered and sat on one side of the church, and the women and children used the other side. The building was constructed of bricks made by skilled slaves. The first pastor, the Reverend Albert Shotwell of West Point, Georgia, rode the stage to Auburn twice a month to hold services. "The Auburn Church promised him two hundred dollars a year and 'all over that amount they could raise,'" according to Malcolm McMillan's Auburn Presbyterian Church: one hundred years. "Shotwell was a northern man by birth but a graduate of Gwinnett Institute in Georgia and Columbia Theological Seminary." Following Shotwell as pastor was a former missionary to the Cherokee Indians, Timothy Root (circa 1854-56), and after him came Robert Bell of Florida, Indiana (1856-58). "Although no records exist of the slavery issue in the Auburn Presbyterian Church, one wonders about the position of a northern man in a southern town in this period of bitter controversy over slavery," McMillan said. "This is especially true since [Bell] had been educated at Farmers College, Ohio, and Western Theological Seminary. Both institutions were in an area where abolitionist sentiment was very pronounced, and Western Theological Seminary was a hot-bed of abolitionism. . . ."

During the nineteenth century, when not in use as a Presbyterian Church, the building served as a Confederate hospital, as classrooms when the main building of the college burned, and as a temporary worship place for the Episcopalians. In 1976 it became the University Chapel.

—Photo: Lee County Historical Society

Simeon Perry, the surveyor who first laid out the town of Auburn, had this home built for his family in the early 1850s near what is now East Drake Avenue across from the present Girl Scout Hut. It was typical of the raised-cottage style found in antebellum New Orleans, but, unlike many other houses of that period, it had closets. It became the E. F. Cauthen family home during part of the twentieth century until the house was severely damaged in the 1953 tornado. "It was like hell broke loose," recalled Maryline Cauthen Westenhaver. Chimneys fell in, the roof gave way, and "you could see daylight where the upstairs was. Shingles were flying across the yard like a snowstorm."
—Photo: Maryline Cauthen Westenhaver

◀ The Auburn coach factory announced in 1852 its return to the manufacture of coaches, wagons, and buggies after the plant had been rebuilt following a fire.
—Photo: AU Archives

▶ The Auburn Water-Cure apparently held out hope to the sufferers of many illnesses in pre-Civil War days. The hospital was at Gay Street and Glenn Avenue, conveniently near the depot. The same 1853 issue of the Auburn Gazette also advertised the merits of Eureka, or German Elixir, prepared and sold at one dollar a bottle by local pharmacist W. R. Jones. Seven citizens, including the president of the Auburn Masonic Female College, offered testimonials to the multipurpose medicine.
—Photo: AU Archives

AUBURN COACH FACTORY

THE undersigned having rebuilt their very extensive establishment, that was consumed by fire, beg leave to announce to their patrons and friends in general, that they are ready to receive and execute all orders that are given in their business in the most workman-like manner; and as for durability and beauty, they flatter themselves that they can be surpassed by none, for they superintend the construction of all vehicles that are made in their establishment, and (being competent and practical in their branches of business they can say it with safety, and moreover they will state all work that is turned out from their establishment is warranted for twelve months, with proper usage, and if not satisfactory to the warrantee, they will be amply satisfied after the work is returned.

They will always keep on hand an assortment of Carriages, such as Rockaways, Coaches, Buggies, Waggons, &c. And as they have procured the Patent to manufacture Hubbard's Patent Spring Buggy, they intend to keep an assortment of them on hand to suit the hard times. Persons wishing to purchase would do well by giving us a call and examine Hubbard's Patent Spring Buggy. The ease and simplicity of their construction cannot be surpassed. The proprietors of this establishment have been selling their work as reasonable as it can be procured in either, Columbus or Montgomery, and intend to continue to sell at reduced prices, from this time out. Their work is not built simply to sell but to do ample service.

STELTS & ALLAN.

ISAAC STELTS,   JOSEPH ALLAN.

Auburn, Ala., Oct. 8, 1852. 34—1y

OLD RAGS WANTED.

AUBURN WATER-CURE.

THIS Establishment is now open for the reception of patients. The location is pleasant and healthy, being on the great Southern Mail Route in Eastern Alabama, and is about a hundred yards from the depot, immediately adjoining the Railroad.

The efficacy of the Water Treatment in all acute diseases, as Fevers, Scarlatina, Measles, Small-Pox, &c., is so complete and rapid as to seem almost miraculous; while in chronic diseases, i. e. all diseases of long standing, as Gout, Rheumatism, Dyspepsia, Neuralgias, Scrofula, Consumption, &c. &c., it is the only effectual mode of arresting the progress of the disease and eradicating it from the system.

In the peculiar diseases of Women, the Water-Cure is a sovereign remedy, where all other remedies have failed, and in child-birth it procures immunity from untold suffering.

Patients should bring one quilt, a comfortable, two pair blankets, two sheets and several yards of linen diaper for bandages.

Terms according to treatment and attention required, payable weekly, invariably.—Consultation fee, $5

DR. W. G. REED, } Physicians.
L. AURELIA ELY, }

N. B.—Fowlers & Wells' publications on Water-Cure, &c., for sale.

Feb. 18, 1853 vol. 1–52 –1y.

Auburn Masonic Female College.

CIRCULAR.

The internal arrangements and appliances of this flourishing institution will enable it to compare favorably with any seminary in the land. If spacious and well-arranged buildings, with richly furnished rooms—a full board of experienced teachers, an ample supply of Philosophical Apparatus and Musical Instruments, the administration of such discipline as secures general order and habits of uniform regularity—are indications of the proper organization of a large institution of learning, and afford any promise of success, then has our College claims worthy of public consideration.

Our rates of tuition, by comparison, will be found to be lower than those of any similar institution in this or any adjacent State.

Our music pupils receive from four to seven lessons per week, under a system which cannot fail to be successful.

Our pupils receive four lessons per week in Penmanship, in classes, under the instruction of an experienced teacher.

Besides weekly reviews, the last Friday in each month is devoted to a thorough review of the month's labors, in all the departments. These reviews are all public.

The scholastic year, commencing on the first Monday in October, statedly, and consisting of two consecutive terms of twenty weeks each, closes with a public examination beginning on the Friday before the 15th July, statedly, and closes on the following Wednesday, which will be commencement day.

A boarding-house for young ladies has been established in connection with the College, under the superintendence of B. F. Johnson, Esq., where the pupils will be under the immediate care of the President.

FACULTY.

D. S. T. DOUGLAS, M. A., *President,*　　MRS. D. S. T. DOUGLAS, *Principal Music Department.*
REV. JOHN P. LEE, M. A., *Prof. &c.,*　　MRS. J. P. LEE, *Ornamental Department, Modern Lan-*
REV. WILLIS B. JONES, *Prof., &c.,*　　　　[*guages, Penmanship.*

BOARD OF DIRECTORS.

N. J. SCOTT, *President,*　　J. W. ECHOLS, *Vice Pres't,*　　J. W. W. DRAKE, *Secretary,*
J. F. WHITE, *Treasurer,*　　JAMES W. KIDD,　　　　ADDISON FRAZIER,
J. G. W. WHALE,　　　　　F. W. DILLARD,　　　　WILEY W. MASON,
JOHN W. JONES,　　　　　H. N. LANGFORD,　　　W. T. DAVIS,
　　　　　　　　　　　　ROBERT T. McFARLAND.

PRINTED AT THE AUBURN GAZETTE OFFICE.

▲ *Schooling for their children helped attract wealthy planters to Auburn in the 1840s. This circular in 1852 advertised the opening of Auburn Masonic Female College at Gay Street and Magnolia Avenue, the present site of AuburnBank. The college enrolled 106 students the first session in such courses as ancient languages, literature, mathematics, ornamental needlework, and wax works. Its president, the Reverend D. S. T. Douglas, taught moral and mental philosophy. Fees ranged up to twenty-two dollars per five-month session for seniors, with additional charges for extras such as music lessons. Board, including laundry and fuel, was fifty dollars a session. The Female College was likely a factor in helping bring East Alabama Male College to Auburn. The Civil War ended the prosperity of both institutions.*

—Photo: Billy Jack Jones

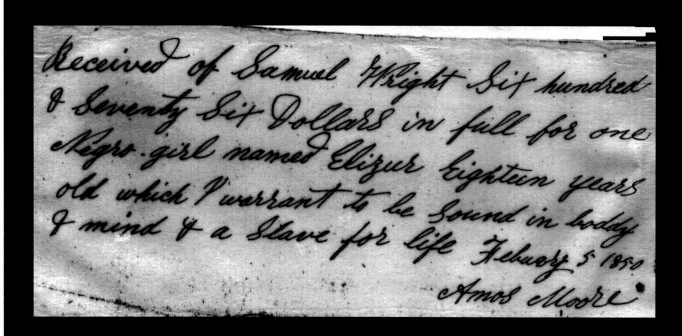

Received of Samuel Wright Six hundred & Seventy Six Dollars in full for one Negro girl named Elizur Eighteen years old which I warrant to be Sound in body & mind & a Slave for life February 5 1850

Amos Moore

▲ Samuel Wright bought an eighteen-year-old slave, Elizur, in 1850 for $676, probably to work on his plantation about eight miles south of Auburn. "The treatment of slaves was generally good because the negro (sic) was property and was cared for as such," Meriwether Harvey wrote in her API senior thesis in history in 1907. But she also said "a great many" slaves ran away, always helped by other slaves who slipped food to them. Most runaways apparently were tracked down with fox hounds. A slave "caught away from home without a pass" was given ten to thirty-nine lashes with a leather strap. One woman who owned 150 to 200 slaves said she never had a runaway. Northern traders sold slaves in Auburn. "Children were auctioned for from $450 to $1,000 to pick the cotton which sold from 7 to 12 cents a pound," Ann Pearson wrote in Lee County and Her Forebears. "The negro [sic] families were seldom separated" in Auburn, Harvey wrote. Pearson noted that stories of cruelties did exist, however, "one of an owner cutting off the ears of a slave as punishment." And Harvey said one owner was fined three times for mistreating his slaves, "especially for failing to supply them with sufficient food and clothing." "On the brighter side," according to Pearson, "many slaves were devoted to their owners, taking, even after freedom, their surnames." Most slaves in the Auburn area, like their masters, were Methodists, but there also were many Baptists. Harvey said, "There was only one known Presbyterian slave in the town." She learned of only two slaves in or near Auburn being taught to read, one of them by white children.

—Photo: John Peavy Wright

pied the same lot where Yancey had taught, the home of AuburnBank (Auburn National) in 1996.

Antebellum Auburn became a good place to shop. By the mid-1850s, Edwards wrote, this town of about one thousand people had eight large dry-goods stores, a jewelry store, grocery stores, pharmacies, a cabinetmaker's shop, a bank, and two tailor shops. But liquor sales were prohibited. Auburn also had a shoe factory, and the Rip Van Winkle Somnific Mattress factory. A carriage factory had burned earlier in one of the many fires over the years.

A log post office was opened in 1837 in what is now Samford Park across from where the University Chapel stands today, Mary Reese indicated, with Billy Owsley the postmaster. But George B. Nuckolls, appointed in 1839, was the first of twenty-three postmasters listed on Auburn postal records. Stagecoaches carried the mail before the Montgomery-to-West Point railroad arrived in 1847. The train station became the hub of social, business, and political conversation. Trains later passed through Auburn carrying Confederate soldiers, guns, and food during the Civil War. "The first depot agent was Mr. Sanford Thornton, whose wife was famous for being the mother of twenty-five children," Mary Reese wrote.

From the beginning, hotels played a part in the growth of Auburn. In about 1837, Samuel Nunn reportedly fed and housed patrons in a log inn near where Hargis Hall is today. W. M. Freeman advertised rooms for rent and land for sale in an 1838 Columbus, Georgia, newspaper. By

THE AUBURN GAZETTE.

▲ *Near the mid-1850s, Auburn had three weekly newspapers—the* Gazette, *edited by Drake and Price; the* Herald, *by Holifield and Reese; and the* Young Ladies' Mirror, *by students at the Female College. All were printed on the second floor of a wooden building near the present Main Gate to the campus. By February 1854, the editor and co-publisher of the* Auburn Gazette, *J. W. W. Drake, had left the newspaper business, but he continued to use its services. An advertisement bearing his name as director-secretary of the Female College warned that if all due tuition accounts were not paid before the next return day, the college would sue to collect them.*

—*Photo: AU Archives*

ers. It advertised a water treatment for fevers, scarlatina, measles, smallpox, and women's diseases.

The town's pivotal news story of the decade before the Civil War was its struggle for a Methodist male college. Auburn raised $100,000 in earnest money, claiming other assets such as four churches, two academies, train service on one of the three railroads in the state, and the absence of both saloons and yellow fever. But Greensboro had $300,000 and the necessary votes at the Alabama Methodist Episcopal Conference. Auburn lost temporarily, but kept working. On February 1, 1856, a week after the chartering of Southern University at Greensboro, the Legislature incorporated East Alabama Male College at Auburn over the governor's veto.

The new Methodist institution opened in 1859 in a new four-story building called Old Main, where Samford Hall is now. No one could have imagined that this tiny liberal arts college would become today's Auburn University. The college began with six professors and fifty-one trustees. Eighty students tackled a curriculum emphasizing Latin and Greek courses, with about a hundred boys in the preparatory division, the former Slaton's Academy. Fees were $54 for the year. Room and board, "exclusive of washing and lights," ran $10 to $12.50 per month, a big outlay in those days.

Students lived in the best homes in Auburn, including those of college President William Jeremiah Sasnett and trustees' President John Bowles Glenn, both Methodist ministers. Sasnett had gained the reputation, while a teacher of English literature at Old Emory at Oxford, as one to whom "a mighty problem in philosophy made a precious morsel." The students shared a pleasant social life with the young ladies of the Female College.

Yet, the most farsighted young men and women may have viewed the future with foreboding as secession debate heated the Female College chapel (now Langdon Hall). A large crowd heard a company of all-day speakers, including Ben Hill, Seaborn Jones, Bob Toombs, and Alexander Stephens of Georgia, W. G. "Parson" Brownlow of Tennessee, and David Clopton and Thomas Judge of Alabama. Fire-eating William Lowndes Yancey of Alabama arrived late but in time to carry the day for the secession advocates.

Auburn had more than a philosophical interest in the resolution of the slavery issue. "Just before the Civil War there were about 1,000 white people and 700 Negro slaves in Auburn and its immediate neighborhood," according to Meriwether Harvey's study. Plantations growing cotton and other crops averaged 640 acres, with from thirty to sixty slaves on each. A Mr. Buchanan had the greatest number of slaves, about 250. Miss Harvey said that only about six families in Auburn owned no slaves. Auburn was in Macon County, and, according to the 1860 U. S. Census, there were 8,625 whites, one "free colored," and 26,802 enslaved

1856, some people rented rooms at the McElhaney House. It was located near the middle of town at the brow of the hill on College Street, where the Baptist Student Union later was built. The Rail-Road Inn, down the hill from the McElhaney, offered food and lodging for eighteen dollars a month. Two talented "daguerreans," known today as photographers, had galleries at the inn. Many Montgomery people vacationed at these two hotels during the fever season on the Alabama River, columnist Pearson wrote in an *Auburn Bulletin* account of this period. A nearby Water-Cure Hospital also helped make Auburn a resort for health seek-

◀ Confederate soldiers once stood muster on the spacious grounds of this home called Sunny Slope, facing what is now South College Street. The 14th and 18th Alabama Confederate regiments were organized here in 1861. William F. Samford, known as the Penman of Secession for his nationally published prewar writings, owned the house and plantation. He was an ordained minister, the editor of an Auburn weekly newspaper, and a cotton planter. His son William James became governor and the man for whom Samford Hall was named. Sunny Slope was bought by the Emrick family in 1890 and while the farm of more than two hundred acres had become a subdivision, Mrs. Verl R. Emrick still lived in 1996 in the home on a seven-acre tract.

—Photo: Rick Helmke

▼ "Pebble Hill" is what Nathaniel J. Scott called this house after building it in 1847 at the end of what is now East Magnolia Avenue. Scott and others from Harris County, Georgia, had helped settle Auburn in the 1830s. He was one of the four men named to divide the new town into lots. He became Auburn's first state legislator. Scott helped found the Auburn Masonic Female College that opened in 1852, and later in the decade helped establish East Alabama Male College, which eventually became Auburn University. The story is told that during the Civil War the Scotts buried their silver near a spring on their one hundred-acre property. Wilson's Raiders watered

their horses at the spring but didn't find the silver. But the Scotts had sold the property by that time, one source said, and the new owners' "slaves had buried some of the silver, some of which was never found and some stolen later." Pebble Hill became the Scott-Yarbrough House in the first half of the twentieth century after Dr. Cecil S. Yarbrough bought the place and moved his family there. Yarbrough was a physician and served three terms as mayor of Auburn. In the 1970s, the house was sold to the Auburn Heritage Association for restoration. Auburn National Bank acquired the property and in 1985 gave it to Auburn University. Pebble Hill became the University's Center for the Arts and Humanities.

—Photo: Rick Helmke

▲ *Virginia Howe, the sixteen-year-old wife of William Howe of the antebellum* Auburn Gazette, *died and left a heartsick husband. Howe couldn't bear for her to be buried in the cemetery, so the story goes, and she was placed in a grave in their front yard on West Magnolia Avenue. Soon, however, William fell in love with Virginia's beautiful sister, who agreed to marry William only if Virginia were moved to Pine Hill Cemetery. This is Virginia's second grave.*

—Photo: Rick Helmke

▲ *Built in 1848 of virgin heart of pine on what is now North College Street, the Halliday-Cary-Pick House stands on land acquired from a Creek Indian in 1839. Wooden pegs hold together the solid mahogany spiral staircase in the center of the house. The staircase doesn't have the central supporting post found in similar staircases of this type and period. "Each step supports the other steps in an arch," one writer wrote. "Support of the stair is impossible until the last step is in place, just as an arch is impossible without its keystone." This picture was made about 1935, approximately eighteen years before Lieutenant General Lewis A. Pick and his wife, Alice Cary Pick, restored the house. Mrs. Pick, the last of three Cary children, was still living in the house in 1996 and still sleeping in the bed in which she had been born ninety-two years earlier.*

—Photo: Library of Congress

Negroes and mulattoes in Macon. In the four counties from which Lee was carved in 1866, there were 48,030 whites, 70 free colored, and 100,435 slaves in 1860.

After the war broke out, most of the students joined the Confederate Army. Two camps in Auburn trained six groups of Confederate soldiers: namely, the Auburn Guards and the 14th, 18th, 37th, 45th, and 48th regiments. James F. Dowdell, who in 1866 became the second president of East Alabama Male College, commanded the 37th. The college closed its doors to classes from 1861 until 1866, but served as a Confederate hospital from 1864 to 1866. The women of Auburn helped care for the sick and wounded in Old Main and in churches.

In the early 1860s, "Auburn was almost a deserted village," a man who lived there as a small boy recalled. ". . . There were vacant buildings and grass-grown streets . . . " as a result of the war. And finally the Federal troops arrived in person.

The raiders of Major General Lovell H. Rousseau burned the Auburn train station and other depots in July 1864. They also twisted and melted the tracks as part of

▲ William Lowndes Yancey, a fiery Southern orator before the War Between the States, made speeches in antebellum Auburn advocating secession from the Union. The Yancey family spent many summers with the Nathaniel Scott family at Pebble Hill, now known as the Scott-Yarbrough House.

—Photo: Alabama Department of Archives and History

▲ The Frazer-Brown-Pearson Home, Noble Hall (photo 1940s), was completed in 1854 as the Addison Frazer family home and headquarters of a two thousand-acre plantation two and one-half miles northeast of the center of Auburn. "Frazer became a wealthy owner of one hundred slaves, owned a grocery store in Auburn, and also served on the Board of Trustees of the Auburn Masonic Female College," Ann Pearson and her father, A. M. Pearson, owner of the house, wrote in A History of Noble Hall. The Pearsons wrote: "The house survived trying times during the Civil War. Though not near heavy fighting, it is reported that Mrs. Frazer took in and cared for sick and disabled soldiers. Once, it is said, when a party of Yankees came through, she gave the Masonic sign and saved the provisions, but the soldiers took the horses and mules." In 1972, Noble Hall became the first structure in Lee County to be named to the National Register of Historic Places.

—Photo: Ann B. Pearson

▶ When John Hodges Drake III, right, was sixteen years old, he left East Alabama Male College after the 1860-61 school year to join the Confederate Army as a drummer boy. Accompanying him to war as his servant and bodyguard was Ephraim Drake. The ex-slave and his former master, both grown gray-haired in the intervening fifty-seven years, sat together and reminisced in 1918. Dr. Drake served for more than half a century as Auburn's college physician, a record not likely to be broken.

—Photo: Carrie Samford Giles

▲ Professor John M. Darby lived with his family in this house built where the President's Home is today. Darby taught chemistry concurrently at Auburn Masonic Female College and East Alabama Male College. He had the young ladies of the Female College recite chemistry with the male students. One of Auburn's agricultural leaders, John Frederick Duggar, and his family lived in the house from the 1890s until it burned in about 1937. Duggar served as third director of the Agricultural Experiment Station and the first director of the Cooperative Extension Service.

—Photo: AU Special Collections

▲ East Alabama Male College began classes in 1859 with the Reverend William Jeremiah Sasnett, thirty-nine, of LaGrange, Georgia, as Auburn's first and youngest president. The college had a fifty-one-member Board of Trustees, eighty college students, one hundred preparatory students, and a new four-story building where Samford Hall now stands. Although the war closed the college in 1861, Sasnett remained president until his death in 1865.

—Photo: AU University Relations

ENTIRELY NEW! ENTIRELY NEW!!
WHAT IS IT?
That Wonderful Purifying Agent,
Prof. Darby's Prophylactic Fluid.

IT is a Chemical Union of materials, provided by Nature herself, for rendering pure the air we breathe. Its action is in obedience to fixed laws.

QUICK-SHURE, POWERFUL.

It purifies dwellings, sinks, kitchens.
It removes all offensive odors.
It cures burns with instant certainty.
It is the best preparation ever used for fresh wounds.
It destroys all vegetable and animal poison.
It relieves in a few seconds the bites of insects, bees, etc.
It scatters boils when forming.
It soothes boils when formed, and heals them rapidly.
It is good for carbuncles, ulcers, corns and sores.
It cleanses the teeth and purifies the breath.
The worst symptoms of Typhoid and Scarlet Fever are mitigated by the use of this Fluid; it has been known to check the spread of Typhoid Fever in families and upon plantations.
Leading physicians are using it in Charleston Columbia, Savannah, Augusta, Atlanta, Macon, Columbus, Montgomery, Selma. Mobile and New Orleans.
Hospitals, corporations, ship masters, manufacturers, planters, physicians, furnished by the gallon at reduced rates.
For sale by druggists and country merchants generally, from whom orders are respectfully solicited.
Try at least one bottle. Price 50 cents.—Follow directions.
☞ Manufactured only in the Laboratory of
Sept 24,18,1y   DARBY & PRICE,
Auburn, Ala.
BERNHARD WARD & Co., agents Centreville.

Professor John M. Darby and his partner, W. H. C. Price, manufactured a patent medicine-disinfectant in a building near the present site of the AU President's Mansion. The glowing purple fluid sold throughout the Southeast for fifty cents a bottle. This advertisement appeared in the Central Enquirer at Centreville, Alabama, on May 12, 1860. Darby's "Prophylactic Fluid" was "extremely helpful to hospitals and surgeons in the war and unsurpassed as an antiseptic by any competitor in any country," H. M. Hamill, who attended Auburn after the Civil War, wrote many years later. Legend has it that Darby refused to divulge his secret recipe for the fluid until the professor, on his deathbed, gave it to his son.

—Photo: Alabama Department of Archives

▲ *William James Samford in 1860-61 attended East Alabama Male College, setting a family pattern of attending what is now Auburn University. In 1862, he enlisted as a private in the Confederate Army and was soon promoted to sergeant major and then to lieutenant. Samford campaigned in Tennessee and Kentucky before being captured in 1863 at Baker's Creek in Mississippi. After the war, he farmed near Auburn until he completed law studies he had begun as a prisoner of war on an island in Lake Erie. Samford later served in both houses of the Alabama Legislature and in Congress. While a state senator, he wrote the law appropriating money to help rebuild Old Main, which burned in 1887. Samford Hall was named for him in 1929. In 1900, Samford became governor. As he lay dying in 1901, his last words were, "I am face to face with death and am not afraid."*
—*Photo: Carrie Samford Giles*

▲ *This plaque near the depot symbolizes Auburn's share in the excitement of Jefferson Davis' circuitous train trip from his plantation Brierfield in Mississippi through Chattanooga and Atlanta to his inauguration at Montgomery in February 1861. "Bonfires blazed along the way in his honor and he made some twenty-five speeches to cheering crowds at railroad stations. At Auburn . . . he reviewed the Auburn Guards, the first troops to be so honored by the president-elect," reports the* Alabama Confederate Reader *by Malcolm McMillan. One of the guards, Private Joseph D. Robinson, later said Davis made a recruiting talk. In 1893, Auburn cadets formed an honor guard when Davis' body was moved from New Orleans to Richmond. The United Daughters of the Confederacy unveiled this marker near the train station on March 30, 1914.*
—*Photo: Paul Kennedy Sr.*

◄ *Private Joseph D. Robinson of Chambers County posed for this picture as he prepared to leave East Alabama Male College for service in the Confederate Army. He had come to Auburn as a freshman in 1860 after inheriting two slaves, two mules, and $3,140 from a neighbor in Shawmut. He lived at Dr. McElhaney's house and studied such subjects as Latin, Greek, algebra, geography, and composition. Robinson, who lost part of an ear to Yankee shot, fought at Corinth, Shiloh, Vicksburg, and elsewhere. "I could follow pig trails in Mississippi blindfolded," he later told his grandson.*
—*Photo: Forrest C. Word*

Sherman's plan to prevent war supplies from reaching the Confederate soldiers in the Battle of Atlanta. The small Auburn post delayed but could not stop Rousseau's Raiders, Malcolm C. McMillan records in the *Alabama Confederate Reader*. There was only so much that eighteen men on horseback with shotguns, including convalescents from the hospital at Old Main (or thirty to forty men, one source said), could do against first about 300 and then an estimated 2,500 invaders. The raiders destroyed war materials such as gunpowder, lead, and potash taken from Auburn businesses, the *Montgomery Weekly Advertiser* reported. They probably looted a drugstore on the lot later occupied by Toomer's. Rousseau apparently spared buildings from destruction, except for government property. From Confederate supplies, his troops were issued clothing, shoes, food, and the much-prized tobacco, Northern Colonel W. D. Hamilton wrote some half century later. Then Auburn people, white and black, were told to "help themselves to what they wanted," the cavalry officer recalled. But an account in the *Montgomery Daily Mail,* soon

after the raid, said the raiders "opened all the stores [in Auburn] and told the Negroes to help themselves, which they did."

Headed east, Union troops came again on April 15, 1865, the day Lincoln died and six days after Lee had surrendered at Appomattox. They shot one recently mustered-out Confederate soldier near Elam churchyard, where he is buried. One account said he was shot apparently "without good reason." Another said, "Union soldiers thought he was reaching for a gun." The pillagers were part of General James H. Wilson's Raiders, who captured Montgomery, and Columbus, Georgia, and other cities. Many of Wilson's men and horses drank from a spring east of what is now the Scott-Yarbrough House (Pebble Hill) at the east end of Magnolia Avenue. Some soldiers camped overnight. The Yankees cut up carpets from the house, then occupied by the C. W. Pope family. They used the carpets for horse blankets, and took other things, according to a descendant of the family. The war ended, but hard times lay ahead for Auburn.◖

▼ *Sherman's assault on Atlanta meant reopening this building, Old Main, and other facilities of the closed East Alabama Male College for care of Confederate wounded. The State of Texas helped pay for the services, and the place became known as the Texas Hospital.*

In July 1864, more than four hundred Texans were treated there. Many Texas soldiers never made it home from east Alabama and are buried in Pine Hill Cemetery.
—*Photo: AU Special Collections*

We copy the following from a letter from Hon. John R. Baylor to the News:

I visited Dr. Bryan's Hospital, at Auburn, where there are four hundred sick and wounded soldiers. The Doctor kindly showed me through the different wards, and even the kitchen. I found it far ahead of the other hospitals, and the people of Texas ought to contribute liberally to that hospital, for it is for Texas soldiers, and contributes greatly to the comfort of our unfortunate sick and wounded. The ladies at and in the vicinity of Auburn are doing all in their power to aid in taking care of our men, and they deserve the thanks of our people for their devotion to our wounded and sick soldiers. Dr. Bryan has done his part nobly, and deserves the gratitude of our State.

We need but add that Dr. Bryan has written us that he is in need of funds, which we hope the people of Texas will not be slow in supplying. We have already received several thousand dollars for the purpose, and have the promise of a liberal donation from the State.

▲ *The work and needs of the Texas Hospital at Auburn during the Civil War were pointed out in a letter reprinted in the* Daily Telegraph *of Houston, Texas, on August 17, 1864. What was the Texas Hospital doing in Alabama? The name ties back to 1862, when the Confederate Congress required that hospitals be named for states to appeal to state pride in financing them.*

—Photo: Texas Library

▲ *This flag on the wall at Draughon Library belongs to the 37th Alabama Regiment, organized at Auburn in 1862. One of the first six professors at East Alabama Male College, Captain W. F. Slaton, helped form the regiment. The 37th fought at Shiloh, Vicksburg, Lookout Mountain, Missionary Ridge, and in the 1864 Georgia campaign. Surrender came at Bentonville, North Carolina, in 1865 with three hundred of the regiment's original eleven hundred present.*

—Photo: AU Special Collections

◀ *Ninety-eight unknown soldiers of the Confederacy were buried near this monument in Pine Hill Cemetery. Many are believed to be Texans, patients who died at the Texas Hospital in Auburn. Seventy-one soldiers are buried in marked graves in the cemetery. White-gloved Agricultural and Mechanical College cadets with rifles formed an honor guard to commemorate the dead on Confederate Memorial Day in 1895, two years after the Ladies Memorial Association placed the monument there.*

—Photo: AU Archives

The first big wedding in Auburn after the Civil War took place in the Drake-Samford House on October 31, 1865. Future Alabama Governor William J. Samford, a twenty-one-year-old former Confederate soldier, married Caroline Elizabeth Drake, eighteen, in her family home on North Gay Street. The railroad tracks had not been repaired after Federal troops had destroyed them during the final year of the war, and Caroline Drake had ridden to Columbus, Georgia, by horse and buggy to have her wedding dress made. After the wedding, more than one hundred guests ascended this curved staircase for supper. As a special treat, the bride's mother, Mrs. John Hodges Drake II, served the last of the pre-war coffee, previously used only in case of sickness.

—Photo: AU Archives

▼ Among the oldest buildings in the Auburn area are those at Pinetucket, on a hill off Wire Road and a few hundred yards east of Shug Jordan Parkway. The one-story frame home shown here and three other structures were built between 1835 and 1850 by Lewis Allen Foster. The home, a simple Greek Revival Cottage, is of heart pine with sills 12 inches square and 16 inches square. The outbuildings include a carriage house, barn, and art cottage. Mrs. Mary P. Norman, great, great, great, great niece of Lewis Allen Foster, inherited Pinetucket from her grandmother, Mrs. Leda Foster, in 1988. Mrs. Norman said Lewis Foster purchased the property in 1835 and began work on the home within the next few years, certainly by 1840. The Alabama Register of Landmarks and Heritage, however, dates construction of the home and outbuildings at 1850. Barely visible in this 1996 photo is a plastic sheet covering an area of the roof damaged by Hurricane Opal. The storm also uprooted about thirty trees on the six-acre tract, including many huge old oaks and pecans.

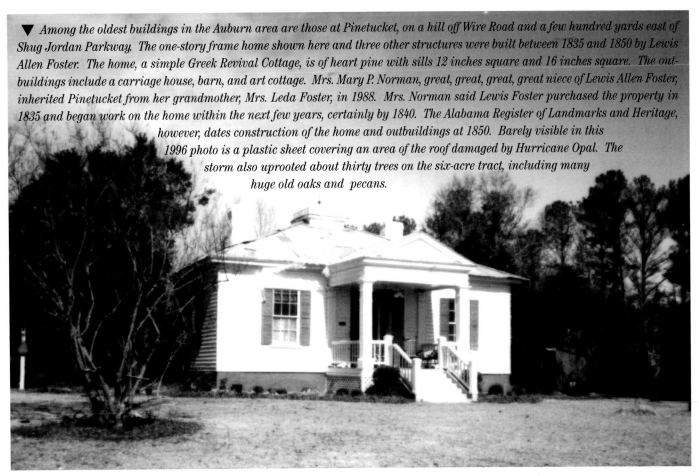

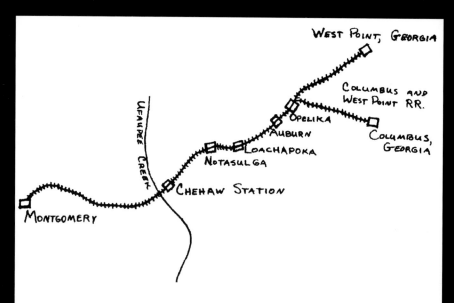

▲ *Many Confederate soldiers rode the Montgomery & West Point Railroad until Rousseau's Raiders destroyed a large part of the line in 1864.*
—Photo: John Peavy Wright

▲ *General James Henry Lane, professor of civil engineering and drawing at Auburn from 1882 until his death in 1907, had become a brigadier general in the Confederate Army in 1862 before he was thirty. Lane fought in every major battle of the Army of Northern Virginia, was wounded three times, and finally surrendered his brigade at Appomattox. "His horse was shot from under him" in Pickett's charge at Gettysburg, the* Plainsman *said.*

An Auburn friend, James P. C. Southall, used to talk with Lane about the war. Southall wrote: "The saddest day of his life, (Lane) said with tears streaming down his cheeks, was that black night after Chancellorsville when his men inadvertently shot Stonewall Jackson riding towards them in the dark. Their proudest day was when General Lee mounted on Traveller took off his hat and bowed his head as the remnants of Lane's division marched past him after having been all day under fire in the 'bloody angle' of Spottsylvania Courthouse . . ." (quotation reprinted from Southall's Memoirs of The Abbots of Old Bellevue *with permission of the University Press of Virginia).*
—Photo: AU Archives

▲ *Auburn's depot lay directly in the path of Major General Lovell H. Rousseau's Federal raiders in July 1864. Their goal: to wreck the Montgomery & West Point Railroad. About three hundred of Rousseau's troops burned the station after skirmishing with a few local militiamen and soldiers from the Confederate hospital. The invaders destroyed other depots and approximately thirty miles of track from just southwest of Chehaw to a point northeast of Opelika.*
—Map: Glenda Logue based on John H. Harper's "Rousseau's Alabama Raid"

OATH OF ALLEGIANCE.

The State of Alabama,

MACON COUNTY.

I, William W. Wright,

do solemnly swear that I will henceforth faithfully support, protect and defend the Constitution of the United States, and the Union of States thereunder; and that I will, in like manner, abide by and support all laws and proclamations which have been made during the existing rebellion with reference to the emancipation of slaves. So help me God.

SWORN TO and subscribed before me, this
9th day of August, 1865.

A. N. Hamm
Judge of Probate

No. — 43

W. W. Wright

▲ *W. F. Glenn, a famous Methodist minister when this photograph was made, took first honors in the first graduating class of the East Alabama Male College in 1860. He also is remembered as the Confederate soldier who hastened his wedding because of a storm. Glenn and his fiancee, Flora Harper of Auburn, had planned to wait until after the war to marry, but a tornado destroyed her home on December 27, 1864, injuring the young couple and causing her family to decide to move to its Mississippi plantation. Glenn didn't want his intended so far away from him, so they married on January 31, 1865, at the Methodist Church of Auburn.*

—Photo: AU Archives

the Zankees come over to us under flag of truce to gather up their dead & wounded where we whiped them out on Saturday, & I tell you there was a many a dead one lying on the field too, Gen Rodes granted them permission to come half way to our lines & detailed some of our men to carry the dead that far to them. it was rather an unusual sight too to see our men & the Zankees meet & shake hands & appear as friendly as brothers. our boys giving them tobacco for coffee & canteens. their friendship was cut short though the flag of truce was out at 5 Oclock & every man had to get back to his post they didn't get up near all their dead. they were lying thick over the field yesterday evening

▲ *George W. Wright, a Confederate soldier who before the war had attended Slaton's Academy at Auburn, wrote home from the Virginia front on December 17, 1862. He told of surviving heavy enemy fire in a battle fought to reinforce Longstreet near Fredericksburg, and of a strange interlude that followed. The letter was to his older brother, William W. Wright, who after the war owned the Wright's Mill property where Chewacla Park is now.*

—Photo: John Peavy Wright

This was one of the first artificial fishponds in Alabama, built by James Stanley Newman in what is now the Donald E. Davis Arboretum just south of the President's Home. Newman stocked the pond, and when this photograph was taken in 1885, he and his children fished there. It later was known as Darby's Pond after John Darby, who manufactured patent medicine in a nearby building. Newman built several other ponds in Auburn for livestock and fishing.

—Photo: Ernestine Walker Sherman

Chapter 2

New Life
for the
Loveliest Village

ast Alabama Male College had closed in prosperity at the start of the war, but it reopened as a financially crippled institution in 1866. The president's annual salary was halved from $3,000 to $1,500, and a professor's pay was first reduced from $2,000 to $1,250 and later cut again to $800 a year. Yet, despite the hardships, the little liberal-arts college survived until 1872. In the eight years that classes were taught there, EAMC graduated future teachers, ministers, physicians, farmers, merchants, lawyers, politicians, and others.

In 1872, the college, ironically, lost its name but saved its life through a federal law passed during the war. The Alabama Legislature decided in 1868 to use this law, the Morrill Act, to create a public land-grant college. The new institution would offer the technical training in agriculture and mechanical arts needed to help Alabamians rebuild their postwar economy. Its curriculum also would include other scientific and classical studies and would require military instruction.

With Auburn out of money in 1871, its faculty had recommended deeding the building, equipment, and grounds to the state for use as a land-grant college. The trustees and the Methodist Conference regretted having to give up their little college; but, agreeing that it could not survive by tuition fees alone, they authorized the transfer. The state, which had land-grant money but no campus, accepted Auburn's offer over those from Tuscaloosa and Florence. Lee County legislator Sheldon Toomer, the father of the man for whom Toomer's Corner later was named, wrote the bill that passed on February 26, 1872, making Auburn the home of the Agricultural and Mechanical College of Alabama.

The state had not escaped the hard times following the Civil War, and neither did its new creation, the A&M College (also called AMC), historians Malcolm McMillan and Allen Jones recall in *Through the Years*. For eleven years the school did not receive a state appropriation. It existed on the annual tuition fee of $50 a student and the $20,280 that the state paid each year in depreciated currency as interest on Auburn's land-grant endowment. President Isaac Taylor Tichenor's workload illustrates the sparse funding. For A&M's first five years, he also served as the only professor of agriculture and directed the farm experiments.

Enrollment had increased to 104 students in the fall of 1875, to 108 in 1876, and to 238 in 1877. "Attendance commenced to drop after the highwater mark of 279 in 1879," an Auburn graduate later wrote. "This was entirely due to the fact that efforts to make the college scientific were not acceptable to the Trustees, the Faculty, or the Students. The old literary education was still in vogue in the South despite the fact that . . . the Morrill Act intended to make the A&M College scientific."

The town also had its ups and downs. "In the late seventies," Dr. Bennett Battle Ross, dean of chemistry, wrote in 1926, "it was stated that only one house had been constructed in Auburn in a period of ten years. But in the last year or two of the decade a building boom reached the town, and some seven or eight new houses were erected in

◄ *Dr. James Ferguson Dowdell, nearly forty-eight, Methodist minister, former Alabama congressman, and retired Confederate Army colonel, served as president of East Alabama Male College during hard times following the Civil War. After the institution reopened in 1866, Dowdell's pay was halved and his faculty members also took salary cuts to help keep it operating despite declining enrollments. Dowdell resigned in the face of criticism in 1870, and a faculty government ran the college its last two years. The Methodist Church turned the property over to the State of Alabama for use as a land-grant institution in 1872.*

—Photo: AU Archives

a space of two years." At the same time many water oaks and elms were planted to replace storm-battered chinaberry trees.

Despite the new houses, Auburn remained a village in the late 1870s. There were no stock laws. Horses, mules, cows, hogs, and goats roamed the streets. A combination calaboose and market stood in the middle of Main Street (now College) just south of Magnolia Avenue until a prisoner burned the building to escape.

From the beginning, the new land-grant college resembled both a military school and a church school. Cadets drilled in gray uniforms and black hats. President Tichenor, who had been a fighting Baptist chaplain at Shiloh, required that they abstain from gambling and drinking spiritous liquors. Mustaches were taboo. Cadets awakened to the beat of a drum at 5:30 a.m. and, if they lived within a mile of the campus, reported for roll call. They attended chapel services each morning and had to stay off the streets during class hours. At 6 p.m. they returned to their rooms and were supposed to be in bed by 10. They were allowed to go on dates only on Sunday evenings. Many A&M cadets later became soldiers. Auburn had thirty-five commissioned officers in the Spanish-American War, second in number among universities only to Cornell.

Dr. William LeRoy Broun, short in stature but an academic giant, led the college to the forefront of the South's scientific institutions in the 1880s and nineties. But he resigned once for a year before his plan was accepted for expanding laboratory and vocational instruction while retaining liberal-arts values. Broun's replacement as president, David F. Boyd, about fifty-nine, convinced the faculty and trustees to make the changes. Broun then returned. Broun, a physicist and classical scholar, commanded the Confederate Arsenal at Richmond during the Civil War.

Broun's emphasis on science apparently attracted more state money for A&M's shoestring budget. He used the fer-

▲ Newly freed black men and women built the Ebenezer Missionary Baptist Church before 1870 on what now is known as Baptist Hill on East Thach Avenue. A white land owner, Lonnie Payne, gave the property to a member of the congregation the year the Civil War ended. Hand-hewn logs, felled on the Frazer plantation northeast of Auburn, were hauled by mules to the construction site. The church has figured prominently in Alabama's black Baptist history. After the congregation moved to a new building on Pitts Street in 1969, the Auburn Heritage Association restored the old structure. It and the parsonage behind it were purchased in the early 1980s by the Auburn Unitarian Universalist Foundation for its center.

—Photo: Auburn Heritage Association

▲ Isaac Taylor Tichenor, about forty-seven, became Auburn's third president in 1872. The former Confederate chaplain and distinguished Baptist minister charted the transition from Methodist liberal arts college to state land-grant institution. He proclaimed the need for providing scientific training in agriculture and engineering and for better use of the state's resources to achieve "any great and permanent improvement in the condition of our people . . ." But during his ten years as president, the new Agricultural and Mechanical College of Alabama received no state funds other than the interest on the college's meager endowment. Tichenor wanted the South to flourish agriculturally and industrially. He felt it was necessary for Negroes to be educated as well as whites. They have "got to be educated by somebody," he said, "and if we do not want the Yankees to do it, as we certainly do not, we must do it ourselves." Near his final year at Auburn, Tichenor sometimes exchanged information with Booker T. Washington, who had recently established an agricultural school at Tuskegee. "During that year Mrs. Kate Dill, Tichenor's daughter, recalled that her father would often drop everything he was doing and go to help Washington," Joel Colley Watson said in his study of Tichenor's work at A&M College.

—Photo: Auburn Bulletin

▲ *James Stanley Newman, a Virginia scholar, agriculturalist, and Civil War hero, served as first director of Auburn's Agricultural Experiment Station from 1883 to 1892. His experiments on 226 acres of washed-out, red land at Auburn helped nearby farmers so much that those regions of Alabama with other types of soils requested and eventually acquired experiment stations. In 1985, research was in progress at the Main Station at Auburn and twenty-two other locations.*

—*Photo: Alabama Agricultural Experiment Station*

State Agricultural and Mechanical College.

AUBURN, ALABAMA.

NEXT SESSION BEGINS SEPTEMBER 25, 1878.

AMENDED FACULTY FOR 1878-79.

REV. I. T. TICHENOR, D. D., President and Professor Moral Philosophy.
COL. R. A. HARDAWAY, A. M., C. E., Commandant and Professor of Engineering.
J. T. DUNKLIN, A. M., Professor Ancient Languages.
W. C. STUBBS, A. M., Professor General and Agricultural Chemistry and Physical Science.
OTIS D. SMITH, A. M., Professor Mathematics
W. H. CHAMBERS, A. M., Professor Agriculture.
P. H. MELL, Jr., A. M., C. E., Professor Nat. History and Modern Languages.
REV. G. W. MANSON, C. E., M. E., Principal Preparatory Department.
E. R. RIVERS, C. E., Instructor.
C. C. THACH, B. E., Instructor.
J. H. DRAKE, M. D., Surgeon.

SIX INDEPENDENT COURSES—Agriculture, Literature, Science, Engineering, Surveying, Book-keeping.

An Excellent PREPARATORY SCHOOL is provided, with graded classes, free of tuition. English, Arithmetic, Book-keeping, Latin and Greek, thoroughly taught in this school. Special attention given to Penmanship and Grammar.

DEPARTMENT OF MILITARY SCIENCE AND TACTICS.

By the act of Congress for the endowment of Agricultural and Mechanical Colleges, in prescribing the required studies, the words, "*including* military tactics," are used. The act is designed to be faithfully carried out, by imparting to each student, not physically incapacitated to bear arms, practical instruction in the school of the soldier, of the company, and the battalion. The duties of guards, outpost and picket service, are practically taught. The College is provided by the State with breech-loading cadet rifles, swords, and accoutrements.

The following uniform has been prescribed for dress, viz: Frock of Cadet gray, three rows of College buttons; gray pants and black hat, trimmings black. A very neat and serviceable dress suit can be obtained here, not to exceed $25, and a fatigue suit, not to exceed $18—sufficient, with proper care, for one

year's service. This is less expensive than the usual clothing. All students are required to wear this uniform at all times during the term. In attendance upon drill, and guard, students lose no time from academic studies.

The drills are short, and the military duty involves no hardship. The military drill is health-giving exercise, and its good effects in the development of the *physique* and improvement of the carriage of the Cadet is manifest.

Each Cadet from Alabama, or elsewhere, at the beginning of each term, or half year, must deposit with the Treasurer—

Contingent Fee, ... $5 00
Surgeon's Fee, ... 2 50
                                    _____
Total College Fees, per term, . . . $7 50

EXPENSES PER TERM.

Tuition, free.
Board and Lodging, ... $40 50 to $58 50
Washing, ... 4 50 4 50
Fuel, Lights, and Attendance, . 9 00 9 00
Surgeon's Fee, ... 2 50 2 50
Contingent Fee, ... 5 00 5 00
                                    _____ _____
Total, ... $61 50 to $79 50

Cadet uniforms are furnished in Auburn at the lowest possible rate.

Board, washing, fuel, lights, and attendance, are paid at the beginning of each month.

Two hundred and thirty-eight Cadets in attendance.

LOCATION.

The College is in a high and healthful region, being eight hundred and twenty-one feet above tide-water.

For further information send for Catalogues. Address any member of the faculty, or

I. T. TICHENOR, President.

—*Photo: AU Archives*

tilizer tax passed in 1883 and funds from the federal Hatch Act of 1887 to build an Experiment Station for agricultural research under J. S. Newman. In 1891, a Broun recruit, A. F. McKissick, taught the first electrical engineering course in the South at Auburn. McKissick also pioneered the use of medical X-ray, demonstrating its value by pinpointing a bullet in a man's leg for successful surgery. In 1892, another young A&M professor, Dr. C. A. Cary, taught the region's first class in veterinary medicine.

During the twenty Broun years, Auburn officially recognized fraternities in 1883; powered electric lights in Langdon Hall in 1886; replaced the burned Old Main with Samford Hall in 1888-89; became the first state college or university in Alabama to admit women students and fielded its first football team in 1892; established the Alumni Association in 1893; began a student news publication, the *Orange & Blue*, in 1894 (renamed the *Plainsman* in 1922);

published its first *Glomerata* yearbook and organized the band in 1897; instituted the "Wreck Tech" pajama parade in a march to the depot in 1898; and persuaded the Legislature to officially change A&M's name in 1899 to Alabama Polytechnic Institute. Both names had been used in the college catalogue since the mid-1880s. Auburn's first three women students were Kate Conway Broun, the president's daughter; Willie Gertrude Little, whose father was Auburn's mayor, a farmer and a businessman; and Margaret Kate Teague, who lived in Auburn with her aunt, Mary Teague Hollifield.

Figures show the institution's growth under Broun. In 1882, it had six full-time professors and 125 students. Broun died at age seventy-four in 1902 while dressing to go to the office. At that time, Auburn had nineteen professors and ten assistants, 403 male students and nine coeds. Yet, President Broun's "greatest genius," wrote a later president,

Hilltop House, which stood adjacent to the site where Comer Hall was built in 1909, served as the first Experiment Station headquarters as well as the home of the James Stanley Newman family. Finding a rundown forty-acre college farm to work with, station Director Newman began to make improvements and soon added one hundred acres. "By June 1885, Newman could boast of a total of 132 completed experiments with another 348 in progress." This picture was taken in 1885 after the greenhouse had been added at left. The house reportedly had the first running water in Auburn, pumped from a nearby pond into a water tower just off the kitchen and bathroom.
  —Photo:
  Ernestine Walker Sherman

▲ *Looking north on Gay Street from Magnolia Avenue in a bygone era, one saw trees, homes, and a quiet dirt road. The house left of the intersection, at the site occupied many years later by the Kopper Kettle, was the home of Dr. and Mrs. N. T. Lupton. Lupton, a chemistry professor, founded in 1887 a popular club that was named the Lupton Conversation Club after his death five years later. Across Gay Street was the John Wills home, later the Kappa Sigma Fraternity house and in 1996 the location of AuburnBank (for years Auburn National Bank). This property earlier had been the site of the Auburn Masonic Female College.*
  —Photo: AU Archives

▲ *Old Main—for nearly three decades, except for the long Civil War interruption, it served as the center of learning for East Alabama Male College and later A&M. It is shown as it appeared to students in* *1883, four years before it burned and was replaced by a new main building, later named Samford Hall. Old Main's twin towers and three sets of front steps differed from Samford's clock tower, lower tower,* *and two front entrances, but these were lesser details. On a more important level, both Old Main and Samford Hall seemed to signify stability, strength, and integrity.*
—Photo: AU Archives

◀ *Ashes and scorched bricks remained of Old Main after a fire on June 24, 1887, destroyed the building, consuming classrooms, administrative offices, the library, a museum, military arms, scientific apparatus, and a valuable portrait of Daniel Webster. Rumors flew that the loss might be the end of the Agricultural and Mechanical College. President William LeRoy Broun issued a circular assuring that the institution would open as usual for the fall semester; and it did, with Langdon Hall partitioned for classrooms. Bricks from Old Main were used to help lay the foundation for a new building on the same ground.*
—Photo: AU Archives

▲ *Fire has been a threat to Auburn train stations. Lightning struck this one and burned it in about 1904. Forty years earlier, Federal troops had put the torch to the town's first station. Annie Terrell Basore, as a child, saw the second fire from her home across Mitcham Avenue. "We were sitting on a side porch, and a lightning stroke came down," she said. "It killed a mule and burned the depot."*

—Photo: AU Archives

▶ *The main building, later named Samford Hall, is shown under construction in 1888-90 after Old Main burned. Samford housed administrative and faculty offices, and classes were taught there from 1890 until about 1969. While Samford was being built, classes were held next door in Langdon Hall, hidden from view here by the Chemistry Building (now Hargis Hall) at right. Hargis was completed while the main building was still under construction. Young George Petrie taught six courses—French, English, history, Latin, German, and Greek—on the first floor of Langdon above the temporaray mechanical laboratory.*  *"The lathes, the saws, and the planer roared all day, a discordant symphony beneath the professor's lecture rooms, (and) a continual warning of the hereafter," Petrie later said.*

—Photo: AU Archives

▲ *Little Allie Glenn and her brother, Tom, were born on a plantation west of Auburn in the 1860s. She later served as API treasurer for forty-seven years, following in the footsteps of her father and grandfather as the institution's check signer.*

—Photo: Elizabeth Glenn Smith Wilder

▲ *A group of Episcopal girls posed for a picture in the late 1880s or the early 1890s. They were, left to right, bottom row: Jean Ross, Lucy Pou, Kate Broun, Fannie Toomer, Redrie Ross. Top row: Bessie Broun, Lizzie Dowdell, Agnes Ross, Kate Lane. The first Episcopal Church building in Auburn had been built in the early 1850s on West Thach Avenue just east of the present Mary Martin Hall. Between 1885 and 1890, the communi-*

cants moved into a new wooden chapel on East Magnolia Avenue and changed the church's name from Holy Trinity to the Church of the Holy Innocents. In 1931, a brick church replaced the wooden one. The next move was to a new building on South Gay Street in 1958. The name Holy Trinity replaced that of Holy Innocents. The Magnolia Street chapel eventually became St. Dunstan's Episcopal Student Center.

*—**Photo:** Ernestine Walker Sherman*

Ralph B. Draughon, "lay in his ability to select and bring to the faculty a remarkable group of young men, many of whom were destined to shape the institution and guide it for fifty years after his death."

In 1895, A&M student Miller Reese Hutchison invented a hearing aid that later helped relieve the deafness of Princess Alexandra of Great Britain. "Hutchison was called in his day an inventive genius second only to Thomas A. Edison," the *Auburn Alumnews* said. "The Mobile native, who worked as Edison's chief engineer, had more than 1,000 patents to his name, including the Acousticon for the deaf; the dictograph; and the Klaxon horn, a precursor to the modern-day car horn." When API's first radio station went on the air in 1913, its 2 1/2-kilowatt apparatus was a gift from Hutchison. The station, with call letters 5VA, operated from Broun Hall and later was heard as far away as Indianapolis. The station's antenna was moved in 1927 and served as a flagpole located between Samford Hall and the library.

The village population grew from 1,018 in 1870 to 1,440 in 1890. In the early nineties, Professor Arthur St. Charles Dunstan installed the first streetlights—kerosene lamps on high posts—the better to expose the nocturnal pranks of college boys. But the new system backfired. Cadets "would put gunpowder at the base, attach a fuse and light it at the burner, scamper away, letting time and powder destroy the lamps."

In 1894, open wells remained in the business district on what are now East Magnolia Avenue and College Street. But the town council no longer let livestock roam the downtown streets. Owners had to pay fifty-cent fines, plus feeding costs, for violations. To protect the oak trees there, the council made it unlawful to "willfully destroy any shade tree or fasten a horse or animal to any shade tree, awning, post or fence except regular hitching posts." The town marshal held offending animals in custody until their owners paid fines ranging from one dollar to ten dollars.

The council also set business license fees in 1894, including the charges of fifty dollars to operate a cock-fighting pit, twenty-five dollars for circuses performing in town,

▲ Langdon Hall looked like a church in this picture, taken several years after it was moved to the campus in 1883. In fact, it had been built before the Civil War as a chapel of Auburn Masonic Female College. It originally stood near the present intersection of Gay Street and Magnolia Avenue. It was named in 1889 for Charles Carter Langdon, who had been mayor of Mobile, Alabama secretary of state, and a trustee of the college from 1872 until his death in 1889.

—Photo: AU Archives

▲ This picture of the old Auburn Methodist Church and parsonage was taken after the parsonage was moved from Gay Street to Magnolia Avenue in the late 1880s. The two-story frame church was built in about 1850 and rebuilt at the turn of the century. The changes included removing the balconies in which slaves once sat during services, lowering the building, and encasing it in brick, Letitia Dowdell Ross wrote in her history of the church. But one source said the church was lowered to one story about 1890.

—Photo: Auburn United Methodist Church

◄ Workers remodeled Langdon Hall in about 1892, bricking its outside walls, removing its steeple, and adding columns and a portico. Behind Langdon, in foreground, was the engineering campus of that era—a machine shop, foundry and forge building, and a dynamo building.

—Photo: AU Archives

and ten dollars for fortunetellers. It cost C. P. McElhaney ten dollars to operate a livery stable. From 1865 to 1900, Bragaw's Drugstore became Auburn's oldest business, according to the *Orange & Blue*. R. H. Bragaw then sold the business to druggists B. D. Lazarus and his stepson/partner Shel Toomer, "the only registered prescriptionist in town." Lazarus and Toomer had run a nearby drugstore since about 1896.

To illustrate changing property values, the Toomer's Corner property sold for $100 in 1868, $40 in 1875, and $95 in 1887. J. M. Thomas, the purchaser in 1887, built a two-story building there and sold the property to Toomer for $7,000 in 1906. In another instance, in 1899, an Auburn merchant paid $988 to a contractor to build his family a new home.

The generally healthy little town suffered a siege of smallpox in the late 1890s. In 1898, the council required citizens to be vaccinated by the health officer, Dr. J. H. Drake, at a charge of ten cents. In 1900, the council forbade circulating false reports that smallpox or other contagious diseases existed in Auburn. Violators would be fined at least five dollars. It also became unlawful for those exposed to an infectious disease to appear in public "without a certificate from the mayor or a physician."

On a happier note, Auburn people in the Gay Nineties enjoyed the literary and musical programs of the N. T. Lupton Conversation Club, entertained out-of-town guests at house parties, and took pleasure in candy pulls, dominoes, buggy trips, and wagon hayrides. They served large meals for visitors during Commencement Week in June. A

◄ John Frazier Heard, a Civil War veteran who became an Auburn merchant, planter, and builder, installed the clock and bell in Samford tower in 1889. Heard (shown with his wife) used a portable steam hoist to lift the 4,200-pound bell up the six stories to the tower. "Originally a janitor would tug a rope to ring the bell on the hour and at ten minutes past the hour for classes and at other times for church services," according to the AU Report. Until an electric motor was installed in 1941, "the clock had to be wound by hand," recalled Heard's grandson, A.H. Swope, in 1971 after years of maintaining the clock. By the 1990s, a computerized clock took its place. The old clock's face was replaced, but the original numerals restored. The 1889 brass bell continued to strike the hour. In addition, an electronically operated carillon sounded the Westminster Chime. Heard owned 333 acres of land south of Samford Avenue as well as a flour mill and a blacksmith shop.

—Photo: Frances Vowell

▲ Cadets, the few coeds, and other town girls enjoyed outings in the 1890s carefully supervised by faculty members and their wives. When night fell at Wright's Mill, old timers recalled, young couples were required to hold a lighted candle within sight of the chaperones. Identifiable at lower left is Professor A. F. McKissick, with fishing pole, bait can, and fish. He taught the first electrical engineering course in the South at Auburn.

—Photo: AU Archives

◀ A notation on the back of this picture calls Clifford Lewis Newman "Auburn's greatest pitcher." From the fall of 1883 to the spring of 1887, he lost only one baseball game, and that to Columbus, Georgia, professionals. Newman beat the Columbus team two of three games. He pitched righthanded and was a switch-hitter. Since the cadets played only intramural baseball in the 1880s, it is not certain which team Newman pitched for against Columbus. But he is shown wearing an Opelika uniform in 1885. Newman was a distinguished graduate in chemistry and agriculture in 1886, according to the college catalogue. Auburn lost its first intercollegiate baseball game, 13-3, to Georgia, in 1892, Brenda Mattson reported in her biography of George Petrie. Until that year, cadets had been prohibited from leaving town while school was in session. Before the game was played, Auburn persuaded Georgia to let teachers as well as students play.

Another considered by many who saw him as perhaps "Auburn's Greatest Pitcher" was Willard Nixon of Lindale, Georgia, who won sixteen games and lost four in 1947 and 1948. He pitched a no-hitter against Mercer in his first college game and finished 6-2 as a freshman, then went 10-2 in leading the Tigers to the 1948

SEC Eastern Division title. The Alumnews quoted the Philadelphia Inquirer as calling Nixon in 1948 "the finest college pitcher since Spud Chandler at the University of Georgia in the early 1930s." The Plainsman recorded Auburn's 6-0 victory over Ole Miss in March in which Nixon "struck out an SEC-record twenty batters and faced only twenty-nine in a two-hit performance." Four days later, he pitched a no-hitter and struck out eighteen of thirty batters as Auburn beat Tennessee 6-0. He also had two one-hitters (Tennessee 14-0, Georgia 6-1), and two two-hitters in addition to the one against Old Miss (Vanderbilt 4-1, 13-0). For the regular season, Nixon allowed 42 hits in 94 innings, 4.02 hits per nine innings. The Glomerata said, "The six-foot-two rangy right hander had an average of fourteen strikeouts per game." As a batter—he played right field when not pitching—he had 27 hits in 58 trips for a .466 average. Nixon signed with Boston after his sophomore season and for nine years from 1950 was a Red Sox pitcher. He worked 1,234 innings in 225 games and won 69 and lost 72. Auburn coach Danny Doyle resigned to become a Red Sox scout in the Southwest a year after Nixon was signed.
—Photo: AU Archives

◀ "One of the favorite places of picnic groups of yesteryear was Moore's Mill, which long ago burned," the Lee County Bulletin reported in 1956, a century after the founding of today's Auburn University. The mill was on Moore's Creek south of Auburn. The cadets standing near the mill wheel are William H. Eagar and William L. Noll, 1901 API graduates in electrical and mechanical engineering. They roomed together with the J. M. Thomas family at Auburn and married the twin Thomas daughters in a double wedding at the Thomas home. Eagar married Mary Belle, and Noll married Annie.

—**Photo:** Annie Noll Ellis

▲ *Backs to the wall and rifles at the ready, Auburn cadets struck a martial pose in 1888 for photographer Tresslar at* 10 Court Square in Montgomery. Military training had been an essential part of the curriculum since the founding in 1872 of *the Agricultural and Mechanical College of Alabama as a land-grant institution.*
—Photo: Ernestine Walker Sherman

◀ *This First Baptist Church building was erected in 1892 about where the south end of the present Sunday School Annex extends. It faced on College Street and also had an entrance on Tichenor Avenue. The first of two earlier churches that Auburn Baptists built on the same lot was used as a Confederate hospital. "A violent storm in 1864 unroofed the Baptist Church," Miss Leland Cooper wrote in her church history. "But the roof rested on the tops of the pews and not a soldier nor volunteer nurse was injured, neither did any get wet by the downpour of rain that followed the cyclone."*
—Photo: AU Archives

▲ One of Auburn's most unforgettable citizens, Robert Wilton Burton (at front gate), built this house on East Magnolia Avenue with money he earned in the 1880s writing four stories for a children's magazine. He proudly called it his Four-Story Cottage. Burton also published newspaper articles and wrote enough poems to be dubbed "the poet laureate of Auburn." He amused patrons of the bookstore that he opened in 1878 (the town's first) with rhymes and jingles on matters of public interest, chalking the verses on a blackboard in front of the store. The gentlemanly Burton served twenty-five years as a town councilman, eighteen as secretary of the API trustees, and many more as a leader in the Presbyterian Church. He died at age sixty-eight in 1917. His bookstore lasted ninety years before closing in 1968. The Four-Story Cottage on East Magnolia Avenue gave way to an apartment complex in the 1990s, but was salvaged. Evans Realty donated the structure to the Alabama Council on Human Rights. It was taken in sections to Opelika, reassembled, and became the community Family Services Center.
—Photo: Gladys Steadham Stewart and AU Special Collections

▲ Looking south in the 1890s from Samford Hall, one saw a rural setting, complete with barn and lot. At right, where Mary Martin Hall now stands, was the home of Professor P. H. Mell. At left, near the horizon, was the Experiment Station. The long, one-story frame building in the center was the town's first bowling alley, built in 1888 Barely visible, to the viewer's left of the barn, was a cyclone pit, a reminder of the several damaging storms that have struck Auburn since its founding in the 1830s.
—Photo: AU Archives

▲ *Robert S. Hammack, a Ridge Grove farmer, helped supply several Auburn boarding houses with fresh milk, butter, eggs, and chickens at about the turn of the century. Hammack, shown with his second wife, Lou Wright Hammack, also ran a cotton gin, a grist mill, and a general store. Hammack's granddaughter Leland Cooper recalled those details in her ninety-third year. Hammack's workman displayed what was "definitely a mule" on the left and what was probably a mule on the right, according to a long-time Lee County mule watcher.*

—Photo: Leland Cooper

∾ ∾ ∾

(Dewey Bedell told in 1980 how his father had been raised in a slave family on a Ridge Grove plantation and was set free at age twelve. "He took his name from the Bedell family that owned the farm, and he worshipped in a section reserved for slaves in a church where Farmville Baptist now stands," said Bedell, one of the first blacks to serve on an Auburn city board. Later the freed slaves built their own church west of Farmville where Bedell's father is buried. "A lot of slave owners never got rich," Bedell told reporter Judith Nunn. "When freedom came, they didn't have much, and some sold off land while others were able to hold on to it." Untrained for other work, his grandfather "kept on working on the Bedell plantation for several years until he was able to make a living," Dewey Bedell, eighty-nine, recalled in 1996. Over several years, his grandfather traded bales of cotton to acquire his own small farm. Few former slaves could afford horses and mules, so they plowed mostly with steers. One man "plowed a cow all day, and then milked her at night," Bedell said. His grandfather gave his father a steer for a wedding gift.)

typical breakfast that week included fried, broiled, or smothered chicken accompanied by orange juice, grits, scrambled eggs, sliced cold cuts of ham and lamb, rolls, muffins, and toast, and sometimes creamed Irish potatoes.

Bicycle races were held on a foot path alongside the railroad from Auburn to Opelika. "We had to dismount four times and carry the bikes over two [trestles] and two cattle gaps," George Petrie recalled. "Even so the record was fifteen minutes from Auburn to Opelika, including stops."

College-oriented Auburn and Opelika, a commercial center, shared in that decade their then coldest recorded temperature—seven degrees below zero on February 13, 1899.

Motor cars, airplanes, and moving pictures were around the corner as Auburn neared the turn of the century. But not all citizens welcomed even the prospect of bringing running water and electric lights to the fair village. "Oh, don't let's change dear old Auburn. I do so like its rural rusticity," Professor C. C. Thach pleaded. ∾

▲ These men helped shape Auburn's academic future in the 1890s, led by President William LeRoy Broun (seated, center). More than half left their names on buildings or streets or both. Left to right, front row: Charles C. Thach, professor of English and political economy, and later president; General James H. Lane, professor of civil engineering and drawing; Otis D. Smith, professor of mathematics and later acting president; Broun, president and professor of physics and astronomy; Patrick H. Mell, professor of botany and geology, and later second director of the Agricultural Experiment Station; Colonel Alexander Bondurant, professor of agriculture; Charles A. Cary, professor of physiology and veterinary medicine, and later dean of veterinary medicine. Middle row: J. M. Stedman, professor of biology; John Jenkins Wilmore, professor of mechanical engineering, and later dean of engineering and mines; Charles H. Ross, professor of modern languages and English; George Petrie, head professor of history, and later dean of the academic faculty and dean of the graduate school. Back row: Anthony Foster McKissick, professor of electrical engineering; Bennett Battle Ross, professor of chemistry, and later dean of agricultural sciences, chemistry and pharmacy; Colonel John H. Wills, commandant and professor of military science and tactics.

—Photo: AU Archives

▲ John M. Thomas (seated, third from left) built the Thomas Hotel in 1899-1900 on the main street about half a block northwest of Toomer's Corner. He had moved his family from Georgia to Auburn in 1878, at his wife's suggestion, so that their children could be educated there. His own formal education at a Georgia college had been cut short by the Civil War. Thomas built several other downtown buildings, probably including the Toomer Building. Courthouse records show that Thomas bought that lot for $95 in 1887. No mention is made of a building being there. In 1906, Thomas sold the property to S. L. Toomer for $7,000, "the same being the lot conveyed to said J. M. Thomas by G. W. Dixon and wife, on June 1st, 1887, on which now stands a two-story brick house, occupied by S. L. Toomer, Heard and Swope, and Miss Ward in Lee County, Alabama . . ." The Thomases and their sons and daughters posed for this family portrait in 1894. From left, seated: James Leonard, Ernest, Mr. Thomas, Ercel, Mrs. Thomas, Willie. Standing: twins Mary Belle and Annie, Fannie Lou, Albert, Nan.

—Photo: Annie Noll Ellis

◀ *"A librarian was appointed in 1877, according to the college catalogue of that year. The library was destroyed along with Old Main in the fire of 1887. When Samford Hall was built on the same site, the library was placed in it and by 1894 contained some 8,000 volumes."* (From Through the Years: Auburn from 1856 by Malcolm McMillan and Allen Jones)
—Photo: AU Archives

▲ *Campus mail carrier Josephus Bell, a former slave, had been a handyman at the college for nineteen years when this picture was taken in about 1897. A fiddle player, he is supposed to have written this rhyme about the speed of the train on the dummy line (A similar jingle is attributed to Robert Wilton Burton):*

Some folks say the dummy won't run
But I want to tell you what the
dummy's done done;
Left Opelika at half past one—
Pulled into Auburn with the
setting sun.

—Photo: AU Special Collections;
Auburn Alumnews

▲ *Auburn's white public school pupils learned reading, writing, and arithmetic before the turn of the century in this one-story building on Tichenor Avenue that had housed a chair factory. This school, the Auburn Female Institute, offered college courses for young ladies, but admitted boys and girls to its primary and intermediate classes. In 1899, the old wooden building gave way to the new two-story brick school at left. The brick school held grades 1-11 of public schooling for whites until a separate high school was built in 1914. "A black public school was built during the late 1890s, probably a one-room school of only a few grammar grades on Foster Street," Ann Pearson wrote in* Lee County and her Forebears. *It was followed by a larger school at Bragg and Frazier streets. An older black citizen told Pearson that Booker T. Washington, founder of Tuskegee University, "came to dedicate the three-room frame school at the corner of Bragg that until the early twenties had only grades 1-7." Called the Auburn Public School, it finally taught nine grades before the first black high school to be built opened in 1929, offering at first ten grades and eventually twelve.*
—Photo: AU Archives

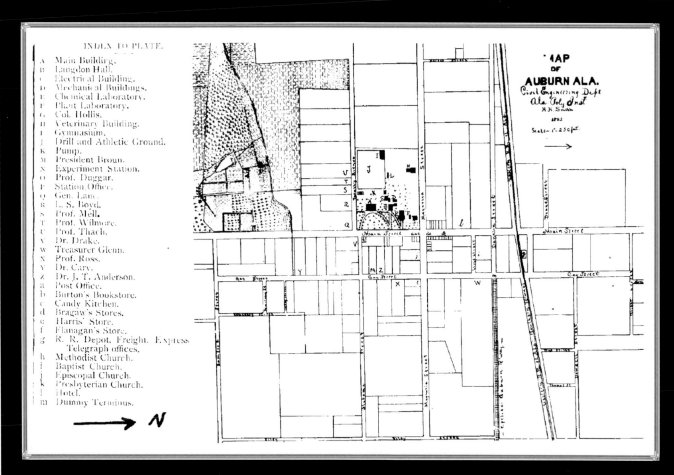

MAP OF AUBURN ALA. Civil Engineering Dept Ala. Poly. Inst. H. H. Smith 1893 Scale 1":250ft.

N

▲ *This 1893 map-index locates homes of professors, stores, and buildings and shows the Opelika-Auburn railway—the dummy line—on what now is East Glenn Avenue. At one time the line ended about two miles from Auburn where C. P. McElhaney met the dummy with a hack. This made the trip convenient for Auburn people shopping in Opelika. Round-trip fare was thirty-five cents. At peak usage, the train ran nearly every hour, but by 1899, its equipment had run down, and the dummy line ceased operation.*
—Photo: AU Archives

◄ *Auburn students accumulated demerits in the 1890s for such violations of rules as unexcused absences from classes and military drills, failure to attend church, improper dress, and long hair. For several decades, cadets with excessive demerits walked penalty tours in front of the main building with rifles on their shoulders. One student facing this punishment explained to his visiting mother that he couldn't spend time with her because he was guarding the college.*
—Photo: AU Archives

▲ *Grammar school students of the Auburn Female Institute posed at the schoolhouse on Tichenor Avenue in 1898. Left to right, front row: Will Hurt, John B. Steadham, John Rutledge, Cecil Boykin, Wilmot Wright, Norwood Anderson.*

Second Row: Miriam Burton, Otis Thach, Ercel Thomas, Nettie Hurt, Lizzie Hawkins, Mary Rutledge, Emma Rutledge, Mary Hudson, Elmer Haynie, Ernest Thomas. Third Row: Miss Sallie Trawick, Ruth Earle, Melanie Earle, Mary

Myhand, Principal George W. Duncan, Walter Anderson, Elwyn Cary, Macy Jones, Frank Lipscomb, Sam Haynie. Back row: Joe Bell, C. P. Wright.
—Photo: AU Archives

This train wreck probably took place in 1897 a few hundred yards east of the Gay Street crossing and behind what later became the home of Luckie and C. R. "Red" Meagher on East Glenn Avenue, based on a notation on the back of the picture and the steep embankment at that location.
—Photo: Mrs. J. W. Cullars

► Auburn's first fraternity, Sigma Alpha Epsilon, came to life secretly at night in a cornfield behind Old Main to escape the disapproving eyes of faculty members in the summer of 1878. The idea spread among the students, and before 1880 both Alpha Tau Omega and Phi Delta Theta chapters also had been formed. The SAEs disbanded from 1880 to 1886, leaving the other two as the oldest continuing fraternities on campus. By 1883, when Kappa Alpha was chartered, the college had lifted its ban on fraternities. In 1897, Auburn's president himself, William LeRoy Broun (with mustache and goatee), posed with his fellow SAEs for this picture printed in the first Glomerata. Other widely known faculty members shown were Bolling Hall Crenshaw (middle row, third from left); to the right of Broun, Robert J. Trammell; then John Jenkins Wilmore. A future electrical engineering, professor, W. W. Hill, sat in front of Broun's left hand.

—Photo: AU Special Collections

▲ The time was right in the Gay Nineties for a bicycle club in Auburn. The high wheeler, with its large front wheel and small back one, had been replaced by a safety model with wheels the same size. Air-filled rubber tires had been around since 1890. Therefore, fresh air, exercise, and pleasure seekers such as George Petrie, fourth from left, and B. B. Ross, sixth from left, organized a group of riders.

The club eventually built a bicycle path from where Gay Street ended at Samford Avenue to Wright's Mill (Chewacla Park). Others in front of the McElhaney House were, from left: Charles Ross, Bob Trammell, J. M. Stedman, Mrs. Petrie (who with her husband had ridden a tandem bike on part of their honeymoon trip in Virginia), A. Foster McKissick with daughter Ellison in basket, and John J. Wilmore. The pet dog was muzzled.

—Photo: AU Archives

▲ Shouts of "Rah, rah, ree, Alabama AMC" may have inspired Auburn to a muddy 10-0 victory over the University of Georgia in the Deep South's first major intercollegiate football game, played February 20, 1892, before a crowd estimated at 2,000 in Atlanta's Piedmont Park. Georgia had "tuned up for the contest by clobbering Mercer, 50-0, January 20," Jesse Outlar wrote in Between the Hedges. Auburn refused to be intimidated by Georgia's touted blocking or by the splendid Tally Ho—the horse-and-buggy equivalent of a Rolls Royce—decked out in Georgia's colors.

Rufus Thomas Dorsey plunged for Auburn's first touchdown, and Jesse Locke Culver ran fifty yards for the second. Frank Allemong Lupton converted once. A touchdown counted four points

and a conversion two. One year and two days later at Lakewood Park in Birmingham, 5,000 saw Dorsey score the first touchdown in a college game in Alabama as Auburn whipped its cross-state rival from Tuscaloosa 32-22.

The Auburn team for the Georgia game included a few young instructors as well as students. The team lived it up in Atlanta, staying at the fashionable Kimball House. After all expenses were paid, including the hotel bill, Auburn netted $29.20 on the game.

The papers of Dr. George Petrie, first coach and father of Auburn football, became the property of the Auburn University Archives. They include in Petrie's own handwriting a meticulous accounting of expenses for that 1892 football game.

Members of the squad, left to right, front row: Clifford Le Roy Hare, Professor Charles H. Barnwell, Dorsey, Richard Billup Going, Lupton. Second row: Robert Mailard Stevens, H. H. Smith, Henry T. Debardeleben, Professor Anthony Foster McKissick, Culver, Alexander Dowling McLennan. Third row: Walter Evan Richards, Arnold Whitfield Herren, Seaborn Jesse Buckalew, Francis Marshall Boykin, George William Dantzler, Union Anderson Culbreath, George Y. McRae, Eugene Hamilton Graves, Raleigh Williams Greene, David Edwin Wilson, Charles Henry Smith. Back row: Professor George F. Atkinson, Bob "Sponsor" Frazier (mascot), Petrie.

—Photo: AU Archives

▲ *This was a Georgia Tech-Auburn football game, probably that of November 7, 1896, which would have been the first intercollegiate football game played at Auburn. If so, Coach John W. Heisman's home team whipped the Atlantans, 40-0, on a field between Samford Hall and where the Foy Union now stands. No hel-* mets, but a few face masks, protected the players. Right end Edgar Graham led Auburn with three touchdowns; left end L. E. Byrum scored two; and running back John Purifoy scored one touchdown and set up another with a brilliant 32-yard run. Heisman later coached Tech.*
—Photo: AU Archives

▲ *John W. Heisman, father of the forward pass, originator of the hidden ball play, and the man for whom the Heisman Memorial Trophy was named, officially won twelve games, lost four, and tied two as Auburn's football coach from 1895 through 1899. In 1971, Tiger quarterback Pat Sullivan became the first player from an Alabama school to win the Heisman Trophy. Auburn tailback Bo Jackson became the state's second Heisman winner in 1985.*

Heisman "railed and snorted in practice, imploring players to do their all for God, Country, Auburn, and Heisman," Edwin Pope wrote in Football's Greatest Coaches. *"In later life, thinking back on his Auburn Years, (Heisman) observed: 'I never had a team at Auburn that I did not love, nor did I have one quarrel with any player during the whole five years . . . ,'" reported Wiley L. Umphlett in* Creating the Big Game: John W. Heisman and the Invention of American Football. *Before arriving at Auburn, Heisman coached at Oberlin and Buchtel (now Akron). He left Auburn for Clemson and later coached at Georgia Tech, Pennsylvania, Washington and Jefferson, and Rice. His complete record was 190 victories, 70 losses, and 16 ties, Umphlett said. A Heisman aphorism: "Better to have died as a small boy than to fumble this football."*
—Photo: AU Archives

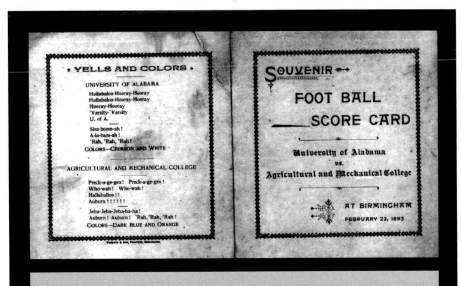

Auburn defeated Alabama, 32-22, in the first football game between the schools. An estimated 5,000 people, including female fans who were shocked by the rough play, attended the game at Lakeview Park in Birmingham on February 22, 1893. Later that year, Auburn beat Alabama a second time, 40-16. These games began a series that would lapse after 1907, be renewed in 1948, and become the state's premier sports event.

—Photo: AU Archives

◀ Most of them running in their stocking feet, six sprinters started the 100-yard dash in 1894. The Auburn Alumnus later said this race was part of Auburn's first track meet, but Dean George Petrie said running events had been included in the first field day in 1889. The 1894 winner, Hinds Peevey, fourth from left, ran in tennis shoes. Other contestants were, left to right: Billy Chears (who didn't place despite his new regulation spike shoes), Harry Smith, "Snow" Perkins, "Dutch" Dorsey, and Jule Dunham. When starter "Beaut" Edwards fired his gun, the youths began the race without benefit of a starting stance or starting blocks.
—Photo: AU Archives

▶ Auburn tennis players of yesterday must have had a gentlemen's agreement to keep the ball in play. Otherwise, they could have spent their afternoons chasing balls where the backstops should have been. Thank goodness, at least, for the picket and white rail fences around Samford Park.
—Photo: AU Photographic Services

◀ David M. Balliet, centre rush at Princeton, succeeded Dean George Petrie in December 1892, and became the only Auburn football coach to post a perfect career record. He coached in only one game, when Auburn played Alabama for the first time and won 32-22 in February 1893. It was Auburn's only game that winter. When fall arrived, G. R. Harvey, a former Cornell fullback, had become coach. Balliet had come to Auburn a month after the Tigers, under Petrie, had lost to Trinity (North Carolina) 34-6 and to University of North Carolina 64-0.
—Photo: AU Archives

▶ (opposite page) Auburn beat Alabama 32-22 on February 22, 1893, before five-thousand fans at Lakeview Park in Birmingham, in the first football game between the two schools. R. T. Dorsey scored three touchdowns and Tom Daniels two for the Tigers. This picture, taken during the first half by photographer John Horgan, Jr., shows Auburn in its "flying wedge" formation. The teams met a second time that year, on November 30 at Riverside Park in Montgomery, and Auburn won 40-16.
—Photo: The Linn Henley Research Library, Birmingham; Birmingham Publishing Company; AU Archives

▲ Spectators crowded the running lane to get a good look at a jumper descending in sight of the new main building, later named Samford Hall. Foot races and baseball games were popular diversions at Auburn near the end of the nineteenth century. Dean George Petrie said a wheelbarrow race helped make Auburn's first field day a success in 1889. Contestants borrowed the wheelbarrows workers had been using in construction of the building to replace Old Main after it burned. The blindfolded youths pushed as fast as they could for 100 yards. One youth "ran into a tree and tore his pants off." Many years later, Petrie recalled that the student had "completed the race in what remained of his trousers, and thus introduced 'the running costume which has since been adopted by all the leading colleges,'" Brenda H. Mattson reported in her Petrie thesis.

—Photo: AU Photographic Services

▲ The Old Rotation is an agricultural experiment in progress continuously since Professor John Frederick Duggar started it in 1896. It consists of thirteen plots on one acre of land a few hundred yards southeast of where the Hill Dorms were built and near the southwest edge of Davis Arboretum. Each plot is a different crop rotation of cotton with corn, summer legumes, winter legumes, and fertilizer nitrogen. The Alabama Historical Commission marker states it is "(1) the oldest, continuous cotton experiment in the United States; (2) the third oldest continuous field crop experiment in the U. S.; and (3) the first experiment to demonstrate the benefits of rotating cotton with other crops to improve yields and utilize nitrogen-restoring legumes in the cotton-production system. It continues to document the long-term effect of these rotations in the same soil." Duggar, was the third director of the Agricultural Experiment Station and first director of the Cooperative Extension Service.

—Photo: AU Archives

▲ Toomer's Corner (at right of large tree) has long been a center of Auburn life. "In the past this was where people congregated to talk, to hear the news of the town, to discuss politics and college happenings," said Ellen Beard and Alice Cary Pick Gibson of the Auburn Heritage Association. It also is a place to celebrate. "It's wonderful to see so many happy people," a Georgia visitor said when caught up in Toomer's Corner madness after Auburn's football team defeated Alabama in 1982.

The photograph was taken about the turn of the century, after the "safety bicycle" with same-sized wheels was invented in about 1885 (see one bicycle near the drugstore and another behind the man at far left) and before a water tank was erected a little northeast of the drugstore in 1908. The building had been brick veneered by this time. Three Sloan's Liniment advertisements appear on buildings, including two on the drugstore where Coca-Cola is also advertised. The store sold 237 gallons of Coke syrup in 1903, a Coca-Cola archivist said. He said the soft drink

may have been sold in small quantities in Auburn during Coke's earliest sales, which began in 1886.

Toomer Drugstore is the oldest business in town. It probably was one hundred in 1996 if you count the time that Toomer was in partnership with his stepfather before becoming the sole owner in 1904. But their business wasn't always where Toomer's Corner is today. Until 1900, Toomer and Lazarus operated their drugstore on the same side of the street but several doors north—where Lipscomb Tiger Drugstore later was located. Their competitor R. H. Bragaw operated a drugstore on the corner. When he retired in 1900, he sold his business to Lazarus and Toomer, and they moved there, according to the Orange & Blue. A drugstore probably operated on the Toomer site as far back as before the Civil War. During the war, a druggist reportedly supplied medicine to wounded Confederate soldiers from a store there.

The Toomer Building itself is more than a century old, but apparently was not built in 1851 as once believed.

Research shows that a country store was built on the corner in 1851 and indicates that the building was restored near the turn of the century. But it is likely two buildings were involved—the 1851 store and the present building. It is not known when the 1851 store was removed. But Arthur St. Charles Dunstan, an Auburn student beginning in 1886-87 and later head of API's Electrical Engineering Department for fifty-two years, noted the old store's absence and the new store's presence. He wrote in reminiscences, as paraphrased in the Lee County Bulletin, "A group of Negro boys formed a military company and drilled on the vacant lot on which Toomer Drug Company is now located. The [military] company was known as the Auburn Black Guards." Leigh Stafford Boyd, A&M class of 1892, an authority on Auburn fraternities and son of a former Auburn president, wrote in 1933 that some fraternities in the 1880s and 1890s had used halls above downtown stores. He said: "The ATOs moved in the spring of 1888 to Auburn's first big business building, newly con-

Chapter 3

Party Lines, Electric Lights, and Motor Cars

structed on the northeast corner of Main Street and Magnolia Avenue in the middle of town, the SAEs moving in also. This building had a large audience hall on the second floor and was known as Thomas Hall, as Mr. John Thomas owned the building." Thomas, a builder, bought the land in 1887 for $95 with no building mentioned in the deed. But when Thomas sold the property to Toomer in 1906 for $7,000, the deed said a two-story brick house "now stands" on the land. Yet, in 1995 the Lee County Tax Assessor's Office records that the Toomer Building was constructed in 1860. But one of the appraisers said 1860 was an estimate made probably in the 1970s.

In the 1890s, within sight of the drugstore, open wells stood in the roads for watering horses and mules pulling buggies and wagons. Uneven boardwalks linked the stores. In the first decade of the twentieth century, a few town boys entertained passersby with guitar and mandolin played on the outside steps leading to Toomer's second floor. About this time, cadets hung a human skeleton above the intersection

after a football loss. The skeleton ordinarily was used in veterinary instruction. When the town's first concrete sidewalk was poured beside the drugstore in about 1912, an old alumnus recalled, a bright, but untraveled API cadet had not seen concrete before. He kicked at the concrete, then said: "It sho' is good that they built a town there; they never would have gotten rid of that rock."

In 1916, the council prohibited driving buggies, wagons, and cars on the sidewalks and made it illegal to leave horses and mules unhitched and unattended on the streets. The fines: one dollar to ten dollars. In 1925, the council changed Main Street to College Street and the next year approved paving College from Magnolia to north of the railroad. In 1929, the Toomer Building became a guide for pioneer aviators. American Legionnaires painted "AUBURN" on the roof in twelve-foot letters along with a large arrow pointing north. With more cars on the road, the town's first traffic light was placed at Toomer's Corner in 1938. The University's Department of Music got its start in

a room over the drugstore in the 1940s. In 1945, the news that World War II had ended was celebrated at Toomer's Corner. Students hitchhiked to the south and west from the curb at the Main Gate, across from Toomer's. In 1952, Shel Toomer, after observing more than half a century of pep rallies, parades, initiations, victory celebrations, and political speeches at his corner, sold the business to Auburn native and fellow druggist McAdory Lipscomb, who bought the three-store Toomer Building in 1974. When did students begin "rolling Toomer's Corner" with toilet paper? "The 'toilet paper over the wires' tradition didn't really begin until about fifteen years ago," Lipscomb told reporter Jackie Walburn in 1978. But the corner had been a convenient place for victory celebrations for decades before that. "It's stayed popular for whoopin' and hollerin' because of tradition and the 'small town atmosphere of Auburn.' The students want to get together out in the open . . . and Toomer's Corner is the best place for that," Mrs. Walburn quoted Lipscomb as saying.

—Photo: AU Archives

"The central object, indeed, the heart of Auburn, is the college. The college, in fact, is Auburn—the town being an aggregation of residences and business houses connected more or less with the life of the college . . . There are no manufacturing interests, no saloons, no places of outside attraction—the life is entirely collegiate." W. D. McIver's words appeared in the *Montgomery Advertiser* of March 2, 1902. How true they were.

Students and white townspeople walked the same dusty (or muddy) streets, swatted at the same flies and mosquitoes, shopped in the same stores, lived in the same homes except for a few old places used as fraternity houses, enjoyed outings at the same Wright's Mill hideaway, cheered the API football team together on a rocky field behind what is now Samford Hall, observed the same "blue laws" against the sale of soda water and ice cream on Sundays, gathered at the same depot for hellos and goodbyes, mailed letters at the same Post Office south of Toomer's Corner, listened to the same preachers, and attended the same Commencement Week activities. Negro residents, of course, were segregated, even when working for whites in close relationships.

For years the college and town endured a common complaint—an inadequate water supply. On campus, cadets drank from a cistern at the rear of Samford Hall. Backyard wells served townspeople. In 1908, the college

erected a 75,000-gallon tank behind Toomer's Corner and began piping water into it from Binford Springs, two miles south of town. Within a year, seventy subscribers, including boardinghouse operators, were buying API water. Daring students climbed a narrow hundred-foot ladder to paint class numerals and football scores on the tank. In 1924, workers dammed Moore's Creek and formed Lake Wilmore as the main water source. This met the needs until Lake Ogletree was built in the early 1940s. In 1996, Auburn averaged using five million gallons of water a day.

The town also had the college to thank for its first electricity. As early as 1886, the college had generated power to light Langdon Hall. By 1908, an electric line had been extended to API's first dormitory, the new Otis Smith Hall for men next door to what is now the University Chapel. About the same year, the trustees agreed to sell the surplus voltage generated in the powerhouse behind Langdon. Its early customers were eleven residences, two churches, nine stores, and two fraternity houses in the summer of 1909. In 1996, there were about 23,000 electric meters in the Auburn area.

Some electrical engineering majors helped pay their college expenses by working in the power and waterworks building. One later recalled shoveling coal to fire the boiler for the generator that powered the town's lights. He turned off the electricity at eleven o'clock every night, leaving any later studying to be done by kerosene lamp. Another EE

◀ *Sheldon L. "Shel" Toomer, a halfback on Auburn's first football team, an 1893 graduate in agriculture and an 1897 pharmacy graduate, became the man for whom "Toomer's Corner" is named. Besides operating a drugstore there for more than half a century, Toomer owned a hardware store, helped found the Auburn National Bank and served as its president for nearly fifty years, and was the president of the Auburn Ice & Coal Co. He served on the City Council for more than two decades, spent three terms in the Alabama Legislature, was an API trustee, and was for thirty years an Episcopal vestryman.*

The same year Shel was born (1872), his father, Opelikan Sheldon Toomer, helped push a bill through the Legislature that established the Agricultural and Mechanical College at Auburn. After Shel's death in 1957, the Lee County Bulletin *reported: "He was the last of the 'old crowd' which largely built and directed the business, civic, educational, and church community that is Auburn today."*

—Photo: AU Archives

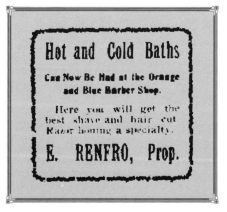

▲ *Barber E. Renfro, whose advertisement appeared in 1906, was one of several Negroes to operate businesses downtown over the years. He cut the hair of white customers in his shop and black customers in his home.*

—Photo: AU Special Collections

▶ *John Reese, a drayman, lent Shel Toomer five hundred dollars with which to enter the drugstore business at Auburn with his stepfather in the late 1890s, retired Editor Neil O. Davis said in a 1980 Founder's Day talk centering on Toomer's Corner. Although Reese didn't make much money hauling trunks for students in his one-mule sideless wagon or in other hauling jobs, he offered to help when Toomer needed a loan. Toomer was pleasantly surprised when the drayman brought several fruit jars stuffed with cash and handed him five hundred dollars. Reese's daughter-in-law, Susie Reese, ninety-five, said in 1996 that her father-in-law, John Reese, told his son, Henry (her husband), the story about Toomer and the money. And Toomer had told the story himself.*

—Photo: Bernice Reese Whitaker

⌘*⌘*⌘

(Susie Reese learned to sew when ten years old and began sewing for pay at nineteen. "She has sewn for such families as the Rosses, Toomers, Thomases, Lipscombs, Draughons, Beards, and Davises and is considered an expert in the field," Grace Jones wrote in the Auburn Bulletin *in 1980. She gave up most of her sewing when she reached her nineties. But her customers and old friends kept coming to see Mrs. Reese, called by one "a much loved person." Her late husband was "remembered by long-time friends as being the 'right-hand man' for Jeff Beard [later athletic director at Auburn University] when Beard ran a feed and seed store on north College Street in the mid-1930s...," Grace Jones wrote. Henry Reese and his son, Mitchell, later were paint contractors.)*

◀ *Many API cadets became skilled at escaping compulsory church attendance on Sunday. Some skipped roll call in front of Langdon Hall with permission of their sergeants. Others pretended to be Roman Catholics during the years that Auburn didn't have a Catholic Church. Some marchers broke ranks and hid in or near "buildings, alleys, lumber piles, empty boxes and barrels, signboards, trees, and dense undergrowth," recalled an API student of 1908-13. During the opening prayer, a few jumped out of church windows. It is not known where the cadets in this undated photograph were headed, but they were in a hurry. The building, now the University Chapel, was Auburn's First Presbyterian Church from about 1851 to about 1917.*

—Photo: AU Archives

graduate remembered also running the engine that filled the water tank. On Saturday nights he kept refilling the tank until two or three o'clock Sunday morning, giving students and townspeople water for baths.

Three of Auburn's earliest cars were owned by: Dr. J. H. Drake, college physician for more than fifty years, a red Hupmobile; Dr. O. M. Steadham, a private physician and druggist, a Rambler with a crank on the side; and Professor Thomas Fullan, a homemade car. In 1909, Homer Wright put in the town's first gas pump on Main Street (now College), about a hundred yards north of Toomer Drugstore.

Fullan built his car from an old buggy and guided it with a lever. Retired General Robert Knapp as a boy saw Fullan drive his newfangled vehicle up on the sidewalk in front of the Episcopal Church to avoid a mud hole. When Knapp followed on his bicycle, the town marshal stopped

◀ *Holland M. Smith disliked the dull military routine as an Auburn cadet about 1900. But he read everything the college's small library had to offer on Napoleon's tactics, learning principles that served him well as Marine General "Howling Mad" Smith. He also was a prankster, Mike Jernigan wrote in the* Alumnews. *His favorite prank began by helping move an outhouse into the street at Toomer's Corner under cover of darkness. The cadets then took a human skeleton from a vet school lab and seated it in the outhouse. The next day, townspeople "who were curious enough to open the door were startled to see the skeleton leaning forward on the seat, a piece of paper in one hand and his chin in the other," Smith said.*
—*Photo:* Auburn Alumnews

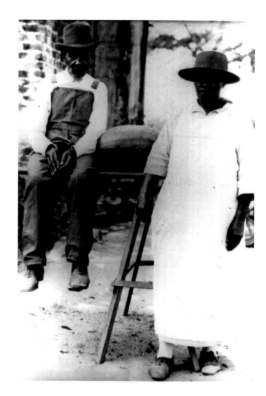

▼ *Shel Toomer, in bow tie, posed with employees of Toomer Drugstore in 1907, the year after he bought the building. The soda fountain attendant appears to be F. R. "Crow" Wright, and at right is Rufus Lee Jenkins, a longtime employee who retired in 1940. Wright apparently worked only briefly for Toomer. He was a clothing salesman in the Southwest for many years and in the 1940s operated a* bowling alley in Auburn. *Jenkins was a pharmacist and also served as bookkeeper for both the drugstore and Toomer Hardware Store. Jenkins' daughter, Carolyn J. Jones of Valley, Alabama, said Toomer was her godfather and Wright was best man in her parents' wedding. She recalled in 1996 that her father said he had worked at Toomer's "for nearly forty years, so he must have worked there before* Mr. Shel bought the store from Mr. Lazarus." *Jenkins was born at Smith Station. Mrs. Jones said he was a private in the Alabama Volunteers in the Spanish-American War and later was a member of the API football team.*
—*Photo:* Carolyn Jenkins Jones;
AU Archives

"*Uncle Jack Card, born a slave, became a land owner, a good farmer, and a champion melon producer,*" *states the caption for this picture in* Lee County and Her Forebears. *The story goes that Card, riding with his young master on Stage Coach Road between Loachapoka and Auburn before the start of the Civil War, spotted a long leather purse containing* $1,500 to $1,700. *It was turned over to the family, and he was promised freedom at twenty-one. Card said the war came and set him free, but that he never got a reward for finding the purse.*
—Photo: Lee County and Her Forebears ; with permission of Lee County Historical Society

▼ *A view south from the main building in the late 1890s or early 1900s showed the white fence that lined what is now Samford Park. At lower right was a stile that students used to cross the fence. At left, across today's Thach Avenue, was the home of General James H. Lane, on what became the northeast corner of the Draughon Library grounds.*
—Photo: AU Archives

▶ *The newly completed Thomas Hotel offered its first guests in 1900 shade trees in the front yard, rocking chair space on the porches upstairs and down, and fireplaces inside. It was located just north of where the Tiger Theatre later operated on College Street for more than a half century. The J. M. Thomas family kept forty boarders at a time in the early years, including many college students, but later reserved most of the twenty-two rooms for travelers. Rates ranged from $1 per night at first to a top charge of $3.50 before the hotel was torn down in the early 1960s.*
—Photo: Annie Noll Ellis

▲ *Auburn coeds of 1900-01, left to right, front row: Mabel Heard, Mollie Hollifield, L. M. Washington, Emma B. Culver. Back row: Annie L. Wright, Lucile Burton, Kate Lane, Toccoa Cozert, Sallie Ordway, Ethel J. Harwell.*

Auburn's first coeds were admitted in 1892, and Willie Gertrude Little, Kate Conway Broun, and Margaret Kate *Teague were among the first to attend a state institution of higher learning in the Southeast. At commencement exercises in 1894, Alabama Governor Thomas Goode Jones escorted each coed to the rostrum to receive her degree "amid thunderous applause."*

—Photo: AU Archives

▲ *John Hodges Drake was a horse-and-buggy doctor who helped care for Auburn students and townspeople for more than half a century. As college physician, he never missed a day at work from 1873 until shortly before his death in 1926. A former patient who moved away from Auburn said he never had a "better and more conscientious physician," recalling that Dr. Drake had seen him through incipient tuberculosis and his wife past near-fatal pneumonia.*

Drake heard every conceivable kind of ache, pain, symptom, and complaint offered as excuses from students who needed his approval to miss roll call, drill, or class. His favorite remedy for the alleged ailments was two C. C. pills, a potent purgative that he required the students to swallow on the spot. He then would inspect their open mouths. Students learned to put the pills under their tongues and keep talking until they could get outside and spit.

—Photo: Joan Askew

him for violating an ordinance. Brought before Mayor Julius Wright's court in the back of his hardware store, the young cyclist pleaded that he had thought he could do the same thing as 'Fessor Fullan. "Robert," the mayor said, "ain't no law against automobiles." Fine: Fifty cents.

Auburn chugged slowly into the automotive age. Dr. Drake, a confirmed buggy rider, never learned to drive his Hupmobile, Leland Cooper said, relying on a chauffeur for that chore. Grocers such as John Turner Hudson continued to hire Negro draymen to make home deliveries in sideless wagons. As late as 1914, a runaway mule caused a commotion in the middle of town. The animal, in front of Zuber's shoe store on Main Street, appeared to be asleep but suddenly bolted and turned over a meat wagon, veered east on Magnolia Avenue, and jumped through a plateglass window at Wright Brothers' Bookstore. The mule "ruined quite a quantity of meat, necessitating its sale to the dormitory," according to the student newspaper, the *Orange & Blue*.

In 1910, young H. A. Vaughan "had ridden a horse—actually it was a mare—from his home in Demopolis in West Alabama to attend Alabama Polytechnic Institute, clear across the state, to study agriculture," his son, J. T. Vaughan, dean emeritus of veterinary medicine, wrote in 1995 in the *CVM Quarterly*. "He never related how many days the trip took. That depended on where he stopped and who he visited on the way. . . . When Daddy completed his degree in 1914, he located in Macon County as its first county agent during the tick eradication campaign under the direction of Dean Charles Allen Cary, who was also the state veterinarian. The elimination of Texas tick fever may be considered as the first step toward making cattle-raising a profitable industry in the state."

As car travel began to catch on, Gladys Steadham Stewart recalled, "Ladies wore linen coats and big hats with a veil. It was considered a great thing to go to Opelika without changing gears." In wet weather, though, "We used to get stuck between Auburn and Opelika."

▲ *Bandmaster M. Thomas Fullan and the API band posed in 1901 at their favorite concert site, in front of Langdon Hall. Fullan, Auburn's John Philip Sousa, formed the cadet band in 1897 and* *led it for about ten years. He also played cornet and violin in the college orchestra. Besides having musical talent, the engineering professor has been called a mechanical genius. He converted a buggy* *into one of the town's first cars, built a merry-go-round for children, and ground the lens for his own telescope.*
—Photo: AU Archives

Auburn gave Orville and Wilbur Wright a hand before 1910, recalled the same General Knapp, an aviation pioneer himself. API engineers Fullan and John J. Wilmore showed the famous brothers how to disassemble their aircraft, and move it in a two-horse wagon from one airfield to another fast enough to meet a military deadline. The Wrights boarded in Auburn for several months, Knapp said.

Auburn entered the party line era on December 1, 1904, with a grand total of thirty-seven hand-cranked telephones in the new Southern Bell Exchange. Emma Smith, a widow with two young daughters, operated the switchboard in her home over a store several doors north of Toomer's Corner and eventually the location of Lipscomb Drugstore. Mrs. Smith knew everybody and called for help in town and family emergencies, including rounding up the volunteer firemen and phoning doctors in the middle of the night. Lula Dunstan recalled years later that once when she

and her husband were eating breakfast, "Emma called and she said, 'Lula, did you know your next-door neighbor's house is on fire?'" The surprised Mrs. Dunstan looked out and, sure enough, saw the house burning.

By 1925, Auburn had 333 telephones. The number had risen to 1,427 near the end of World War II. The exchange switched to the dial system in 1959, and by 1976, Auburn had 20,188 phones—but no Miss Emma.

The town and college welcomed celebrities such as former President Theodore Roosevelt, who made a brief campaign talk from the rear of a train in 1912. Auburn gained its first two-bathroom house as a side benefit of William Jennings Bryan's lecture visit in about 1913. Bryan's hosts, Professor and Mrs. B. B. Ross, built a second bathroom in their house on South Gay Street for his use.

By 1913, the YMCA had begun showing silent movies at Langdon Hall nearly every week with admission five and

Mules and wagons awaited their turns at the cotton gin at the southwest corner of the Glenn-College intersection early in the twentieth century. To the right, across Glenn, was a blacksmith shop. The old gin closed sometime before 1920. It was replaced in the mid-twenties by a new gin on Opelika Road. G. H. "Monk" Wright said the replacement ginned more than 2,500 bales of cotton in 1925.
—*Photo: AU Archives*

Dr. and Mrs. I. S. McAdory posed with their tandem bike at their home on West Magnolia Avenue. The McAdorys frequently rode around town with their little daughter, Freddie Scott, sitting in a small seat behind her mother. Mrs. Mac was a long-time spokesman for the Women's Christian Temperance Union. Dr. Mac was the trusted lieutenant of Dr. C. A. Cary and succeeded him as dean of veterinary medicine after Cary's death in 1935.

When Cary fell from the roof of a house he owned and broke his leg, the story goes, "He sent not for a medical doctor but for Dr. McAdory, who took him to the Veterinary Building and set the bone. Thereafter, until he recuperated, Dr. Cary admitted no one else except Dr. McAdory to his room." Cary lived the rest of his life—many years—with a distinct limp from the accident.

—*Photo: Carolyn Ellis Lipscomb*

ten cents. On some summer nights, the pictures were shown in Samford Park to escape the heat. The movies had to pass the inspection of three professors' wives before they appeared on the screen in Langdon. Pep rallies (known as "mass meetings" in those days), play-by-play reports of football games via telegraph, sermons, speeches, plays, classes, and even some funerals took place in Langdon Hall.

One Sunday morning at roll call before 1910 in what is now Ross Square, API's prize jersey cow was found "thirty feet up in the air on a platform with a railing around it." For three or four days, men had to "climb up there and feed, water, and milk her." College officials didn't know how to get her down. Finally the president said nobody would be punished if the cow was brought down. To put her up

there, cadets had built a low platform and put the cow on it. They then built another platform two feet higher and moved her to that one. They kept raising the platforms until the cow was thirty feet in the air. The students then removed one platform, leaving professors wondering how the cow got up there. To lower her, they rebuilt the second platform and reversed the procedure.

After President Broun died in January 1902, Otis D. Smith, senior member of the faculty, served as acting president. When Smith stepped down on June 9, 1902, his son-in-law, Charles C. Thach, forty-two, an English professor, the same day became the first alumnus chosen Auburn's president. Thach served into 1920. Professor P. H. Mell, who, according to a Thach opponent, had been "an aspi-

▲ *Supplementing the standard drums as noisemakers at this uptown pep rally in about 1905-07 were at least one dishpan, a metal lid, water buckets, several washtubs, king-sized drumsticks, uniden-* *tified horns, and a variety of megaphones. Who knows what was in the barrel! Nearly everybody wore a hat or a cap. Peering from under a derby third from far right, back row, is football coach Mike* *Donahue. The people looked serious, but they undoubtedly livened up again once the picture had been taken.*
—Photo: Mrs. William Hardie II

rant" for the presidency, soon left to become Clemson's president.

Thach helped add badly needed buildings, including in 1906-1910 the first separate engineering building, Broun Hall. Late in that decade, a Carnegie grant made possible Auburn's first separate library building, now named Mary Martin Hall for a longtime librarian. It was built on the former site of Professor P. H. Mell's home near Faculty Avenue, today's West Thach Avenue. By 1912, the new library had about 15,000 books; by 1996, its successor, Draughon Library, contained more than 2.2 million volumes. In 1915, the college completed a president's home barely in time for Thach's granddaughter Nellie to be born there. The home later served as the Social Center, renamed Katharine Cooper Cater Hall.

Under Thach, Auburn developed its third major division, the Cooperative Extension Service, to complement its academic and research functions by spreading agricultural information. In 1911, home demonstration work grew out of the girls' tomato clubs. The college also began training teachers for vocational agriculture and established a School of Education. In 1907, Auburn formed the first Department of Architectural Engineering in the South. The same year, veterinary medicine, founded in 1892, became a separate school.

During most of the Thach years, a scrappy little Yale graduate from County Kerry, Ireland, helped keep the alumni happy. As Auburn head football coach from 1904 until his resignation in 1922, with a one-year hiatus in 1907, Michael J. Donahue won 99 games, lost 35, and tied 5. Mike's Tigers claimed three Southern Intercollegiate Athletic Association football championships. The *Atlanta Journal's* Ed Danforth later wrote: "You were nobody until you had beaten Auburn. That was the place card for the head table." Donahue also coached baseball, basketball, and track teams; in his spare time, he taught freshman English and mathematics and helped run a clothing store. In 1918, Mike Donahue took on a new task, refereeing the boxing matches between soldiers when the campus became an Army camp. ⌃

◀ *Derby hats apparently were as common in downtown Auburn about the turn of the century as they later were in a Charlie Chaplin movie. Not only were Professors B. B. Ross and C. A. Cary (right) wearing derbies, but a small boy was being swallowed by one. At far right, out of view, was Toomer's Corner. Behind the professors on what is now North College Street were hitching posts for horses and mules. At far left was W. A. Cullars' grocery store. Just past the center trees were the roofline and chimneys of a building about next door to the old Tiger Theatre site of 1996. Located on part of the theatre site in Auburn's early days was Harper's grocery, the town's first store.*
—Photo: AU Archives

A view east from the main building about the turn of the century disclosed a neighborhood with cowlots, chicken yards, and garden plots. College Street (foreground) was unpaved near where Ingram Hall, formerly Alumni Hall, *stands today. Ingram Hall was named for W. T. Ingram, who worked at Auburn University for forty-eight years. He began as an auditor in 1925 and became business manager and treasurer. He was known for his integrity and for* *requiring a careful accounting of University expenditures. At the Gay-Magnolia intersection (upper left), the Methodist Church had recently been rebuilt.*
—Photo: AU Archives

A three-story brick annex, initially used for pharmacy instruction, was built in 1896-97 at the rear of the first Chemistry Building, later called the Music Building and in 1978 named Hargis Hall. The annex also provided space for classes in chemistry, mechanical engineering, and drafting before it was removed in 1964. Photo circa 1900.

—Photo: AU Archives

▲ This was probably the second covered bridge built over Chewacla Creek near Wright's Mill (now Chewacla Park). The first had to be replaced because it had been built too low and was damaged when flooded by heavy rains, according to historian J. Peavy Wright.

—Photo: AU Special collections

▲ *Measuring levels and rods have symbolized civil engineering students since before this 1901 class posed with two professors. At left, with beard, is General* *James H. Lane. In the derby is O. D. Smith, acting president in 1902. To the right of Smith is Paul S. Haley, an Auburn trustee from 1917 until his death in 1968.* *The ten-story Haley Center is named for him.*

—Photo: AU Archives

▲ *Picnicking at Wright's Mill clubhouse in the late nineteenth or early twentieth century. A few steps away, where a water-powered gin and sawmill had been located probably in the 1840s, was the Gin-Saw* *Hole, for many years a popular place to swim. The clubhouse was approximately one-half mile west of the Wright's Mill site. Alas, the place lost most of its appeal in about 1912 when the city leaders, while* *providing a badly needed waste-disposal system, diverted sewage into Town Creek, which fed the Gin-Saw Hole. Nothing remains of the clubhouse except pleasant memories.*

—Photo: Frances Vowell

▲ Faculty houses like the one in the foreground typically stood near the campus and had lightning rods, wells, and cowlots at the turn of the century when this photograph probably was made. Based on the map-index in Chapter 2, this house apparently was occupied in 1893 by the family of John J. Wilmore, later dean of engineering. The Wilmore house stood across Mell Street from the house of Patrick H. Mell, professor of botany and geology. Mell became president of Clemson University. The Mell house fronted on Faculty Avenue, now named West Thach Avenue. The windmill probably pumped water into the tank at right to help meet the college's water needs until a larger tank was erected behind the Toomer Building in 1908. The Mell House gave way in 1908-09 for construction of the Carnegie Library, now Martin Hall. Near where the photographer stood to take this picture was the property of Professor Charles C. Thach, API president. The Thach house was replaced in 1915 by a new President's Home, later renamed Social Center, then Cater Hall.

—Photo: AU Archives

◄ Dean C. A. Cary, standing at left, posed in 1909 with seniors and juniors in the recently created School of Veterinary Medicine. The first class to receive D.V.M. degrees from a school in the Deep South included W. M. Howell, who practiced at Clio, and James E. Threadgill, who practiced at Enterprise. The 1910 class included F. P. Woolf, who later taught at Auburn; B. H. Moon, a USDA veterinarian based in Alabama, Tennessee, and Iowa; and B. T. Simms, director of the USDA Regional Animal Disease Lab at Auburn 1938-45 and then chief of the Bureau of Animal Industry in Washington, D.C.

—Photo: 1909 Glomerata;
AU Special Collections

This photograph of the first veterinary building on campus was made about 1902, but it had been used by then in veterinary instruction for almost a decade. The building stood near where Ramsay Hall and the Textile Building are now, facing West Magnolia Avenue. Sometime after 1917, it was moved across Magnolia to a lot facing the site of the present Drake Student Health Center. Workers had to cut down a huge oak tree near the Toomer Street-Magnolia intersection to allow passage of the building. This picture probably was taken from an upstairs window of Broun Hall.
—Photo: George D. Ingram

▶ A rearing mule warned vet students of the perils of large animal practice at a Saturday clinic in the early 1900s. Cadets from Ag Hill also observed the action. The clinics weren't the only outside activity. Dr. C. A. Cary and his chief assistant, Dr. I. S. McAdory, didn't have room to perform surgery inside, so they operated underneath a chinaberry tree. By 1907, Cary was dean of API's School of Veterinary Medicine and state veterinarian. He helped rid Alabama of Texas tick fever despite the sometimes armed opposition of farmers to having their cattle dipped.
—Photo: George D. Ingram

▼ Once each year a sham battle took place between the two battalions on campus, highlighting Auburn's military training. This battle was photographed in the early 1900s. "It was all made as real as possible except that each rifleman was given five blank cartridges that could be fired to his best advantage," wrote W. K. Askew, a 1917 graduate. "The battle was the crowning event and culmination of all of the constant drilling, marching, reviews, inspections, parades, and particularly the rivalry between the battalions." Such training helped put Auburn men in great demand when the United States entered World War I in 1917.

One wonders what distracted the two boys as skirmishers charged toward Auburn's first gymnasium that was used exclusively for physical training. The one-room frame building was constructed in 1895-96 at a cost of $1,848. The 300-yard area between it and Samford Hall to the east was used for football, baseball, and military drill. Before this gym was built, Professor George Petrie and an assistant in the Mechanical Arts Department fashioned a roughly equipped gym in the attic of Samford Hall.
—Photo: AU Archives

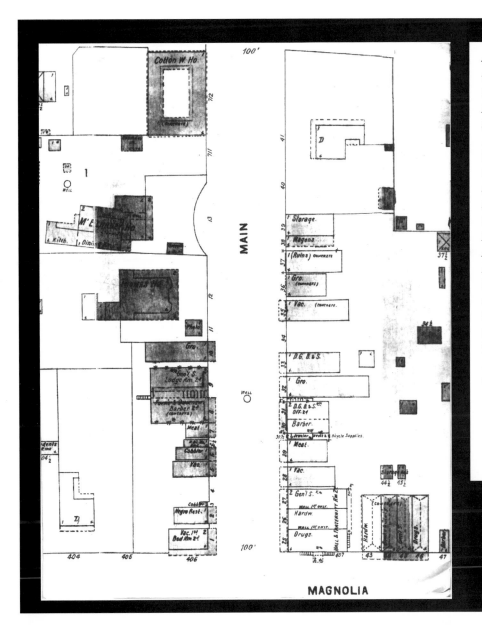

This was Auburn's main business district in 1903. Toomer's Corner, of course, was at East Magnolia Avenue and Main Street (renamed College Street in the 1920s). Across Magnolia from Toomer Drugstore were a confectionery, two grocery stores, and a stationery shop. Just south of the stationer's on Main was the Post Office. The vacant building across Main from Toomer's had housed W. A. Cullars' grocery in the 1890s. Down West Magnolia from that building was McElhaney's livery stable. Between the cotton warehouse at upper left and the railroad tracks (off the map) was the J. M. Thomas cotton gin. The town of 1,600 fought fires with an unorganized bucket brigade in those days.

—Map: University of Alabama Special Collections, Sanborn Map Company, and Lee County Council of Governments

Professor Charles C. Thach taught this class in the main building, possibly in 1900. His elevated desk and the benches for the students contrasted with the lecterns and individual desks of most classrooms today. Thach continued teaching after becoming president in 1902, the first alumnus to serve as Auburn's chief executive. Miss Leland Cooper, a 1907 graduate, recalled having taken junior and senior English under the president. "He had a lot of funny mannerisms," she said. "One was he'd talk and scratch his nose." She said Thach liked major figures such as Shakespeare and Milton, and he spent more time on them than on less renowned writers.
—Photo: AU Archives

▼ The new Lee County Training School opened with ten grades on West Glenn Avenue in 1929, and eleventh and twelfth grades were added during the next two years. The two-story, red-brick school replaced the Auburn Public School at Bragg Avenue and Frazier Street. That school had only seven grades, raising concern in the black community that "far too many young people were forced to end their education in seven years," Mrs. Susie Hughes Giddens wrote.

"The City of Auburn did nothing to help," but the Rosenwald Fund provided money to be matched locally for building the new school. Mrs. Giddens was valedictorian of the first graduating class at Lee County Training School in 1932, and the young man who later became her husband, John H. Darnell Giddens, was the salutatorian. The school was closed in 1932-33 by the Depression and then reopened the next year. Its first- through sixth-graders later moved to the Boykin Street Elementary School, and those in grades seven through twelve went to J. F. Drake High School in about 1957. "The old . . . building remained standing for quite a few years," Mrs. Giddens wrote. "Many club parties and dinners were held" there before it finally "became the victim of the bulldozer."

—Photo: Susie Hughes Giddens

▲ The remodeled Presbyterian Church, circa 1900. Gone were the front porch and the centered cupola, replaced by a steeple and an arched foyer. Presbyterians worshiped there until 1917, when they moved to their new church at Gay Street and Thach Avenue. This structure served as headquarters for the YMCA and YWCA, then for forty years as a theatre for the Auburn Players before being restored in the 1970s and becoming the University Chapel.
—Photo: Lee County Historical Society

LEE COUNTY TRAINING SCHOOL

▲ Many API cadets pretended to be Roman Catholics in the early 1900s to escape compulsory church attendance. Because the town had no Catholic Church, students who were Catholics were excused from parading in uniform to services each Sunday. Attendance was required of students of other religious persuasions. The surprising increase in Catholic numbers reported at the college caught the attention of the bishop of the diocese, who, so the story goes, decided a mission was needed. Sacred Heart Church, the predecessor of St. Michael's, was built in 1912 on East Magnolia Avenue. In 1943, the Reverend Patrick J. Doran (on the front steps) became the first resident pastor of the parish, previously served by Vincential Fathers from Opelika. He served until 1960.

—Photo: St. Michael's Church

▲ Two ladies wearing hats and long dresses strolled beside a picket fence across unpaved Gay Street from the Auburn Methodist Church in 1910. The house on the corner across Magnolia Avenue from the church earlier was the Wills home and at this time the Kappa Sigma Fraternity house. In the nineteenth century, the Auburn Masonic Female College stood on that lot.

—Photo: Lee County Historical Society

▲ Miss Leland Cooper, left, and Mrs. Marion K. Ashby, both of Auburn, were pictured in a 1978 issue of Auburn Football Illustrated ready for Homecoming. The story states that they were among seven petite coeds who, seventy-one years earlier, "became Auburn's first, although admittedly unofficial, female cheerleaders." The occasion was during halftime of the 1907 Auburn-Clemson game. "They dashed from the wooden bleachers," the story goes, "that early November afternoon with Auburn nursing a slim, 6-0 lead ... Each of the group had sewn one blue letter of the word, V-I-C-T-O-R-Y, on the bill of her orange cap. Wearing light-colored uniforms, they rendered a pep song or two to lend vocal support to the struggling Auburn team." It must have worked. Auburn won 12-0. Miss Cooper recalled, "We did not have permission to do what we did. We just did it. We seven were the only girls enrolled at Auburn at the time and we wanted to do our part. We thought football was wonderful and we loved Coach Mike Donahue and the Auburn team." For the record: the first officially recognized Auburn female cheerleaders were Doris Greene and June Tooker in 1937.

—Photo: AU University Relations

Old Broun Hall on the south side of Magnolia Avenue, a few hundred yards down the hill from Toomer's Corner, became API's fourth major building and its second largest when what became its east wing was completed in 1906. The central section and west wing were added in 1910. The three-story structure was named for President William LeRoy Broun and served for more then eighty years as a classroom building and for many years as home of military ROTC units. It was razed in the 1980s, and the Harbert Center for Civil Engineering went up in that location. But a new Broun Hall for Electrical Engineering was built several hundred yards southwest of there behind Thach Hall. The columns from Old Broun were saved and used as the entryway at the ROTC building, Nichols Center, on Donahue Drive at Thach Avenue in 1986.

—Photo: AU Archives

▶ This group—Auburn's first official varsity basketball team— won three games, including victories over Georgia Tech and Tulane; lost by two points to the Columbus (Georgia) All-Stars; and tied the Birmingham Athletic Club, 14-14. The year was 1906 and football coach Mike Donahue also coached the basketball team. Under Donahue, basketball practice was a contact sport. "He never bothered calling fouls— said it slowed up the game," Charles W. Woodruff, a player on the first team, told the Alumnews fifty years later. Left to right, front row: Dee Gibson, Seymour Hall, Donahue, Bob Ware. Back row: Bill Hardie, Bill Lacey, Frank Jones, Henry Whitaker, Charles W. Whitaker.

—Photo: AU Special Collections

▲ This family produced two long-time Auburn mayors. The father, Julius W. Wright (with mustache) was mayor 1907-16 and 1918-22. He also operated a hardware store just east of Toomer Drugstore. Wright's little son, George Herbert "Monk" Wright, seated in front of him, was mayor 1944-55, 1956-60, and 1964-68. Photographer W. R. Abbott of Opelika took this family portrait on the front steps of the Wright's Samford Avenue home in 1905. Family members were, left to right, top row: F. R. "Crow," Mrs. Wright, Julius, Homer W., Charles P. Bottom row: Annie L., Barbara L., Margaret, "Monk," Lucile, Roselle, and Julius Jr.

—Photo: G. H. "Monk" Wright

◄ A steam-driven tractor ploughed this Experiment Station field in 1906 or 1907.
—Photo: AU Archives

▲ If Tom Sawyer and Huck Finn had ever been Boy Scouts, they probably would have looked a lot like the members of Auburn's newly founded troop on this hike in 1911. The scouts had their picture taken by scoutmaster A. L. Thomas just after they had crossed the bridge and made a left-hand turn on the Auburn side of Chewacla Creek. They were camping for a few days at the Wright's Mill clubhouse. The Auburn troop had been organized the year after the first American scout troop was formed in 1910.

One of the boys, George Alfonso Wright, when in his eighties, identified the scouts: in front with rifles, Melvern Baker, left, and James Lipscomb, with cocked hat. Left to right, front row of four: Monk Wright, Harry Thach, Alfred Boyd, Robert Beasley. Second row: Fox Howe, George Alfonso Wright (with bangs), Clary Boyd, Ewell Floyd. Next row, George Duncan's face and big hat just clear Floyd's head. Just clearing Lipscomb to the viewer's right are Thomas Duncan, the taller one, and Richard Thach, the shorter one (blond, with hat on the back of his head). On the next row was Robert D. Knapp, tall, wearing leggings and hat tilted to his right. The shorter one to Knapp's left was Bill Donahue, brother of coach Mike Donahue. "Magnifying glass is not strong enough to identify others," Wright said.

—Photo: George Alfonso Wright

▲ *This workman used a wagon, a mule, and two oxen to help move materials used in building Samford Hall in 1888-90. The man held a separate line to each animal. Hitching posts were common in Auburn in those days. At this stage of construc-* *tion, the building is recognizable by its distinctive window trim. For many years, a white picket fence stood on the College Street side and a white board fence on the Thach Avenue side of Samford Park.*
—Photo: AU Archives

Miss Leland Cooper posed in 1912 or 1913 with her first- and second-grade Auburn students. Caroline Drake DuBose of Manhattan Beach, California, second from left in front row, provided the photograph and wrote that the grammar school was located on Tichenor Avenue, later for many years the site of the Post Office. She stated that "many of the students finished college in Auburn," and she provided the following information:

"They are first row, left to right: first grade, boy, cannot recall the name; Caroline 'Bessie' Drake; girl, cannot identify; Dorothy Taylor, father had a jewelry store; Julia Mitchell, father taught in the college; Eileen Donahue, father was football coach for many years; Elsie Gibbs, uncle ran garage; Robert Duncan, father president of Auburn College. Second row, second grade: Mary Foster, father farmer; girl, can't identify; Mary Stodghill, mother had boardinghouse for a long time; the next two girls, can't identify; Sudie Dowdell. Third row: Miss Cooper; Billy Wyatt, father professor in college; Louie Tamplin; John D. O'Neal, mother had boardinghouse; Dick Yarbrough, father a doctor."

—Photo: Caroline Drake DuBose; AU Archives

▲ *API faculty, circa 1914. The group remained motionless to avoid blurring the picture as a circuit camera rotated and recorded this portrait. Dr. A. M. Pearson, professor emeritus of zoology-entomology, provided most of the names. The Glomerata was used to make some identifications*

From left to right, seated: two unidentified; Charles W. Ferguson, instructor, veterinary medicine; William L. Mitchell, instructor, mechanical arts; unidentified; George H. Marsh, instructor, organic chemistry; William B. Stokes, instructor, mechanical arts; Albert L. Thomas, assistant professor, mechanical drawing and machine design; M. Thomas Fullan, professor, mechanical drawing and machine design; Jimmie Jackson, chemistry; James R. Rutland, librarian and professor, English; L. S. Blake, acting professor, pharmacy; Michael J. Donahue, director and professor, physical culture; James T. Anderson; Clifford L. Hare, professor, chemistry; unidentified; Charles R. Hixon, instructor, mechanical engineering; Arthur St. Charles Dunstan, profes-

sor, electrical engineering; George Petrie, dean of academic faculty, professor, history and Latin; Charles C. Thach, president, professor, mental science and political economy; John J. Wilmore, dean of engineering and mines, professor, mechanical engineering; J. F. Messick, professor, mathematics; John E. Wiatt, professor, modern languages; Bennett Battle Ross, dean of chemistry and agriculture, state chemist, professor, chemistry; John F. Duggar, director, Experiment Station, professor, agriculture; George N. Mitcham, professor, civil engineering; James P. C. Southall, professor, physics; Colonel Benajmin S. Patrick, commandant and professor, military science; Bolling H. Crenshaw, professor, mathematics; Warren E. Hinds, professor, entomology; unidentified; Reuben D. Webb, professor, rhetoric and composition; Berner L. Shi, registrar and associate professor, mathematics; Robert L. Brown, professor, geology and mining engineering; W. W. Hill, professor, electrical engineering; Dr. John H. Drake III, college physician; Allie Glenn, treasurer; Mary

Martin, assistant librarian.

From left to right, standing: Ben E. Evans; unidentified; A. R. Gissendanner, assistant, animal industry; three unidentified; Marion J. Funchess, assistant professor, agriculture; unidentified; C. M. Stodghill, assistant, pharmacy; Issac S. McAdory, assistant professor, veterinary science; James A. Parrish, library assistant; Samuel Adler, instructor, chemistry; A. B. Moore, instructor, history; B. A. Wooten, instructor, electrical engineering; Noble C. Powell; Joseph Callaway, Jr., assistant, chemistry; R. W. Riddle, assistant, physics; C. W. Watson, assistant, chemistry; Herbert Martin, chemistry; O. H. Sellers; J. G. Sparkes, assistant, machine design and drawing; unidentified; W. B. Nickerson, instructor, English; C. B. Moore, assistant, civil engineering; John E. "Boozer" Pitts, mathematics; two unidentified; P. P. Powell, instructor, chemistry; George S. Templeton, professor, animal industry.

—Photo: Dr. and Mrs. R. G. Brownfield

▲ These Autauga County cotton planters were probably on their way to or returning from an agricultural meeting at Auburn in about 1915. They were identified by a longtime Autauga resident as J. W. Oliver, Howard Doster, John Wadsworth, Jack Taylor, and John Alexander. "Elbert Williams, a media specialist with the Alabama Cooperative Extension Service [who died in 1991], claimed this photograph was designed to depict the typical large plantation owner, suspicious of book farmers in Auburn," according to the newsletter of the Society of American Archivists.

—Photo: AU Archives

Champions of South
1913

AUBURN FOOT BALL SQUAD.

Hare · Donahue · Bragg · Robinson · Hairston · Wynne · Pendergast · Sparkman · Steed · Pitts · Thigpen · Esslinger · Martin · Harris · Louiselle · Christopher · Newell · Arnold · Bidez · Culpepper · Fricke · Hart · Kearley · Penton · Lovelace · Bragg

▲ The API team of 1913 won every game it played, and Captain Kirk Newell was one of six All-Southern selectees. Pictured left to right are Dean Cliff Hare, faculty chairman of athletics; Coach Mike Donahue; Ed Bragg, alumni coach; Robbie Robinson, captain-elect, All-Southern end; Legare Hairston, freshman end; Jack Wynne, tackle; F. H. Pendergast, halfback; S. S. Sparkman, halfback; G. M. Steed, freshman center; Boozer Pitts, All-Southern center; J. H. Thigpen, All-Southern guard; M. S. Esslinger, tackle; C. B. Martin, guard; Red Harris, All-Southern fullback; William "Lou" Louiselle, tackle; Chris Christopher, fullback; Newell, All-Southern halfback; Ted Arnold, quarterback; Bedie Bidez, fullback; C. W. Culpepper, tackle; Roland Fricks, guard; Frank Hart, fullback; R. I. Kearley, halfback; G. W. Penton, assistant coach; J. B. Lovelace, student manager; Tom Bragg, graduate manager. Not pictured, F. W. Lockwood, All-Southern guard; C. S. Noble, quarterback; E. C. Adkins, halfback; G. E. Taylor, end.

—Photo: AU Archives

▲ Sibbie Moore of Auburn posed with the fanciest car in town in 1914 or 1915. The owner, Felton Little, had electric lights and a self-starter installed in this Ford, eliminating the need for gas lights and cranking the car by hand. This picture was taken in front of the C. E. Little home on the west side of Gay Street, the first house south of the railroad tracks.

—Photo: George Alfonso Wright

▲ These young ladies played on one of the girls' baseball teams at Auburn Public School in about 1914. George Alfonso Wright identified them as, back row, left to right, Madie Dowdell, Marion Hudson, and Marie Jones; middle row, Miriam Lane, Morris, and Lillian Gatchell; front row, Willie Zuber, Maribel Haynie, and Gladys Steadham. They probably posed near the school at the southwest corner of Gay Street and Tichenor Avenue.

—Photo: George Alfonso Wright

▲ *The Experiment Station barn in 1913 stood in approximately what is now the front yard of the President's Home. The house at left with two chimneys was the Duggar home. It burned in 1937, and the President's Home was built on nearly the same spot. Across the street from the barn, where the Swingle Fisheries Building stands today, the college pastured its prize bull.*
—Photo: Maryline Cauthen Westenhaver

◄ *James "Po'k Chops" Drake was Hudson grocery's first bicycle delivery boy, probably in 1914.*
—Photo: George Alfonso Wright

◄ *Snow coated the campus in this view of Ag Hollow made from Comer Hall between 1910 and 1915. A blanket of white lay on the ground now occupied by the Comer Hall parking lot and Draughon Library parking deck and the library itself. Visible on the skyline, from left, were Carnegie Library (later Martin Hall), the smokestack at the powerhouse that provided electricity for town and college, the main building (later Samford Hall), and the water tank.*
—Photo: Maryline Cauthen Westenhaver

▲ *"First public sale of livestock at Auburn, Ala., Aug. 1913," agronomist Edward F. Cauthen wrote of this event in his photo album. Cauthen lived in a house where Duncan Hall is now, a short walk from the Experiment Station barn where the sale took place. Note that many farmers wore hats, ties, and suspenders to the event.*

—Photo: Maryline Cauthen Westenhaver

▲ *Neither rain, sleet, nor ankle-deep mud kept the Auburn Agricultural Extension Service workers from their appointed rounds in 1914. Riding a mule, Dr. Wolf carried the message of diversification, said to give farmers a weapon against the "cotton-devouring" boll weevil.*

—Photo: AU Special Collections

▶ *Bob Frazier, nicknamed "Sponsor," won the affection of Auburn athletes as their mascot, waterboy, trainer, and unofficial cheerleader from the Gay Nineties to perhaps the Roaring Twenties.*

"Bob did everything for the players," a former football substitute recalled. "He cleaned their uniforms, bandaged their injuries, went on trips with them." Sponsor stood in the back row next to Coach George Petrie when Auburn's first football team posed for its picture in 1892. This photograph appeared in the 1905 Glomerata.

—Photo: AU Special Collections

Auburn's outnumbered coeds stuck together in Dr. George Petrie's history class in 1914. They found him a friend and also a hard teacher. Petrie's sister-in-law, Kate Lane (wearing hat), graded papers for him. Petrie trained history teachers and scholars and served on the faculty and administration from 1887 to 1942, with a break in service in 1889-91. He founded the History Department in 1891, introduced tennis to Auburn in 1888 and football in 1892. A visitor said of Petrie, "I could have listened to him all day; it is not difficult to imagine how he inspired students with a genuine love for history."
—Photo: AU Archives

Sheep Lamb, All-Southern tackle in 1911, led the granddaddy of goal-line stands near the end of a scoreless tie with favored Georgia that year. The Bulldogs began their four tries from the one. Lamb made three of the four tackles as Auburn threw Georgia back to the ten-yard line.
—Photo: Tom Wingo Scrapbook

Captain Kirk Newell, a fast and shifty halfback of proven greatness, helped lead Auburn to an undefeated, untied season and the Southern football championship in 1913. This perfect record included the Tigers' first victory against powerful Vanderbilt in seven tries over twenty years. Auburn had not beaten the Commodores since winning 30-10 in 1893. Newell's team outscored its opponents 223 points to 13. The 146-pound back's running ability inspired his blockers. They liked the way he ran behind them, telling them which way to knock tacklers. Newell, in return, declared that Auburn had "without a doubt the best line that the South has ever seen."
—Photo: Ransom D. Spann

◄ *Auburn students promised to get "Tech's goat" at a rally in Atlanta before the 1911 football game. Mike Donahue's lads didn't let them down, defeating John Heisman's team 11-6. Kirk Newell returned a punt 80 yards, and end Ted Arnold intercepted a pass and ran 105 yards for Auburn's two five-point touchdowns. The field was 110 yards long in those days.*
—*Photo: Tom Wingo Scrapbook*

► *Grant Field, 1915. Auburn's eight-game winning streak against Georgia Tech ended with a 7-0 loss, but the Tigers still led the series 15-2. One game was a tie.*
—*Photo: J. Andrew Douglas*

► *A player without a helmet had a toehold on the ball carrier in this football game at Drake Field in 1915 approximately where the upper Haley Center parking lot is now. At least one other player wasn't wearing a helmet, but he did have on a nose protector. Auburn won six games and lost two that year.*
—*Photo: Lee County Historical Society*

▲ *Girls in middy blouses with bows in their hair watch the boys playing a game—perhaps soccer—in about 1914. The public school was nearby at the southwest corner of what became Tichenor Avenue and Gay Street.*

Across the field, cadets and townspeople watched the action. Another picture taken apparently the same day showed the girls playing ball.

—Photo: Ann Graves

▲ *API cadets sometimes referred to the marble soda fountain of Toomer Drugstore in 1913 as "Hugh's Bar" in deference to the man who tended it, the bow-tied Hugh Tamplin. At Toomer's, "a very beautiful soda fountain has been installed . . . ," and on "any warm day it is crowded with students and residents of the city," the* Opelika Daily *News reported in 1907. Young ladies enjoyed going on Coke dates there, but respectable ones avoided the Kandy Kitchen across Magnolia Avenue: it was for men only.*

—Photo: Tom Wingo Scrapbook

▲ *Senior Boozer Pitts, starting at center for four years, climaxed his football career in 1914 by helping Mike Donahue's unbeaten, once-tied Auburn team march through its first unscored-on season. Pitts and three other linemen, Dick Kearley, G. E. Taylor, and J. H. Thigpen, made All-Southern. From 1913 through the sixth game of 1915, linemen like these dominated opponents. The Tigers went twenty-three games without a loss, including fifteen straight shutouts. The twenty-three was an Auburn record until Ralph Jordan's 1956, 1957, and 1958 teams put together twenty-four games without a defeat. Pitts later coached football and taught math at Auburn.*
—*Photo: Tom Wingo Scrapbook*

▲ *Pictured are many Auburn students who rode a freight train to Atlanta to see the basketball team play Ole Miss for the Southern Conference championship in 1928. Auburn lost 32-31. W. R. Moon, at extreme left wearing knit cap, recalled that a train-man opened some empty boxcars at Auburn and told the student hobos, "Boys, just be careful." Moon said the group marched in formation into Atlanta after getting off at East Point. After the game, the students piled into boxcars on a west-bound freight and returned to Auburn. Moon, sixteen, a saxophone player, came to Auburn from Gadsden in 1926 and joined both the Auburn Collegians Orchestra and the API Marching Band. Moon recalled in 1996 that in addition to making every football game for four years, he "made enough playing with the Collegians to more than meet the cost of tuition, books, board and room, and other expenses."*

—Photo: W. R. Moon

Chapter 4

FROM THE MARNE TO WILL ROGERS

Many Auburn men took off the West Point-gray uniforms that they had been wearing to classes and to Ross Square drills in 1917 and put on Army khakis for the duration. After the United States entered the war to make the world "safe for democracy" on April 6, most seniors left for strategic industry and officer training camps, but many of them returned for graduation in June.

▲ *Three coeds in long white dresses appear to be giving undivided attention to Daniel DeKalb Gibson, back to camera, and ignoring the smiles of fellow seniors to their left during 1915 commencement* *exercises in Samford Park. The coeds were, left to right, Hassie Terrell, Fanny Duncan, and Victoria Steele. Gibson, from Lineville, had been president of the freshman class and at this time was pres-* *ident of the senior class and cadet major of the First Battalion. His daughter, Danny Sue, became one of Auburn's first drum majorettes in 1946.*
—Photo: J. Andrew Douglas, API '17

"Two thousand Auburn alumni served in World War I," a university news release stated. One hero was the captain and running back who had led the undefeated Donahue team of 1913 to the Southern football championship. "To save his men, First Lieutenant Kirk Newell threw himself onto a hand grenade that had been tossed into a trench in France," Clyde Bolton wrote in *War Eagle: A Story of Auburn Football.* "The grenade exploded and killed the two men on either side of him. Newell was injured, but a canteen shielded him and saved his life."

Another Auburn man, General Robert Lee Bullard, showed a stubborn streak in 1918 after his troops captured Cantigny, France, near the beginning of the Second Battle of the Marne, called the turning point of the war. Bullard issued the order to hold or die, and his First Division fought off several German assaults, heartening America's French and British allies, and discouraging the enemy. Bullard had

attended the old A&M College in 1880-81 before entering the U.S. Military Academy.

The campus became a military camp in the fall of 1918. Nearly all able-bodied male students over eighteen joined the U.S. Army as members of the Student Army Training Corps, Section A, in a ceremony at Ross Square. They continued their academic studies while preparing for war. API also trained more than one-thousand enlisted men in Section B as "fighting mechanics." They learned such skills as automotive repair, blacksmithing, and radio and wireless maintenance. They slept in Alumni Gym, where Foy Union is now, and in barracks on campus. Willie Harper, later known as "Sam" to hundreds of Auburn agriculture graduates, remembered that as a young man one of his tasks was hauling milk for soldiers housed in barracks where Ross Lab later was built. The college remained on a war footing until after the armistice was signed on November 11. Harper was

▲ United States Vice President Thomas R. ("What this country needs is a good five-cent cigar.") Marshall, with walking cane and dark bow tie, strolled in Samford Park in 1915. At left front, with vest and dark suit, was Alabama Governor Charles Henderson. After reviewing the cadets in regimental parade and commending Auburn's military training, Marshall, his mind obviously also on the war in Europe, said, "I pray God that we will never have to fight." The vice president said the nation looked to institutions like API to develop men with constructive ideas. More than two-thousand people heard him speak from a specially built platform on the steps of Langdon Hall.

—Photo: George Alfonso Wright

▲ The first Confederate flag raised in Auburn came from Betty Dowdell on March 4, 1861, at the Masonic Female College at Magnolia Avenue and Gay Street. Some fifty-three years later, in 1914, the United Daughters of the Confederacy unveiled a memorial tablet at the same site, on the Kappa Sigma Fraternity house lawn. Among those attending were Mrs. B. B. Ross (front row, next to lady in black); Howard M. Hamill, chaplain general of the United Confederate Veterans (second down from Mrs. Ross); and Judge John C. Owen (far right)

—Photo: Carrie Samford Giles

▶ Some sixteen-hundred people attended the dedication of the new Alumni Gymnasium on February 22, 1916. President C. C. Thach (at lectern, lower left), welcomed visitors, including Governor Charles Henderson and delegates from University of Alabama, University of Georgia, Georgia Tech, Clemson College, and Gordon Institute. Alumni raised approximately $50,000 to pay for the building. Auburn varsity basketball teams played in this facility until moving to the Sports Arena in 1948. Students and townspeople flocked to the gym over the years to hear speakers from far and wide—including Will Rogers—and the basketball court served as the dance floor for many a formal for three decades.

—Photo: AU Archives

▲ *The API Band performed during the 1915 Alabama Confederate Veterans Reunion at Selma in front of the Hotel Albert. Two or three years later, several of these musicians were in Europe with the 16th Infantry Regiment Band. P. R. "Bedie" Bidez (third from right), later Auburn's bandmaster, led that Army band across France. Snare drummer F. M. "Taterbug" Taylor (at bass drummer's left) reportedly began to play the cadence for "Touchdown Auburn" as the band entered Germany.*

—Photo: AU Archives

plowing with a team of mules in a hollow near where Jordan-Hare Stadium now stands when he heard whistles and bells signaling that the "war to end all wars" was over.

Before the war ended, however, the feared Spanish influenza that had ravaged Army posts and cities invaded Auburn. Thirteen deaths resulted from the eighty cases of pneumonia that grew out of the seven hundred instances of flu on campus, President Thach reported to the trustees. The ill were given aspirin, fed soup, and kept warm in makeshift hospitals in the gymnasium, Smith Hall, private homes, and tents. Thach praised "the heroic service of about forty women of the community, who, at the peril of their lives, nursed the young soldiers day and night and by their spirit of self-sacrifice . . . constituted the chief agency in the preservation of the lives of these young men, and bringing about the highly gratifying low death rate."

The town underwent changes in the postwar years. After decades of a non-student population of less than 1,500, Auburn claimed 2,263 non-students in the 1920 census and 2,997 in 1930. From 1922 to 1926, workers built 125 to 150 new houses and doubled the number of businesses. Historian Charles Edwards attributed this growth "to expansion of the college made possible by increased state appropriations and the loosening up of credit afforded by the establishment of the First National Bank in 1923." The new bank offered competition for the Bank of Auburn, established sixteen years earlier. Other commercial additions included the Auburn Printing Company, two large planing mills, an ice plant, a steam laundry, and a cotton warehouse and gin. Some businesses yielded a bit to changing times: By 1927, safety razors brought a permanent decline in barbershop shaves with straight-edged razors.

In a private project earlier in the decade, Miller Avenue, linking Gay and Main streets near Ag Hollow, became the first paved street in town. Then in 1926, the Town Council, a blend of professors and businessmen, approved paving Main from Toomer's Corner to the railroad. The paving of other downtown and residential streets followed. In preparing for the twice-daily home delivery of mail in 1926, the council officially named the streets and numbered the houses. It changed the name of Main Street to College. Also that year, API took down the white picket fence that had long been a boundary marker for the main campus.

On October 12, 1920, Mrs. A. L. Dillard, "wife of an Auburn merchant," became the first Lee County woman to register to vote, as provided by the Nineteenth Amendment to the U.S. Constitution. "Her daughter, a Mrs. King, was next in line. A total of 97 Auburn women were added to the voting list at that time," reported *Lee County and Her Forebears*.

Also in 1920, ill health having forced Dr. Thach to retire, the trustees elected a new president, Dr. Spright Dowell, forty-two, former Alabama state superintendent of education. *Through the Years* states that despite strong

Looking east on West Thach Avenue in 1915. The serum plant at left is in front of the sheep barn and just up the hill from the present pharmacy building. The old President's Mansion, to become the Social Center and then Cater Hall, is barely visible on the horizon beyond the frame buildings to the right of Thach Avenue.
—Photo: AU Archives

▲ A large, two-story house across the street from the depot epitomized the boardinghouse years. Mrs. Leila A. Terrell, a widow with three small children, began feeding students there soon after moving in at Mitcham Avenue and North Gay Street.

"When I came to Auburn in 1902, there was no water, no lights, and nothing but dusty streets," Mrs. Terrell said in Trails in History in 1969. "Fences in those days were a necessity about one's home to keep out roaming hogs and cows."

She fed as many as sixty students a day, but usually fewer. Like other boarding house operators, she relied on Negro cooks. One of her diners was Kirk Newell, a football star and later a World War I hero. College boys who ate at her table became "prominent lawyers, doctors, merchants, engi-neers, and soldiers," the Auburn Alumnus reported in 1931. "Mrs. Terrell still calls them all by their first names." Mrs. Terrell stopped serving meals to students in 1944, but contin-ued to rent rooms to them. At least one-thousand students lived under her friendly roof.

Mrs. Terrell "never lost her enthu-siasm for Auburn's football team," lis-tening to games on the radio in the last autumn of her 104 years. Another interest was her prize camel-lia, more than eighty years old and thirty feet in circumference. Her home was more than one hundred years old when torn down in the early 1970s, to become the site of Auburn Bank & Trust Company and later SouthTrust Bank.

Auburn boarding houses peaked by the early 1950s with a high of per-haps twenty-six places. "They all pro-vided three hot meals, served family style, and most had rooms for men," Owen Davis wrote in the Lee County Bulletin in 1973. "Many students who slept elsewhere ate on a monthly meal ticket at a boardinghouse. Still others waited on tables" to earn their meals.

Auburn boarding houses, other than Mrs. Terrell's, included Mrs. Mac's, which "fed up to 250 and had rooms for 30 students," Mrs. Bailey's, Mrs. Brown's, the Blueroom, Crockett's Dorm, the Day House, the Greenhouse, Mrs. Hardy's, Klinner's, Little Henry's, Mrs. Jackson's, Mrs. Lane's, Mrs. Lowe's, Mrs. Marshall's, Mrs. Rutlage's, Thornton's, Windsor, and others.

—Photo: Emily Hixon Gunter

▲ This class made Auburn public school history in 1915, becoming the first to graduate from the new Lee County High School. Until their senior year, the students had attended the public school on Tichenor Avenue at Gay Street. Their new school was on Opelika Road, a few hundred yards from Gay Street on property now occupied by the city's Frank Brown Recreation Center. This school served white high school students until another school was built in 1931 on Samford Avenue. Class members posed facing their old school. Behind them, across Tichenor, was the First Baptist Church. The students were, left to right, front row: Helen Blasingame, Mary Beasley, Alma Smith. Middle row: Robert M. Beasley, Herbert "Monk" Wright, James D. Foster, Elmer Waller. Back row: Alfonso Wright, George Duncan, Duke Haynie.
—Photo: George Alfonso Wright

▲ Mrs. Terrell sat on the steps of her boarding house with her little grand-daughter, Emily Hixon, in the mid-1920s.
—Photo: Emily Hixon Gunter

opposition, Dowell helped streamline the growing institution's administration and regulations to meet postwar needs.

During the twenties, Extension Director L. N. Duncan continued to develop a system of county agents, home demonstration agents, and others of service to farmers, their families, and other rural Alabamians. Duncan went a step further, providing the idea and leadership for the Extension Service to found the Alabama Farm Bureau Federation, an Extension historian said. Duncan's "mission and dream" were to help organize farmers to achieve more bargaining power. In Houston County, for instance, group-selling had brought six dollars a ton more than the local price for cottonseed meal. Some Clarke County farmers had together bought fruit trees for $339 that would have cost about $900 if sold to individuals. Appreciative farmers became more receptive to Auburn advice on scientific agriculture. In addition, organized farmers meant clout with the Legislature for themselves, as in obtaining tax breaks; for the Farm Bureau; and for the Extension Service. County agents of that long-ago era helped organize county Farm Bureaus and reportedly were evaluated partly on how well farmers paid their bureau dues. Opponents accused the Extension Service of practicing politics. Extension replied

that it was not political, but was helping farmers organize to better their lives. But, the historian said, "There's no doubt Extension was heavily, heavily into politics through the Farm Bureau."

In 1921, the college established a separate Department of Home Economics, quickly resulting in a modest increase in female enrollment. After serving from 5 to 18 women students a year from 1909-10 through 1921-22, API registered 67 women in 1922-23 and 108 the next year. But the male students still outnumbered the coeds more than 11 to 1. Smith Hall became a women's dormitory in 1921, housing students, the dean of women, and other female faculty members. For a time in the early 1920s, some male students slept in Alumni Gym and in tents near the gym.

In 1923, Auburn said a sad goodbye to Mike Donahue and to winning football championships until the Jimmy Hitchcock team of 1932. Donahue left the campus after eighteen seasons to coach at Louisiana State University.

In another unhappy event of the 1920s, a longtime resident recalled, 200 to 300 hooded Ku Klux Klansmen, apparently bent on terrorizing the town's Negroes, rode sheeted horses down College Street one night. They stopped near a hillside across the street from Ag Hollow and heard a speech by Dr. Zebulon Judd, dean of education. On

▲ *Lee County High School was built in 1914 on Opelika Road, where the Frank Brown Recreation Center stands today. Newspaper columnist Ann Pearson was told that when J. A. Parrish began his* duties *as principal in 1915, he had "just $2,000 to maintain the building and pay himself and four other teachers." After a new high school was constructed on Samford Avenue in 1931, this building* was used as a recreation center until it was torn down in 1973. This photograph was made in the 1930s.

—*Photo: AU Archives*

another occasion, API cadets ridiculed a hooded merchant who walked down Main Street with fellow Klansmen. They recognized the crippled man by his limp.

Will Rogers' lecture visit in 1928 highlighted the Roaring Twenties for Auburn. An estimated thousand students and townsfolk welcomed Rogers at the depot and paraded the delighted humorist in a flivver decked out as an "aeroplane." Students looked forward to the big dances, to the annual All-Campus Hike and, late in the decade, to "talkies" at the Tiger Theatre. Simple pleasures included hanging out at Toomer Drugstore and washing down the dill pickle and crackers bought across the street at Jones' grocery with a five-cent Toomer's Coke. In those days, hunters enjoyed traipsing after squirrels in what became Cary Woods subdivision.

Meanwhile, President Dowell worked to improve course offerings in engineering and other fields, and he helped raise the money to build the Erskine Ramsay Engineering Hall. During the continuing struggle for operating funds, he set a personal example of thrift by looking for lights to turn off in vacant rooms in Samford Hall. Dowell left Auburn in 1928 under pressure from students, alumni, and others.

"Starting with the ouster of President Spright Dowell in

1928 and the election of President Bradford Knapp to succeed him, [Farm] Bureau leaders have played prominent roles in jockeying for control over [Auburn] policy," columnist Neil O. Davis wrote. Dowell went on to a successful career as president of Mercer University. Knapp was fifty-seven when chosen Auburn's eighth president.

Knapp, former president of Oklahoma State University, apparently had heard the accusations that Dowell wasn't close enough to the student body or to the football team. Knapp threw out the first ball at his first API baseball game, sat on the bench at football games, and wrote a column in the *Plainsman*. He began a fund-raising campaign for a football stadium to replace Drake Field (where the upper Haley Center parking lot is now). But plans for the stadium and for some buildings fell victim to the Great Depression that beset Auburn and the nation. Nevertheless, despite the stock-market crash in 1929, Auburn added Ross Chemical Laboratory, Duncan Hall, and the Textile Engineering Building during Knapp's four-year term. It also began course work in textile and aeronautical engineering. All told, though, Malcolm McMillan says, Dowell and Knapp served through unstable years for the API presidency. Rough economic times lay ahead for the college. ∿

▲ For several decades, as many as six passenger trains a day going each way stopped at Auburn. A lot of students, however, preferred to hop a freight and save the fare, particularly on football trips. One time, alumnus W. K. Askew said, students bribed the engineer of a freight train with corn squeezings to slow down when the train crossed Donahue Drive. Fifty to seventy-five students climbed aboard and rode free to and from Atlanta. A hoboing excursion ended in tragedy in about 1915 when a student suffocated under mail sacks in a baggage car while riding free to a game in Birmingham. The advent of the automobile eventually caused the demise of college hoboing.
—Photo: AU Special Collections

▲ An upperclassman clipped a freshman's hair to conform to the fashion for "rats" in 1916. One freshman that year, J. P. Fuller III, retained a fringe of hair that imitated Dean George Petrie's natural baldness. "My recollection is that the first time Fuller appeared this way in Dr. Petrie's history lecture, he was ordered to leave Langdon Hall and not return until his hair was cut correctly," said Alfonso Wright, also a freshman at that time.
—Photo: George Alfonso Wright

▼ Auburn's Pete Bonner swung with gusto on a baseball diamond in what is now Ross Square. Bleachers lined the bank below Samford Hall and the Thach Avenue third base line. The smokestack of the powerhouse, source of electricity for the college and town, rose above the trees. An inviting gully in right field awaited left-handed hitters. The field also was used for football, soccer, and track. As cadets drilled there on Tuesdays, Thursdays, and Saturdays, a Negro man named Will beat the cadence on a kettledrum. He stood "under a tree near where the flag pole now stands," and "it was said that Will could fall asleep and never miss a beat," wrote W. K. "Happy" Askew of the Class of 1917.
—Photo: AU Archives

◀ *Sarah Evelyn Moore, the only woman in the graduating class of 1916 at API, was the class poet. She wrote, in the class poem, "A center of study and learning, the site of our dear Auburn College. Gather at Auburn each autumn, the Freshmen, as green as the grasses; boys mostly, with just a few co-eds like blossoms amid the deep verdure . . ." A half century later she told the* Birmingham News, *"'When we were there, there weren't but two autos in all of Auburn. You walked everywhere you went. When my husband graduated, he hired the horse and buggy from the local livery stable and we spent the day touring the town.'"*

—*Photo: AU Archives*

▲ *Four shorn freshmen, called "rats," posed as hard-drinking poker players in 1917 at Dumas Ranch, a Magnolia Avenue boarding house. While the props may have been staged for the photograph,* alumnus Lyle Brown said the pranks were pretty rough. "You might come home and find a yearling tied to your bed," he said.

—Photo: Lyle Brown

▼ *Professor W. W. Hill (centerfront, wearing cap and white shirt) and his helpers worked in about 1916 to increase the supply of electricity for college and town. To create the space for new power-plant machinery, they hauled an old engine and generator from the power-house behind Langdon Hall to the train station. They used heavy manila rope, a winch, real horse power, and a wagon with specially built wooden wheels. In the background are Toomer Drugstore, Burton's Book Store, and other buildings. Hill, who taught electrical engineering, also had charge of the town water supply.*

—Photo: Mrs. Winifred Hill Boyd, Jr.

▲ *Smith, Comer, and Samford halls are readily identifiable in this undated photograph taken from the water tower. Only memories remain of Cora Hardy's boarding house, the octagonal-shaped Post Office, and the YMCA-store building on* Magnolia Avenue. Ralph Draughon, future Auburn president, roomed at Mrs. Hardy's as a student. Charles Edwards, future registrar, roomed in one of the college-owned cottages behind the YMCA.

—Photo: Auburn Heritage Association

▲ *During the Spanish influenza epidemic of 1918, this house was used as a hospital across Mell Street from Mary Martin Hall, the API library of that day, recalled Charles W. Edwards, a student in 1918 and college registrar for many years. Students near death from pneumonia were cared for in nearby cottages, said Edwards, who waited on patients as an orderly. Most API students had joined the Army through the Student Army Training Corps, and hundreds of other soldiers* were on campus for technical training. *"So many soldiers were sick" that "nobody under sixteen was allowed in that part of town," Ann Pearson wrote. Oxygen taken from welding outfits used in the technical training was administered to soldiers convalescing from pneumonia in an open air ward, the* Auburn Alumnus *reported. President Charles C. Thach told the trustees that there were some seven hundred cases of flu, that eighty developed into pneumonia, and that there were thir-* teen deaths. *"I am glad to say that the effects with us were not nearly so severe as in many other institutions," Thach said. Many years later, Roger Allen, retired dean of Science and Literature, recalled that he had graduated from API and was serving in the Army near Atlanta during the nationwide epidemic. "I was on details any number of times to carry corpses from the barracks," he said.*

—Photo: AU Archives

◀ *In the days at the end of World War I, travelers stepped down from the train, walked up the hill, and checked in at either the Thomas Hotel (left) or next door at the Jones Hotel. The latter, named the McElhaney House in antebellum days, became Jones Hotel, and in its final years Jones House. Later, a motel and the Baptist Student Union were built on the property. Glenn Avenue cuts through the top one-third of the picture to the home of Miss Mary Cox near the horizon, later the site of Tiger Terrace Apartments.*

—Photo: George Alfonzo Wright

▲ The roof lines of Toomer Drugstore and the adjoining hardware store are in the foreground of this picture of 1918 that shows parts of what are now West Magnolia Avenue and North College Street. The Main Gate and Broun Hall are at left. Broun Hall was demolished in 1983 to make way for a new civil engineering building, Harbert Center. Across from Toomer's are the Bank of Auburn on the corner, a barber shop, Zuber's grocery and general store, George and Mollie Bedell's shoe repair shop and cafe to the right of the tree, a meat market, and Haynie's furniture store.

—Photo: George Alfonso Wright

∽∽∽

(The Bedells were among the Negroes operating stores in the 1920s and 1930s who stayed in business for years, Dewey Bedell, 89, recalled in 1996. His uncle George Bedell's hand-sewn shoe repairs were preferred by some professors because they lasted longer than machine stitching. Across Magnolia Avenue from the Episcopal Church, Ben Jones had a well-equipped shop and was the town's main shoe repairman. His daughter, Newton Jones Lewis, ran a grocery a little west of Ebenezer Baptist Church on Thach Avenue from perhaps 1931 to 1969 or 1970, her son Carl said. Robert "Bob" Foster, offered pressing, tailoring, and dry cleaning, on the west side of North College Street. He would press an API student's uniform while he waited. Foster's wife, Oelia, managed a grocery and beer tavern on Loachapoka Highway, decades later renamed Martin Luther King Drive. Ella White had a cafe on the same road. Mr. Mott had a fish market and ice house on College Street, just past the brow of the hill and about 150 yards north of Toomer's Corner. He brought a wagon load of ice from Opelika each week. Will Grant's cafe was near Mott's place. John Vickerstaff ran a grocery and a market at Drake and Frazier streets. Johnny Gus Frazier had a gocery and a soda fountain on Frazier Street. After Frazier and his wife died, Raymond Byrd operated both places and also a funeral home in the old Frazier house. Dewey Bedell recalled that Byrd used a horse-drawn hearse. Joe Frazier later had a funeral home on White Street and sold it in about 1960 to Peterson and Williams Funeral Home. Byrd's son John ran a barbecue and beer saloon on Loachapoka Highway. Brittain Drake had a grocery at 476 Opelika Road and his daughter Velma later ran the store. Her uncle Glenn Rudd had a car repair shop next door. Both buildings were still there in 1996.)

◀ Auburn's great punter, Fox Howe, kept Georgia Tech out of touchdown range during a scoreless tie on this rainy day at Grant Field in 1923. Despite the wet football, Howe regularly kicked 45 to 55 yards, and his first punt went 82. At least two players were without helmets on this play. Howe wore a shin guard on his left leg.

—Photo: AU Special Collections

103

World War I hero Robert Lee Bullard, third from left, Auburn's and Alabama's first lieutenant general, returned to campus in the 1920s. With him were, from left, Dr. Spright Dowell, API president, 1920-28; Dr. Clifford Le Roy Hare, dean of chemistry, 1930-48, and a teacher for fifty years, for whom the stadium is named; and Dr. John Hodges Drake, college physician for more than half a century.

Bullard was born in Russell County, Alabama, about two months before the Civil War started. He was named William Robert. In 1866, Bullard's home was included in a new county named for Robert E. Lee. "Sometime thereafter young William Robert asked his parents if he could change his name, too. He was baptized Robert Lee Bullard, 'Lee' to his family for the rest of his life," Allan R. Millett wrote in a biography of Bullard. Bullard attended A&M College in 1880-81, but out of money for schooling, he won an expenses-paid appointment and transferred to West Point.

—Photo: John C. Ball, Jr.

Zelda Sayre of Montgomery (photo circa 1919) dated several Auburn students during her stormy two-year courtship with novelist F. Scott Fitzgerald, including star halfback Francis Stubbs. She attended dances on campus and was an ROTC sponsor. Five football players formed a society in her honor, naming it Zeta Sigma. "Part of the ritual was a 'pledge of devotion' to her,'" historian Leah Atkins wrote. Zelda had a newspaper picture of Stubbs in her scrapbook.

Her biographer, Nancy Milford, wrote in 1970 that Stubbs remembered Zelda as "a very popular and beautiful young lady," but "not what is known as wild." She was "very much full of life and pep." So much so, an old Auburn story indicates, that at least once she "danced naked in the Pi Kappa Alpha lily pond." The biographer quoted Stubbs as saying his roommate had fallen in love with Zelda "and kept a life-size photograph of her in his room and thought he was going to marry her right up to the time she married Scott Fitzgerald" (From Zelda: a Biography by Nancy Milford; reprinted by permission of Harper & Row, Publishers, Inc.).
—Photo: Scottie Fitzgerald Smith

On October 1, 1918, nearly all of API's able-bodied male students eighteen or older voluntarily joined the United States Army for what turned out to be short-lived military careers on campus. The student-soldiers numbered 878, according to President Charles C. Thach, and formed the academic section of the Student Army Training Corps. The vocational section was composed of enlisted men sent to Auburn for training in radio, auto mechanics, and general mechanics. Both sections apparently were assembled on the drill field where Ross Square is today for the swearing-in of the student-soldiers. They heard brief patriotic talks from Thach and others. The students received honorable discharges in December following the Armistice that ended The Great War on November 11. Each received "a sixty-dollar bonus check from Uncle Sam," the Glomerata reported.
—Photo: AU Archives

▲ Agriculture students set out on an entomology trip to Opelika in 1918 or 1919. Class member Lyle Brown supplied the identifications. On the truck, left to right, top row: John Deramus, Brown, D. G. Sturkie, Duke Kimbrough, Reuben Johnson. Middle row: A. A. Lauderdale (wearing cap), Sidney Phillips, Clint Jacobs, "Parson" LeBron, G. C. Williams, two unidentified, Glenn Riddell (on top of cab). Bottom row: Herb Bonner, two unidentified, Eugene Maynor (hands between knees), two unidentified, R. L. Martin. Duck Samford was in the cab of the truck.

—Photo: AU Archives

◄ The number of coeds almost doubled in 1922 and totaled sixty-seven, helping lead to the chartering of the first API sorority, Kappa Delta. Original KD initiates were, left to right: Lysbeth Fullan, Kate Floyd, Camille Dowell, Anita Patterson, Emily Hare, Dorothy Anderson, and Lillian Sharpley. They were installed at the President's Mansion. One initiate, Camille Dowell, was the daughter of college President Spright Dowell. Later in the school year, a chapter of Chi Omega also was formed.

—Photo: Mary George Lamar

◄ With an enrollment of about thirteen-hundred students and no men's dormitories, emergency housing was necessary in the early 1920s. Tents, relics of World War I days, were set up outside Alumni Gymnasium. One-hundred beds filled the gym floor.

—Photo: AU Archives

◄ Arthur St. Charles Dunstan, head professor of electrical engineering 1899-1951, had his eye on the ball in this 1920s photograph at Auburn's second golf course, Beasley's pasture. Professors Charles H. Ross and Clifford L. Hare designed the first course at the bottom of the hill and to the south of East Magnolia. "After their enthusiasm lagged," Dean George Petrie recalled, "we transferred the course to the north side of the street . . . Here many an Auburnite got his first taste of the game, and the caddies learned to cry 'In the ditch! In the ditch!'" Perhaps Dunstan couldn't always find his golf ball, but he could find a needle in a garbage dump. He used his own electroscope. Working for medical facilities, Dunstan "tracked down between $60,000 and $70,000 worth of lost radium" before 1949, said Bill Feaster, professor emeritus of electrical engineering. He helped hospitals recover radium needles that had been lost or accidentally discarded. A piece of radium the size of a pinpoint was valued at more than $1,000 in those days. Dunstan spoke five languages fluently—French, German, Polish, Russian, and English. He was teaching himself Greek not long before he died in 1959. His department's many distinguished graduates included Ben S. Gilmer, president of AT&T, and Otis William Bynum, president of Carrier Corporation. "I never met a former student of his who didn't love and respect him," Feaster said.

—Photo: Lyle Brown

▶ *In the summer of 1923, Lieutenant Robert D. Knapp, later an Air Force general, became one of the first pilots to land near Auburn. While stationed at Maxwell Field, he accepted the invitation of his brother, Levi, Auburn postmaster, and set a trainer down in a pasture during a barbecue for World War I veterans. On a later flight to Auburn, he intended to circle low over the Post Office in a wartime bomber,*

the Dehavilland Four (like the one in this picture), then wave and fly back to Maxwell. But the engine failed about a mile from town. Knapp said the plane was in a dive and the speed enabled him to make a 180-degree turn and glide into a cotton patch west of town. The plane had to be trucked back to the base. The shaken but uninjured pilot and a passenger returned by car. Knapp was a combat flyer in World Wars I and II. His mother was pleased because the Wright brothers had told her great things about the future of aviation. But she gave her son this advice: "Fly low and fly slow, Robert."

—Photo: Brigadier General Robert D. Knapp

Alma Mater Song

*On the rolling plains of Dixie,
'Neath its sun-kissed sky,
Proudly stand, O. Alma Mater A.P.I.
To thy name we'll sing thy praise,
From hearts that love so true,
And pledge to thee our loyalty
The ages through.*

*Hail thy colors, Orange and Blue,
Unfurled unto the sky.
To thee, our Alma Mater, we'll be true,
O, A.P.I.*

*Hear thy student voices swelling,
Echos strong and clear,
Adding laurels to thy fame
Enshrined so dear.
From thy hallowed walls we'll part,
And bid thee sad adieu.
Thy sacred trust we'll bear with us
The ages through.*

*God our Father hear our prayer,
May Auburn never die.
To thee, O Alma Mater, we'll be true,
Our A.P.I.*

◀ *The API "Alma Mater Song," as it appeared in the 1925 Glomerata. The words were revised in 1960 when the school became Auburn University.*

—AU Special Collections

▲ *William T. "Bill" Wood, a band member for four years, wrote the API "Alma Mater" in 1924 during his senior year. The band's first capes were bought with $1,100 earned from a series of amateur shows that the Montgomery student directed and staged, the Plainsman said after Wood's death during the 1933 football season. In a ceremony in his memory, the band played the Alma Mater at Langdon Hall, where the students had gathered for a play-by-play report of the Auburn-Tulane football game. Wood is shown in 1924 in front of the Sigma Nu house.*

*—Photo: Glomerata;
AU Special Collections*

Agriculture majors on tractors and veterinary students with a wagon load of skeletons paraded through town on Ag Fair Day in 1924.

—Photos:
AU Special Collections

▶ *Led by the API band, half of the more than fourteen-hundred students and a good number of faculty members took the All-College Hike of 1924. They left Samford Hall early Saturday afternoon and, passing a parked car and wagon on the way, walked approximately one mile north of Auburn. There the games began, including a tug-of-war, pillow fights, a boxing match, and a coed football game. Then came a picnic supper, followed at dusk by fireworks.*
—Photo: AU Special Collections

Cows grazed in front of Comer Hall, probably in 1924. The inside of the building was only two years old that year, having been replaced after a fire gutted Comer in 1920. Nobody knew for sure what started the fire that early Sunday morning in October. Nearly sixty years later graduate Lyle Brown theorized that a still being used to make distilled water in an overnight lab experiment had been the cause. "In those days," he said, "it wasn't uncommon for the town water to be cut off. When that happened, of course, the still kept running and got so hot that it melted down and set the building afire."

Volunteers promptly laid a hose from town, but Phil Hardie, Cliff Hare's son-in-law, recalled that the water hose wasn't long enough to reach the fire. The rebuilt Comer looks much the same today, but the cow pasture lies mostly beneath an asphalt parking lot.

—Photo: AU Archives

▲ Eston Melton was Auburn's first licensed black plumber. "Dude Drake was a plumber before me, but nobody had to have a license then," Melton, ninety, said in 1996. Melton remembered beginning work in Auburn in 1925 pushing a wheelbarrow for twenty cents an hour in helping build Ramsay Hall. For about ten years he handled most of the plumbing and electrical work at API. He either did the work himself or supervised students who did it. He was one of the first employees that Director B. T. Simms hired at the USDA's Regional Animal Disease Lab in 1938. Melton later had his own plumbing company. His striped cap, cigar, and dependable work were widely known. He was a founder of Bell Missionary Baptist Church, driving the first nail in the original wooden building.

—Photo: Eston Melton

◀ Until the 1930s, South Gay Street ended just beyond the Samford Avenue intersection, blocked by a house owned by Alpha Cullars. Edward F. Cauthen and Leslie Wright, who owned property beyond the end of Gay, wanted the street extended. Cullars moved the house after Cauthen paid him eight-hundred dollars to buy brick for a new foundation and after Wright agreed to grade the proposed extension of Gay. This picture, taken from about the Virginia Avenue intersection, looks north on Gay after the deal had been completed. Note the water tower, which stood off Gay, south of Samford. When the street was opened, Levi Knapp's cotton patch at the end of South Gay Street was damaged. The Town Council voted in 1938 to pay him $15 damages.

—Photo: Maryline Cauthen Westenhaver

◀ Car trouble occurred frequently in the 1920s, and a raised hood often signaled a breakdown. Such was the case for Gladys Steadham and her fiance Glenn Stewart in this photo taken near her home on Opelika Road.

—Photo: Gladys Steadham Stewart

▶ Margaret "Cutie" Brown (holding ball) led the API women's basketball team to its third consecutive undefeated season in 1924. She ran, shot and dribbled well enough to have played on the men's varsity, a teammate later recalled. In fact, the women occasionally scrimmaged the men for fun and scored baskets even though they didn't win. The one referee at games with other women's teams tended to let the action get rough at Alumni Gym. But the Auburn women didn't wilt because they were strong from walking everywhere in an era of few cars on campus. From left, after Cutie Brown, were Margaret Lane, Marye Tamplin, Ethel Price, Ruby Powell, Elizabeth Young, Olive Gibbons, and their coach, ROTC Lieutenant R. D. Ingalls. API's first women's basketball team played in 1915, according to the Glomerata.

—Photo: Wilella Plant Ingalls

◀ A group of 4-H Clubbers gathered for a ceremony in the 1920s on the baseball field between Alumni Gym (in the background) and Samford Hall. The youths camped in the tents near the gym that male students had lived in during the school year because of a housing shortage. By the 1950s Auburn employees supervised more than one-hundred-thousand 4-H youths throughout the state.

—Photo: AU Archives

▲ *The WAPI Orchestra filled many hours for Auburn station listeners in the mid-1920s. Two 200-foot towers south of the campus also beamed weather, farm and market news, and lectures from Comer Hall. Most members of the orches-* *tra were students, but Sarah M. Tidmore was pianist, Mary D. Askew (third from left) violinist, and API Band Director Bedie Bidez (at Mrs. Askew's left) saxophonist. The station was started and operated by the Agricultural Extension* *Service to provide information and entertainment to farm families. Home demonstration agents organized listening parties.*

—Photo: John C. Ball, Jr.

◄ *A large stag line watched the dancing at Alumni Gym during one of the three big dance weekends in 1923-24. There weren't nearly enough coeds to go around. The* Plainsman *reported years later that out-of-town girls flocked to these dances.*

—Photo: AU Special Collections

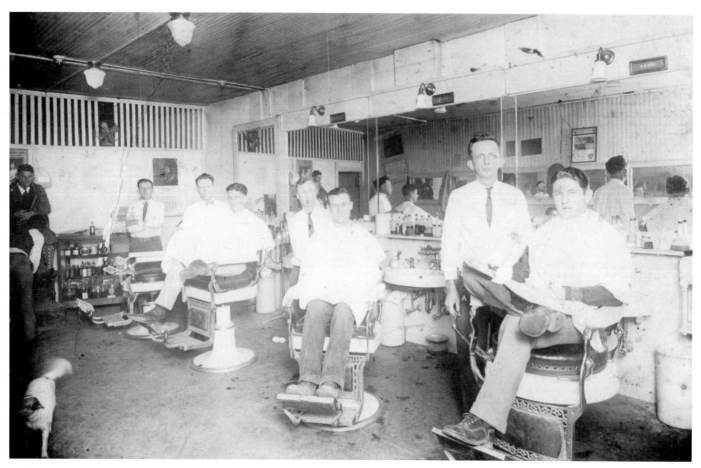

▲ *This barber shop in downtown Auburn two doors north of Lipscomb's Rexall Drug Store offered twenty-five-cent haircuts in 1926 and was a popular place for those needing to read a newspaper or while away some time in conversation. The barbers were, left to right, Judge Hill, Red Sanders, J. B. Richards, and E. E. Harmon. Beginning in 1922, Richards cut hair in Auburn for fifty-three years. Slim Stephens, another long-time barber, worked in this shop several years. For a period, the center of attraction was Hodge Drake, a black entrepreneur with a wooden leg who shined shoes, swept the floor, ran errands, and hustled tips. In a summer of the early thirties, the town's three barbershops got into a price war. "Haircuts were fifteen cents," William Hardie recalled. And one shop "cut it to ten cents. And then one day, one of 'em cut it to five cents. Haircuts for five cents!"*

—Photo: Mrs. J. B. Richards

◄ *Governor Bibb Graves inspected the ROTC unit on Governor's Day in the late 1920s at what is now Ross Square. At left was Alumni Gym. Graves also was on hand in 1930 for the dedication of Bullard Field, used for ROTC drill and intramural football and softball until five women's dorms were built there in 1952. The dedication honored former Auburn student and World War I hero Robert Lee Bullard. The field was also used for polo during the decade leading up to World War II when the Army had horsedrawn artillery units at API.*

—Photo: Leonard W. Thomas

This "A-Day" handshake symbolized a change of leadership at API in March 1928. Leaving to become president of Mercer University was Spright Dowell (right), Auburn president since 1920. Arriving was Bradford Knapp, Oklahoma A&M president, who served at the Auburn helm until 1932. Alumni and faculty members in the background, left to right: J. V. Brown, 1895; J. E. "Boozer" Pitts, 1915; F. R. Yarbrough, 1901, Atlanta; Dean George Petrie; Major J. T. Kennedy; coach G. M. Bohler. Dowell came under fire from students and alumni in 1927, which apparently helped lead to his resignation.
—Photo: Auburn Alumnus ;
AU Special Collections

▲ These houses stood across West Magnolia Avenue from Ramsay Hall before being replaced by Wendy's and McDonald's in the 1970s. At left was the S. L. Toomer home. Toomer's mother, Mrs. W. B. Lazarus, lived next door in a house that had been occupied in antebellum days by William Howe, a poet and newspaper editor.
—Photo: J. Andrew Douglas

▶ Wilbur Hutsell and Snitz Snider were Auburn's delegates to the 1928 Olympic Games at Amsterdam. Hutsell coached the winning 1,600-meter relay team, and Snider competed in the 400-meter run. Hutsell served as an Olympic coach three times and had four Olympic performers from Auburn. The others were Percy Beard, second in the 120-yard high hurdles in 1932; Whitey Overton, 1948 steeplechase; and Jim Dillion, third in the discus in 1952.
—Photo: AU Special Collections

Two 200-foot towers of Radio Station WAPI stood in 1928 in an area south of what is now the Samford Avenue-Donahue Drive intersection. Leonard B. Thomas, a student, climbed one of the towers to take the pictures seen here. Three of the pictures have been put together to form the top panel and two to form the bottom panel. To the left in the upper picture is Drake Field, the varsity football field then and located approximately where the upper Haley Center parking lot is today. The gully at left in the late 1930s became the site of Jordan-Hare Stadium. ROTC horses were stabled in the two buildings running north-south at lower left near where the Sports Arena is now. Perpendicular to the stables was the long shed housing field artillery pieces, caissons, and trucks. John C. Ball, Jr., retired assistant AU purchasing agent, recalled spending "many a night wrapped in a horse blanket" inside the little building in front of the gun shed. He slept there when his father, an Army sergeant with the ROTC detachment, had guard duty. The white sand road extended from the gun shed to Thach Avenue near Alumni Gym and the President's Mansion. Samford Hall is shown directly in front of the water tank that stood behind Toomer Drugstore. Bullard Field, in the middle of the picture, was the site for years for ROTC drill and parades, polo matches and intramural football and softball. To the right of Bullard are the Theta Chi and Sigma Nu houses. Shown directly behind the Sigma Nu house, but actually several blocks away is the Presbyterian Church. At right stands Comer Hall, with greenhouses and other agriculture buildings nearby.

In the picture below, the photographer aimed his camera to the east, down what now is Samford Avenue, and then to the southeast, catching part of the second radio

tower in his second shot. The barn at center
left stood in what became the front yard of
the President's Mansion when it was built in
1938. The prized bull was housed nearby.
The water tank behind the barn was off
South Gay Street. The narrow road at bottom left was an extension of Samford.
— Photos: Leonard W. Thomas
and H. C. Morgan, Jr.

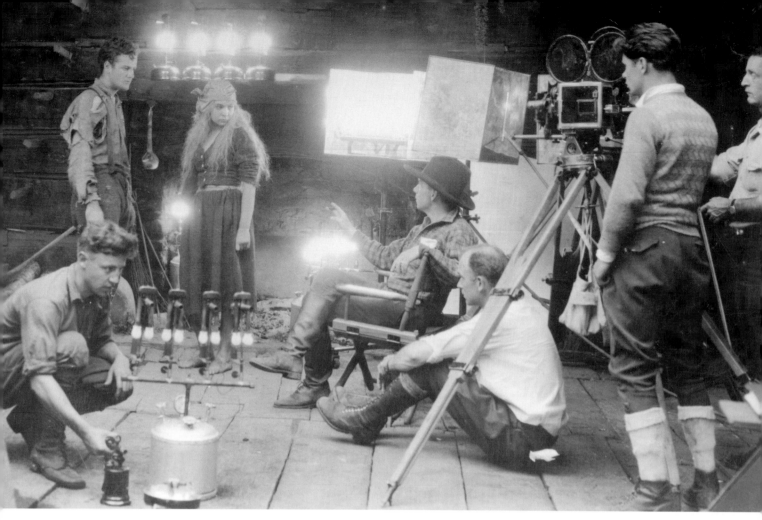

▲ *API athlete Forrest "Fob" James (standing at left) starred in the silent movie, "Stark Love," shown under production in 1927. Filmed in the North Carolina hills with a cast of mountaineers except for James and one or two others, "Stark Love" was called "a work of art" for its realism. When the picture played at Auburn, James was offered several hundred dollars to appear on stage, but he modestly declined. He had been recruited by movie scouts while the Auburn baseball team ate in a hotel dining room during a trip to Knoxville, Tenn.*

The curly-haired, blue-eyed James gave "an amazingly good performance," Photoplay magazine said. James later said he used the movie pay to help "Ebb [his brother] and me get through college, and we had a little left over." When his sons Fob, Jr., and Cal were growing up, they found still photographs in the attic taken from "Stark Love." Fob, Sr., warned that he would tell them only once about making the picture. Cal recalled in 1996 that his father had nearly drowned in a flood scene. He was barely able to save himself and co-star Helen Mundy, a high

school girl recruited for the picture, when a dammed-up mountain stream was turned loose. A mountain girl had been the first choice to play the role that Mundy played, but her hillbilly father denied parental consent, saying, "I'd see her dead an' in her coffin before I see her play actin' for nobody." Mundy later appeared in other movies, but Fob turned down a Paramount contract.

—Photo: Museum of Modern Art; Film Stills Archives, New York City

◄ *Within sight of Samford's clock tower, Auburn whipped Howard College, 25-6, on Drake Field in 1928, the Tigers' first football victory in seventeen games. A dark-jersied Auburn runner gained ground amid players who wore neither face masks nor chin straps and, in a few cases, went without helmets.*

—Photo: Leonard W. Thomas

◀ One of Auburn's winningest basketball teams, the 1927-28 edition, won twenty of twenty-two games, including three victories in the Southern Conference Tournament before losing to Ole Miss 32-31 in the championship game. Cliff "Jelly" Akin and Frank Dubose made All-Southern. Fob James, Sr., captained the team. Left to right, front row: coach Mike Papke, Buck Ellis, twins Fob and Ebb James, Akin, Moon Mullins, manager Elmer Salter. Back row: Al Smith, Louie James (brother of the twins), Dubose. Catcher Ebb James captained the 1928 baseball team that won Auburn's second consecutive conference title. Akin and Ellis were outfielders, and Fob James played first base.

—Photo: AU Athletic Department

▶ Cleveland Adams of Eufaula began his college career in 1928 with a full head of hair under his cap, a Birmingham News scholarship paying $500 a year, extra shoes, and an armload of books. The hair was soon to go as the male members of that freshman class became the last to be shorn en masse before President Bradford Knapp urged the practice be stopped. Adams survived the indignity, majored in textile engineering, and later headed that department. He served on the Auburn City Council, the Planning Commission, as a textile consultant in seventy-seven countries, and on the National Security Council.

—Photo: AU Special Collections

▲ The blue-caped API band walked onto Drake Field in 1928 for the Auburn-Howard football game to be played approximately where the upper Haley Center parking lot is now. A car nearly marked the spot where the War Eagle cage was later built. ROTC students drilled on the ground between the car and the two buildings at rear, the Theta Chi house (closest to camera) and the Sigma Nu House (across Mell Street).

—Photo: Leonard W. Thomas

119

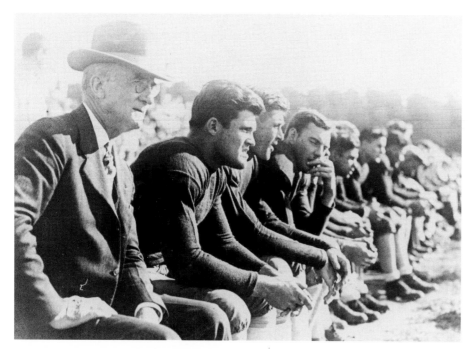

◀ *Auburn's new president, Bradford Knapp, sat on the team bench next to Carl L. Schlich as API beat Howard College 25-6 for its only football victory of 1928. Knapp's presidency didn't survive the critical dollar shortage of the Great Depression and opposition from presidential aspirant L. N. Duncan and the Extension Service, which Duncan headed, according to long-time Auburn Registrar Charles W. Edwards. Duncan became the leader of the experienced triumvirate that replaced Knapp. Years later, Travis Ingram, retired business manager and treasurer, said that Duncan had statewide clout through the Legislature and the Extension Service.*
—Photo: Leonard W. Thomas

▲ *One of the town's earliest fire trucks stood ready for action on East Magnolia Avenue in 1929 not far from the Toomer Building (at rear of truck). The fire station was in the open-fronted building behind the pickup truck. As late as 1922,* volunteers had fought house fires with bucket brigades. This truck helped upgrade Auburn's firefighting resources before being replaced by a later model.
—Photo: Leonard W. Thomas

A new Baptist Church building was under construction on East Glenn Avenue in 1928. Members of the Pastor's Helpers Sunday School Class inspected the progress. They are identified by John H. Jeffers in the Auburn First Baptist Church 1838-1988 as, left to right, front row: J. B. Jackson, unidentified, John T. Hudson, Pastor J. R. Edwards, W. D. Martin, C. E. Little, R. C. Neighbors. Back row: Clifton Jones, Dr. C. L. Boyd, Byron Jones, Professor Callan, Mr. Frisbie, Professor C. E. Cauthen, Mr. Pate, Mr. Kerr, Mr. Newton, two unidentified.
—Photo: Miss Leland Cooper

▲ More than one-thousand students and townspeople crowded around the depot for the arrival of humorist Will Rogers (right) in March 1928. His Kiwanis Club host, Army Captain B. Conn Anderson (left), enjoyed Will's witty, common sense talk that night at Alumni Gym, but Anderson recalled more than fifty years later that he was even more impressed with the compassion of the visitor. Anderson was there when Rogers gathered in his arms and patted on the back a little old lady who had stopped him on campus, saying, "Mr. Rogers, you're such a great man; I just wanted to touch you." And Anderson watched Rogers leave the dinner table to go shake hands with a man in a wheelchair on a truck, who had asked to meet him. Before making his speech at the gym, Rogers stopped outside and passed out dollar bills to students who didn't have the price of a ticket. After the performance, he bought hot dogs for students who kept him up till daybreak in conversation at a downtown diner.
—Photo: B. Conn Anderson

▲ *Farm men and women gathered in front of Langdon Hall in August 1929. The* Auburn Alumnus *said a record number attended Farmers' Week events "to get* practical information about their farm and home problems, and . . . get inspiration concerning a bigger and better rural life." *Nearly everyone wore a hat.* Attendance was promoted in the Digest, monthly publication of the Extension Service.

—*Photo: AU University Relations*

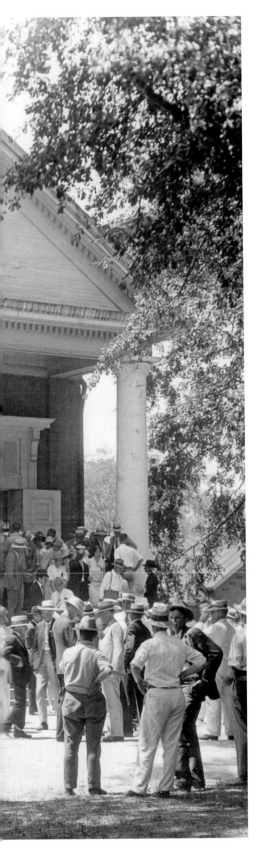

▲ *This "aeroplane" never got off the ground, but it carried Will Rogers in a parade through the middle of Auburn. Students mounted the wings and propeller on a stripped-down car, a flivver in those days, and Rogers rode in it behind the API band and a mounted escort from the local chapter of the national honorary* ROTC *society, Scabbard and Blade, from College Street to Magnolia Avenue, down Gay Street and back to College and the Thomas Hotel. Rogers stopped briefly at the hotel, then toured the town and campus to gather material for his humorous talk that night.*

—Photo: the Auburn Alumnus

▲ *This curb market in the heart of Auburn opened May 3, 1928, and sales to September 1 totaled $2,172, according to information written on the back of the picture. The market was on Magnolia Avenue by the side of the Bank of Auburn* Building at Toomer's Corner. Dr. Cecil S. Yarbrough, mayor of Auburn , and druggist Shel Toomer joined the crowd on this occasion. The picture was made by E. H. Green, Photographers, Auburn, Alabama.
—Photo: AU Archives

API students Alfonso Wright in about 1918 and Leonard W. Thomas in about 1929 climbed the water tank behind Toomer's Corner to record history, and they came up with strikingly similar pictures. The Wright picture, above, shows North Main Street in the foreground. A livery stable was in part of the wide building across the street to the right of Jones Hotel. Beyond the house next door was a cotton gin and then an open blacksmith shop. That puff of smoke in upper left is from a train. A fire on the west side of the street a few years later razed the livery stable, an ice house, a meat market and Grant's Cafe.

The Thomas picture, at right, illustrates the substantial construction in the area during the decade following World War I. At least sixteen structures had been built on West Glenn Avenue (center of picture), most of them private homes, but also at least two boarding and rooming houses, and near the intersection of Glenn and what by now had become College Street a gasoline station, auto shop, and three other businesses. Starting to the right of the Jones Hotel (hidden by trees) and going down the hill, storekeepers had replaced wooden structures, several of which had been destroyed by fire, with brick buildings still in use in the mid-nineties.

—Photo: George Alfonso Wright;
—Photo: Leonard W. Thomas
and H. C. Morgan, Jr.

A Maxwell Field pilot coming in from the west took dead aim and dived his plane at Samford Hall moments before this picture was taken in the 1930s. The water tower at upper left is just behind Toomer Drugstore. The class numeral "34" appears to be painted on the tank. To the left of the water tower at the edge of the picture is the Post Office opened in 1933 at Gay Street and Tichenor Avenue. The word "Auburn" is on the roof of the Toomer Building, painted as a guide to aviators. The building due west of Samford Hall is Alumni Gym, and that is a tennis court on the Thach Avenue side of the gym. Across the street is the

President's Home, later named the Social Center and finally Cater Hall. Up the hill on Thach is the library, surrounded on three sides by homes of faculty members. On the south side of Magnolia Avenue are the recently completed Textile Engineering Building and Ramsay and Broun halls. The first house across the street from Ramsay is the S. L. Toomer home, with a pasture on the downhill side. For several years, cows in that pasture provided the milk that went into ice cream sold at Toomer Drugstore.

Up the hill are three more homes, the most distant that of Dr. and Mrs.

Fred Allison, then a tennis court, and the Lambda Chi Alpha house. By the 1980s, Wendy's Hamburgers, McDonald's, and Anders Bookstore stood side-by-side downhill from the Allison home, which years later became the home of Chi Alpha Campus Ministries. The fraternity house became Anders Bookstore and eventually Magnolia Place, which had several shops and apartments.

Find the intersection of Thach Avenue and Gay Street and you'll see the stately Presbyterian Church with its many columns before it was torn down and rebuilt. Just beyond, on the oppo-

site side of Thach Avenue is the roof of the original Wittel Dorm, opened in 1931. Dave Wittel sold the dorm to the college in 1946, and it became Auburn Hall. But Wittel Dorm lived on. The name was given to a brick structure that Wittel had built on Gay Street at the corner of Thach. It was managed into the 1980s by a son, W. David Wittel. The Andy Pick family acquired Auburn Hall at auction from the University and after renovation opened it in 1983 as student housing with fifty-three modern apartments.

—Photo: AU Archives

Chapter 5

HARD TIMES

*T*he Great Depression emptied pocketbooks and lowered standards of living in Auburn. Faculty members underwent pay cuts in the falls of 1932 and 1933, and for four school years beginning in 1932-33 received only 45, 66 2/3, 85, and an estimated 60 percent of their reduced salaries. An instructor making $1,800 a year before the first reduction could have expected to earn $7,200 over four years. Instead, he probably was paid about $3,000 less than that, based on figures in the *Auburn Alumnus* and in API's financial records. In effect, he worked more than one and one-half years for nothing. "For the period of October 1, 1932 to April 30, 1936 our faculty has earned $515,238.80 which it did not and perhaps never will receive," President L. N. Duncan wrote.

▲ *Pallbearers carried the casket into Langdon Hall where the funeral was held for the "grand old dean of chemistry," Bennett Battle Ross, in April 1930. Ross served as API's acting president in 1920 and 1925. The members of the chemistry faculty were active pallbearers. They included Ross' successor as dean, Clifford Le Roy Hare, the gray-haired man at left. On the viewer's side of the coffin, third from left, was Roger W. Allen, who became dean of science and literature. The second man behind Allen was Carl Rehling, later state toxicologist. After the funeral, students, faculty members, and others, including Governor Bibb Graves, walked in the procession to Pine Hill Cemetery.*
—Photo: AU Archives

The college received about $1.4 million in warrants from the state that for a long time amounted to uncashable checks, said W. T. Ingram, who retired as business manager in 1973 after forty-eight years of AU service. To pay even the reduced salaries, API was forced to issue, along with scarce cash, certificates of indebtedness called scrip, sometimes negotiable with difficulty even at discount.

"Most of the merchants took it because they felt that scrip was better than nothing, but some wouldn't accept it," Ingram told Owen Davis of the *Auburn Bulletin*. "The college didn't particularly lose employees, but it didn't hire any new ones. The depression was nationwide, and there wasn't any place for faculty members to go."

"The college owed everybody," not just its faculty and staff, Ingram said, pointing out that API nearly ended the fiscal year in the hole on June 30, 1932. "The college account was a little below $6,000," he said, "and there was an overdraft on those funds. Only federal money from the Extension Service and Experiment Station let the college escape a deficit."

Ingram later said that Duncan, then director of the Alabama Cooperative Extension Service, didn't like President Knapp's diverting Extension money to API's general fund. This temporary—but probably illegal—transfer of funds was the "key issue" that ended Knapp's presidency, said a former long-time API official, Charles W. Edwards, a Duncan critic. "Bradford was trying to take care of the teachers, you see, and that brought him at issue with the Extension Service; and it didn't help Knapp."

Everyone tightened belts. Once a driver of a meat truck refused to leave a delivery at the kitchen of Smith Hall because he had been instructed to make only cash sales. Consulted about the problem, Ingram told the butcher to take back the meat; the college didn't have the money to pay for it. In 1932, API had to quit providing medicine for ill students. The year before, juniors and seniors in pharmacy had compounded 1,860 prescriptions. On campus, buildings went unrepaired, supplies went unbought, and obsolete equipment served a declining enrollment.

People spent money mostly on necessities, such as food, housing, and medicine. Few bought new clothes. Many walked more. Faculty wives wore darned stockings. Caroline Draughon, whose husband, Ralph, was a young history teacher in the early 1930s, later told reporter Judith Nunn that her family sold its little Ford car to pay the physician who delivered their infant daughter. One professor

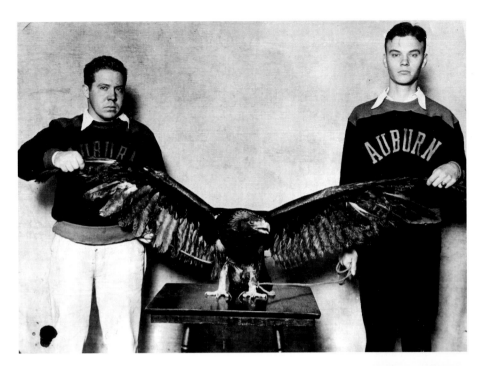

◄ *Auburn's great football cry, War Eagle, took on feathered form in 1930 when this golden eagle was found on a farm near Auburn entangled in thick pea vines. Bought for ten dollars by local businessmen, the eagle was turned over to the A-Club. Cheerleaders DeWitt Stier (left) and Harry "Happy" Davis, later executive secretary of the Alumni Association, helped care for the new mascot, which quickly proved a good omen. Auburn hadn't beaten a Southern Conference football foe in four seasons until the eagle attended the 25-7 victory over South Carolina at Columbia in the last game of 1930.*

—Photo: the Auburn Alumnews

cashed in his life insurance to tide his family over the hard times. More people planted gardens.

When there was no money to meet the API payroll, a laborer in the School of Agriculture later said, "We could get milk from the college dairy and vegetables and fruit from the garden and orchards, so we didn't go hungry." The best-off college employees, though, were Extension, Experiment Station, and ROTC workers on the federal payroll. Their deposits helped both Auburn banks survive the Depression when thousands of others failed, a local bank executive of that era said later.

Several Auburn merchants earned the gratitude of broke customers for extending credit beyond the bounds of safe business practices. "If it hadn't been for Mr. John Turner Hudson, we would have gone hungry," said Mrs. Roger W. Allen, whose husband was a chemistry professor during the Depression and later dean of the School of Science and Literature. When the money crisis finally eased, Hudson had an uncollected $16,000 on his books, and he owed wholesale grocers about the same amount. Many customers repaid every penny when they finally got the money. Others bought new cars but never paid their grocery bills.

William MacD. Moore's meat market went into the red $12,000 and out of business trying to help people through the bad times. Other merchants, including Clifton Jones, also took risks giving credit. Money worries during the Depression helped cause a fatal heart attack for C. J. Young, the operator of a laundry and dry cleaning establishment, according to his daughter, Mrs. L. L. Johnson. Times were hard, indeed.

Yet, many Auburnites later reckoned that the miseries of the 1930s were made more endurable by the knowledge that most other people didn't have much money either, and

▲ *These Auburn women paused in 1930 to look back on their business careers. They were left to right: M. A. "Allie" Glenn, API treasurer for forty-seven years before her death in 1953; Mildred McElhaney, clerk at Burton's Book Store; Wilhelmina B. Lazarus, former boardinghouse operator and mother of druggist Shel Toomer; and Emma Smith, former switchboard operator and manager of the town's first telephone exchange. The women were at Mrs. Lazarus' home on West Magnolia Avenue.*

—Photo: Elizabeth Glenn Smith Wilder

▲ Susie Grant (pictured in 1930) and her husband Will, a Negro couple, ran a cafe downtown in the 1920s and early 1930s. They got up at 4 a.m. to cook breakfast for early customers, and they kept working until they closed at 10 p.m. Mrs. Grant recalled in 1979 that they often served greens, peas, stew meat, and the like to porters and other workers. Their cafe burned in a major fire of the early 1930s, along with other businesses on the west side of North College Street from about the top of the hill north to Glenn Avenue. Included were a fish market, a hat shop, a meat market, a pool room, and a livery stable.

—Photo: Susie Grant

▲ Brittain Drake, right, is shown in his store at 476 Opelika Road in the late 1930s or early forties. His son-in-law, Dewey Bedell, center, clerked there for years, and Bedell's wife, Drake's daughter Velma, later ran the store. The other person is unidentified. Bedell laid brick for the quadrangle dorms on campus and the walkway connecting the dorms. He helped build the foundation for part of

Cliff Hare Stadium and laid brick for the walk and fishpond at the President's Home. He helped build two fraternity houses across College Street from the present Draughon Library site and laid brick for the Bulletin/Eagle building on Tichenor Avenue. Bedell believes he was the first black person to serve on the city Board of Zoning Adjustment.

—Photo: Dewey Bedell

► Auburn Camp Fire Girls gathered at their bus in front of the Thomas Hotel before leaving for Pine Needles Camp at Fairhope in May 1930. One of the campers, Tiny Shi Brownfield, many years later identified the group. Left to right, standing beside the bus: driver Papa Weed and Elizabeth Allison. Seated on the ground: John Scott, Jr., Charles Hixon, Jr., Amy Drake, Hazel Avery, Libba Duncan (leader), Eleanor Lewis, Kay Kennedy, Suzelle Hare, Betty Showalter, Emily Hixon, Virginia Dudley, Tiny Knapp, Frances Smyer in front of Helen Funchess, Ernestine Hill, Frances Wright,

Tiny Shi in front of Sarah Price at right, Virginia Yarbrough, Dot Brewer, Madeline Breedlove. In the bus: Marie Sewell (chaperone), Hulda Rutland, Jule Tisdale, Mary Lydia Williamson, Marjorie King, Eleanor Scott, Louise Shubert, Carolyn Jones, Frances Wilson, Margaret Bain, Doris Chritzburg, Sylvia Shuptrine, Helen Gardiner, Heslope Ham, Bit Mitchell, Elizabeth Wright. Other chaperones were Mrs. L. N. Duncan, Mrs. J. W. Wright, and Mrs. John Scott. Auburn's first Girl Scout meeting was in 1932.

—Photo: Ann B. Pearson

◄ *Glenn Stewart's Shell gasoline station seemed to reflect the business woes of 1933. Stewart stood near a pump with no customers in view. His wife, Gladys, was approaching from the left. Regular gasoline sold for about 20.5 cents a gallon in the 1930s, approximately one-third less than the 30 cents cost of the 1920s. Stewart's station was some fifty yards north of the railroad track on Gay Street. Auburn's first gas pump was installed in front of Homer Wright's drugstore on North College Street in 1909.*
—Photo: Gladys Steadham Stewart

the money that folks did have went a long way. A ham sandwich and a milkshake cost only ten cents each at Benson's Confectionery near Toomer's Corner. A&P coffee sold for seventeen cents a pound and regular gasoline for about twenty cents a gallon. A morale booster in 1937 was the Lee County High School football team, which lost only to a Columbus, Georgia, team, and won the East Alabama championship. The team played home games on API's Drake Field.

In addition to the Depression, Negroes, legally and through custom, endured racial segregation. In the 1920s, 1930s, and 1940s, most apparently accepted it but found it burdensome. "In the twenties, it was pretty tough," an elderly black man recalled. At a white boardinghouse, which probably had a respected black cook, he was fed outside the back door. "You didn't go into a white eating place except to work. You could get a drink at Toomer Drugstore and carry it out, but you couldn't sit and drink it." The system prevailed into the 1960s. "In all those rough times," the man said, "I knowed what to do," meaning he was subservient to whites. He also was skilled at his trade. "I got along with white folks as good as I got along with the colored. There's where I got all my work—from white folks."

An elderly woman said, "We could walk into a store and stand there forever until someone waited on us." If a black woman had to use the bathroom downtown, she had to walk to the train depot, she recalled. Overcoming such indignities, the woman earned bachelor's and master's degrees and taught school—eventually to desegregated classes. She said she loved Auburn. But she couldn't attend API.

Negroes found pleasure in their social lives. They attended church services and church socials, had guests in their homes for meals of vegetables from their gardens and maybe homegrown chicken, and enjoyed dances at the school, one elderly black woman recalled. Some people went to juke joints. Baseball was popular on warm Saturday afternoons. At least a few big-time musicians performed in or near Auburn, including Cab Calloway, probably in the late 1930s or early 1940s.

▲ Percy Beard of Greensboro, captain of the 1929 Auburn track team, later established world records in the 100-meter and 120-yard hurdles six times and won three outdoor and four indoor National AAU hurdles championships. He finished second in the 100-meter event at the 1932 Olympics in Los Angeles and probably would have won but hit the sixth hurdle while in the lead. Beard, coaches Wilbur Hutsell and Mel Rosen, and 1927 NCAA and AAU hurdles champion Weems Baskin were members of the National Track and Field Hall of Fame. Beard served as track coach at the University of Florida for many years. His brother was Jeff Beard, Auburn athletic director in 1951-72.
—Photo: AU Athletic Department

▲ Workmen began preparing this hollow in 1934, during the Depression, to build Auburn Stadium, but federal work-relief money dried up for the project until 1938. The first 7,500 seats, at the bottom of today's lower west stands, were completed in 1939. In the first game in the stadium, Dick McGowen threw a touchdown pass to Babe McGehee, and McGowen kicked the extra point as Auburn tied Florida 7-7 on November 30, 1939. By 1987, the stadium was named Jordan-Hare Stadium and seated 85,214. Missing from the photograph, besides the stadium, are Petrie Hall, the modern pharmacy building, Thach and Tichenor Halls, and Haley Center. At top left is the old veterinary building, later to become the serum plant. At right are Alumni Gym, Ross Hall, and Samford Hall.
—Photo: AU Archives

Many of API's 1,777 to 2,477 male students enrolled during 1931-32 and 1932-33 managed to accumulate the price of tickets for the Sophomore Hop in October, the Junior Prom in January, and the Senior Dance in May. The 250 women students were not nearly enough to go around, so dates also arrived by train from colleges as far away as Virginia, Louisiana, and Kentucky. The couples danced at the Alumni Gym in the 1930s to the big band music of Wayne King, Hal Kemp, Kay Kyser, and Ted Weems. A talented student orchestra, the Auburn Knights, won favor not only at API dances, but also with collegians in neighboring states.

One alumnus recalled the aftermath of a drinking party held near the end of the Prohibition era. A fraternity man who had put himself to sleep with bootleg whiskey woke up the next morning facing a wall two inches away. When he opened his eyes and saw only dull gray, he panicked and screamed that the moonshine had blinded him. His amused roommates turned him away from the wall, and his sight was restored. In 1937, four years after the nation had revoked the "noble experiment," Lee and 24 other Alabama counties voted wet. Auburn approved repeal by 115 votes. In a *Plainsman* poll, 295 students favored the legal sale of liquor, and 73 opposed it. Most didn't vote.

Neil O. Davis, 1934-35 *Plainsman* editor, and his former journalism instructor, Joseph Roop, founded the *Lee County Bulletin* in 1937. It became the town's first newspaper since the nineteenth century to achieve stability, except for student publications. Under Davis, the *Bulletin* (later renamed the *Auburn Bulletin*) became an award-winning newspaper, known for its accurate reporting, its Democratic editorial views, its courage in taking the unpopular side of racial issues, and its championing of the poor and defenseless.

Discouraged by the Depression and under criticism, Knapp resigned in 1932. Knapp was thwarted by API's

▲ These Hughes sisters were in the first graduating class of the Lee County Training School in May 1932. Shown at the Auburn Conference Center in 1995 during the third reunion of LCHS alumni are, left to right, Miss Juanita Hughes, 81, of Auburn, Mrs. Sally H. White, 82, of Chicago, and Mrs. Susie Hughes Giddens, 80, of Auburn. Mrs. Giddens was valedictorian of her class, and her husband to be, Darnell Giddens, was salutatorian. He attended Tuskegee Institute, for many years was postman for the Quad Dorms at API, and was an amateur landscape painter of note. Miss Hughes was the first special diets cook for East Alabama Medical Center at Opelika, and Mrs. Giddens was still working as a domestic in Auburn in 1996.

▲ *Alabama Governor B. M. Miller (left) presents honorary doctor of laws degrees in 1934 to the triumvirate who ran the college during two and one-half of the worst years of the Depression. Receiving the trustee-awarded honors were, left to right, John J. Wilmore, dean of engineering; L. N. Duncan, director of the Extension Service; and B. H. Crenshaw, head of mathematics. When President Knapp resigned in 1932, the trustees decided against naming another president because of the critical money shortage and the controversy over a successor.*
—Photo: AU Archives

▲ *Caroline Drake Samford, age eighty-nine, wife of the late Alabama Governor William J. Samford—for whom Samford Hall was named—played two pieces at the Auburn Centennial Banquet in April 1936. She had played the same pieces near the same spot in concert seventy-five years earlier. Hers had been the first big wedding in Auburn after the Civil War.*
—Photo: Carrie Samford Giles

financial troubles, and "he couldn't manage the Extension Service like he wanted to," recalled W. T. Ingram, business manager and treasurer emeritus. Some trustees sided with Extension people in wanting to name Duncan president, but other trustees, led by Publisher Victor Hanson of the *Birmingham News,* urged broadening the search. Duncan didn't press for the presidency at that time "because he was waiting for Governor [Bibb] Graves to get back in office," Ingram said. Duncan "hit it off" with Graves and "felt like Graves would be on his side." The trustees compromised by appointing a three-member administrative committee with about "140 years combined experience at Auburn": Dean John J. Wilmore of engineering; B. H. Crenshaw, head of mathematics; and Duncan. "None of 'em were afraid," Ingram said. He felt that the men did a "real good" job of guiding the college through the next two and one-half stressful years. They all said pretty much what they thought, "but they all looked to Dr. Duncan for leadership," Ingram said. They recognized that he was more politically connected statewide through the Legislature and the Extension Service. In Ingram's view, Duncan was a kind of behind-the-scenes president. Then Graves was inaugurated governor on January 14, 1935. One month and eight days later, Duncan officially became API's ninth president.

The year after Duncan, at fifty-nine, began his twelve-year presidency, the Southern Association of Colleges and Secondary Schools placed Auburn on probation until full salaries were resumed for faculty members and per-student expenditures were increased. API had hit bottom, and there "wasn't much way for it to go except up," said Ingram,

retired business manager. "But at the same time, I think it took a lot of courage [for Duncan] to get it done." Historians Malcolm McMillan and Allen Jones wrote, "Faced as president with an indebtedness of over one million dollars in a continuing depression, a disgruntled faculty and staff, and growing pressure for physical expansion, Dr. Duncan rallied political support in the state and exploited every possible financial program of the New Deal." Before Duncan died in 1947, API had paid off its bonded indebtedness. In competing for state funds, Duncan used agriculture people and the University of Alabama's president used lawyers as their power blocks, another source indicated. When the college, under Duncan's leadership, was taken off probation in 1938, the Depression had loosened its grip on Auburn.

Duncan headed one of API's biggest expansions in 1938-40, taking advantage of federal programs to erect fourteen buildings and build a 7,500-seat stadium. Drake Infirmary, the President's Home, the Women's Quadrangle, and Petrie, Tichenor, and Cary halls were part of this construction. President Franklin D. Roosevelt visited the campus in March 1939, addressing townspeople, faculty members, and students at Bullard Field (where Dorms 5 through 10 are now). His wife, Eleanor, spoke briefly on campus the following September.

Auburn's economic revival coincided with growing alarm over Hitler's threat to world safety. Many ROTC cadets who had heard FDR's Auburn speech would fight in World War II against the Germans, Italians, and Japanese. ∾

These were the first two API students to own airplanes, the *Auburn Alumnus* reported in 1931. James W. Boyd (left) of Auburn and Jesse F. Stallings of Birmingham already had landed in their share of cow pastures before enrolling in Auburn's new aeronautical engineering program. They stood near Boyd's 180-horsepower Air-Bos biplane, manufactured in Birmingham.
—Photo: AU Special Collections

◄ Solon Dixon (left) of the Mechanical Engineering Department became in 1929 one of the first API professors to own an airplane. With him in this 1930 snapshot was student Tom Pyke. A half century later, Dixon, a 1926 API graduate, and his wife gave to Auburn the 3,500-acre Dixon homeplace in Covington and Escambia counties and $500,000 for construction of a forestry education center near Andalusia. It was the largest donation to the University up to that time by living persons.
—Photo: Mrs. Solon Dixon

Grocer John Turner Hudson, left, opposite page, and butchers Jack Tamblyn, left below, and his partner, William MacD. Moore, were among the merchants who helped many Auburn residents survive the Great Depression. When the college stopped paying faculty salaries, the Lee County Bulletin wrote, Tamblyn and Moore "kept meat on many a professor's table, extending credit of several hundred dollars to individual residents." Their generosity proved financially disastrous, and the meat market finally went out of business. Hudson, shown with clerk John King, center, and student-clerk Billy Hill, managed to stay afloat, largely because ROTC instructors and others on the federal payroll were able to pay cash for their groceries.
—Photos, circa 1926: Clark Hudson;
Dr. and Mrs. J. W. Tamblyn

▶ The Fire Station and City Hall were located in this building just south of the Post Office on Gay Street in the 1930s. City Hall in those days was a little larger than a double garage. The Fire Department consisted of four college students who worked for ten dollars a month and an unfurnished room. When a fire broke out, the first student to arrive at the station drove the truck to the fire. The others climbed aboard en route or got to the scene as best they could. At left was the home of Arthur St. Charles Dunstan, head of API's Electrical Engineering Department for more than half a century.

—Photo: AU Archives

▲ This model A was the first student car to be registered on campus, and it was assigned tag No. 1 in 1938. Its owner, one of a lucky few students with a car in those days, paid a registration fee of fifty cents. In 1994-95, students paid fifteen dollars a year for campus automobile registration, and they registered 13,794 of them. They also bought tags for 296 motorcycles and 1,766 bicycles. Faculty, staff, and emeritus faculty members registered 5,282 cars at a cost of thirty dollars for most, but fifteen dollars for those of retirees and some staff members. The University issued 62,000 tickets for parking violations to students, faculty, and staff members during the year. That was almost six tickets for each of the 10,600 parking spaces on campus.

—Photo: AU Archives

▼ More than 625 freshmen began the ODK Cake Race in 1937, and almost 600 finished. Those with medical excuses weren't required to run the 2.7-mile race. Dropouts along the way were supposed to be turned over to the A-Club's hazing committee. Herbert Drake ran the race in record time and won a huge white cake, and a freshman numeral. The next 24 finishers received smaller cakes. Coach Wilbur Hutsell originated this campus tradition in 1929 to help find talent for the varsity track team. The event was renamed the Wilbur Hutsell-ODK Cake Race in the early 1940s. Winners found that kissing Miss Auburn put the icing on the cake.

—Photo: AU Special Collections

▶ Camaraderie flourished aboard this passenger train, a War Eagle Special taking Auburn fans to Atlanta for the 1939 Georgia Tech football game. Elizabeth "Lib" Harwell and husband-to-be Jack Dunlop, a Delta Sigma Phi fraternity member, are the first couple seated at left. They later were longtime operators of Dunlop & Harwell real estate in Auburn. Other Delta Sigs in the coach include Freddie Bass, foreground, with a hand on his chin; Bert Simpson, sitting on the arm of a seat and facing the Dunlops; and Roger Hamil, to the left rear of Simpson with his hand on his hat. Riding a War Eagle Special to a game in Birmingham or Atlanta: It didn't get much better than that!

—Photo: AU Archives

▶ *A train meant smoke and whistle and steam pulling into Auburn from the nineteenth century until the diesels took over, and finally the passenger train era ended with a 1970 trip of the Crescent Limited. The train meant people and noise . . . mail and pranks . . . maybe even a girl friend aboard for the big dance. It meant coming to college and going home.*

Welcoming the football team back from a road game had become a tradition long before this picture was made in about 1937. Old trainmen didn't forget when students greased the tracks and forced a locomotive to spin its wheels. Or the time in 1916 and perhaps again later when a circus operator offended the cadets with his high-priced and low-grade show near the depot. During the ensuing melee, cadets attached a long rope from the circus tent to a train that stopped to pick up mail. When the engineer got away on schedule, "down came the tent, headed full steam for Opelika and points east."

—Photo: AU Special Collections

▲ *Horse-drawn artillery enlivened ROTC drills on Bullard Field in the 1930s. Horses had been a part of military training at least from the spring of 1921, when* *fifty-three steeds arrived from Oklahoma and silenced a standing joke about Auburn's horseless artillery unit.*

—Photo: AU Archives

▲ *As far back as 1921, the* Orange & Blue *reported that coeds enjoyed the ladies' riding class sponsored by the Military Department. Several were delayed in riding, however, until they had bought or sewn the regulation riding habit required by the dean of women. A* number of townswomen also joined the class. This photo of Emily Hixon was taken by her father, perhaps in 1935. In the background are the stable and gunshed for the horses and equipment of the Army ROTC field artillery unit.
—Photo: Emily Hixon Gunter

▲ *These eleven agriculture students bought identical 1939 Ford Deluxe Tudor Sedans for $700 each when they graduated from API. Salesman Joseph B. Sarver, Jr., later executive secretary of the Auburn Alumni Association for more than 25 years, arranged for delivery at* the Atlanta Ford plant as soon as the buyers had jobs with which to make the payments. When he sold the cars, Sarver was working for Anderson Blackburn, who in about 1930 began managing Auburn's first Ford agency. Sam Teague, later an Auburn city councilman, also worked briefly as a salesman for Blackburn. Blackburn was called "coach" by the football players, and he let them borrow used and demonstrator cars for dates in the 1930s.
—Photo:
Mr. and Mrs. Joseph B. Sarver, Jr.

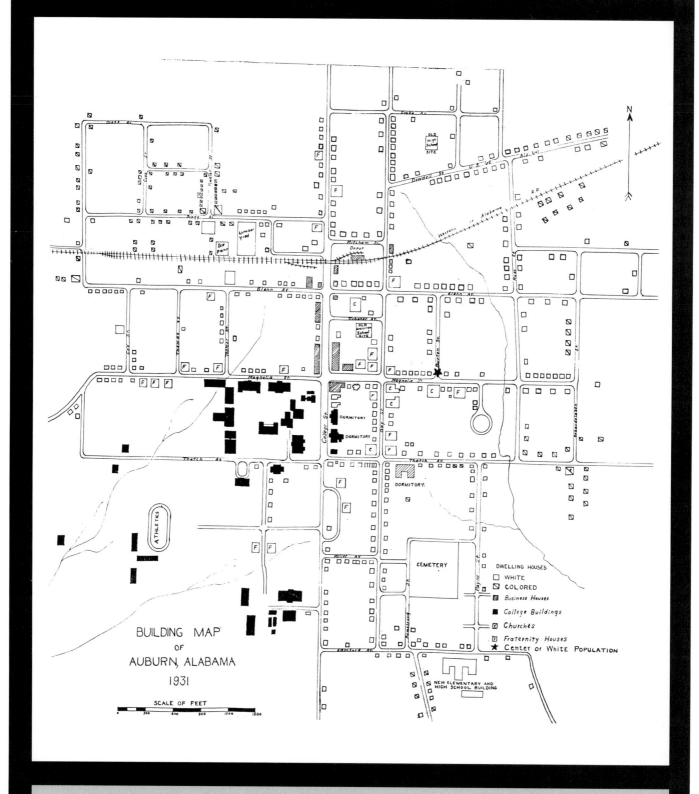

BUILDING MAP
OF
AUBURN, ALABAMA
1931

SCALE OF FEET

DWELLING HOUSES
WHITE
COLORED
Business Houses
College Buildings
Churches
Fraternity Houses
★ Center of White Population

▲ *This map was drawn to show all dwelling houses, business houses, college buildings, churches, fraternity houses, and dormitories in Auburn in 1931. It includes 396 homes of whites and 101 homes of colored.*

Churches identified include only Ebenezer Missionary Baptist and First Presbyterian on Thach Avenue, United Methodist and St. Michael's Catholic on Magnolia, and First Baptist on Glenn. St. Dunstan's

Episcopal is shown on Magnolia, but not identified as a church.

—Map: Leonard W. Thomas and H. C. Morgan, Jr.; enhancement by George Adams

▲ *This group turned out for the Rotary Club's luncheon at the Thomas Hotel in 1937 to honor children of the members. Left to right, front row: Sister High, James High, unidentified, Sammy Hay, Paul Lowery, Margaret Toomer, Charles Hixon, Carlyle Burkhardt, Beverly Ann Burkhardt, Martha Hay, Charles R. Hixon. Second row: unidentified, S. L. Toomer, Fred Allison, Elwood Burkhardt, Shel Toomer, Jr., Albert Thomas, Herbert Martin, Clark Hudson, Kathleen Johnson, John Bruce Martin, John Turner Hudson. Third row: Buck Young, Martha North Watson, Paul Duggar, Frank Duggar, Wilbur Hutsell, J. M. Robinson. Fourth row: Sam Burney Hay, J. R. Rutland, Dryden Baughman, John Turner Hudson, Sr., B. C. Pope, Jr., Billy Martin, Jr. Fifth Row: Albert Thomas, J. W. Watson, Melton Fuller, John R. Moore, E. W. Burkhardt, J. F. Duggar, B. C. Pope, Sr., Roberts Brown, unidentified, I. S. McAdory, W. D. Martin, Sr., J. C. Lowery.*

—Photo: Clark Hudson

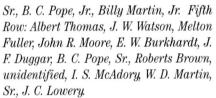

◄ *Enjoying a tea at Mrs. Robert Partin's home on Payne Street in April 1937 were, left to right, Mrs. C. A. Basore, Mrs. A. W. Reynolds, Mrs. Partin, and Mrs. B. B. Ross.*

—Photo: Annie Terrell Basore

▲ Auburn schools have included such teaching legends as Frances Duggar, Mrs. H. M. Lane, Mrs. Glenn Bradley, Frances Trammell, and Lucille Rhodes and such principals as 'Fessor J. A. Parrish, O. B. Hodges, and James B. Douglas. Miss Duggar went without during the Depression to provide chalk, crayons, and poster boards for her children. Miss Rhodes is remembered by those in her classes as the best English teacher a student could have had.

Miss Duggar is shown with her first grade class of 1935-36. Left to right, front row: Mike Meagher, Lynwood Story, Billy Doster, two unidentified, Clarice Manning, Myrtle Elsie Barnes, Darby Dick, Jack Trussell, John Lowery, Reid Lingerfelt, Garvin Cannon, Shay Tidmore. Second row: Carolyn Ellis, Levi Knapp, Buddy Moring, James High, unidentified, John Oliver, Spud Wright, Jenny Pittman, Ted Sargent, Billy Ward, unidentified, Gene Hurt.

Third row: unidentified, Guy Handley, Stanley Fincher, Mary Scarseth, Jeanne Ann Hill, Yvonne Cargile, Sister High. Fourth row: Glenn Marsh, Patty Lou Reeves, two unidentified. Standing: unidentified, James Patterson, Lula Hudmon, Patsy Allen, James Hudson Edwards, unidentified, Lester Teel, Frances Duggar.

—Photo: Carolyn Ellis Lipscomb

◄ "The world's largest bottle" was built five miles north of Toomer's Corner in 1924. It was at the intersection where the extension of College Street (Lee County Road 147) runs into U.S. Highway 280. Painted bright orange, the structure was sixty-four feet tall and forty-nine feet around at its base. It was shaped like a Nehi drink bottle and was a combination home, grocery, and service station. Visitors could see miles of countryside from windows in the neck and from the bottle cap, an observation tower. Although fire destroyed the structure in 1933, decades later the intersection was still called The Bottle.

—Photo: the Auburn Alumnews

▲ A Tom Thumb Wedding sponsored by the Auburn Service Club was presented in Langdon Hall in May 1937. Members of the cast in the picture were, left to right, first row: Billy Adkins, Elna Culver, Patsy Peters (flower girl), Sidney Fuller (groom), Marylyn Bailey (bride), James High (minister), Jeanetta Ware (maid of honor), Sammy Hay. Second row: Lucille High (Queen Mary), Mary Frances Grimes, Lamar Ellis, Evans Young, June Bryant (bridesmaid), Nancy Peters (bridesmaid), Godfrey Bennett (grooms-man), Bettye Brackeen, Mary Beth Robinson (bridesmaid). Third row: Carolyn Ellis, Betty Jean Moreman, Patty Lou Reeves, Louise Young, Anna Louise Fretwell, Mary Jo Reed (Queen Elizabeth), Virginia Young, Martha Ann Newton, and Erline Walker. Performers not in the picture included groomsmen Edward Lee Spencer and Clyde Meagher, bridesmaid Ann Draughon, and bride's parents Gene Hurt and Gene Mullins. Ada Wright sang "I Love You Truly," accompanied by Katherine Wright at the piano. Lamar and Carolyn Ellis sang "Love's Old Sweet Song," accompanied by Gay Ellis at the piano. Winifred Hill played the wedding march.

—Photo: Carolyn Ellis Lipscomb

Auburn's internationally known fisheries began with Farm Pond One in the early 1930s. Leslie Wright's workers and mule teams built the dam for the 1.8-acre pond north of the swine production unit off Shug Jordan Parkway (old-bypass road) at the Bull Test Station. The pond was stocked with bullhead catfish, bluegill bream, shellcrackers, and red-eye bass. When the pond was drained after one year, 293 pounds of fish and 2,225 pounds of tadpoles were collected. To reduce the tadpole population, the pond was restocked partly with large-mouthed bass. Dr. Homer Swingle led the Auburn fisheries program to international stature before his death in 1973. He remarked that in the thirties he simply was trying to find a good place to fish. Under the leadership of Swingle's successor, Dr. Wayne Shell, professors did further research helpful in feeding the hungry in other nations and in developing farm ponds in Alabama. By 1996, Fisheries and Allied Aquacultures had 317 ponds, with thirty research projects ranging from worldwide tilapia to Alabama cat-fish.

—Photo: Mrs. Homer S. Swingle

◄ Two Auburn men convinced the Legislature in 1935 that the state needed a Department of Toxicology and Criminal Investigation at Auburn. H. W. Hixon and Carl Rehling pointed to the FBI's successful use of scientific investigation in solving the Lindbergh kidnapping case and the lack of such analysis in the Scottsboro rape case. Nixon (in white hat) became the first state toxicologist in Alabama. While a helper fanned away flies with a pine limb in 1938, Nixon helped examine a body taken from south Alabama waters to find the cause of death. Rehling, Nixon's assistant and successor as toxicologist, later led the department to national recognition for its use of scientific investigation in solving crimes.

—Photo: Alabama Department of Forensic Sciences

▲ Marching behind a sign that urged the Tigers to claw that Bulldog, Auburn's band paraded before the football game with Georgia in Columbus, Georgia, in 1933. Auburn won, 14-6. The teams continued playing each other in Columbus until 1959, when they began playing on a home-and-home basis to provide more seats than the Columbus stadium offered.

—Photo: AU Archives

▶ As college physician from 1923 to 1939, Dr. B. F. Thomas, Sr., (with cigarette holder) helped trainer Wilbur Hutsell (in cap) take care of the football team. Thomas saw the student body through a number of exhausting health emergencies, including two or three flu epidemics that finally forced the college to close until the students got well.

One year a cadet walked into the office with a case of smallpox, and Thomas had to vaccinate every student at API—between 1,200 and 1,500 of them. Another time he treated two students who had contracted typhoid fever from a contaminated spring near Auburn. During President Knapp's administration (1928-32), Thomas diagnosed a case of scarlet fever and had no place to isolate the student. Knapp let him quarantine the patient over Knapp's garage near the President's Home (now Cater Hall).
—Photo: AU Special Collections

▲ Like a huge three-story sign stating that the Great Depression was loosening its hold on the economy, the thirty-six-room Pitts Hotel took shape in 1936-37 across East Magnolia Avenue from the Episcopal Church. Former Auburn student Jim Howard Pitts borrowed heavily and also put his savings into the $140,000 project. It eventually included forty-four rooms, a restaurant, twelve cottages behind the hotel, and store space to rent. The business flourished until motels became popular. The hotel finally became a rooming house under different management before being torn down in 1975.
—Photo: James Stanfield

▲ *Dr. Joseph Fanning Drake served as president of Alabama Agricultural and Mechanical College at Normal, near Huntsville, from 1927 to 1962. He was born in Auburn and attended elementary school there. J. F. Drake High School, a public school for blacks in Auburn before desegregation, was named for him. He earned a B.A. degree from Talladega College, an M.A. from Columbia University, and a Ph.D from Cornell University. He was president of the Conference of Presidents of Land-Grant Colleges in America, 1935-36. Dr. Drake sometimes returned to Auburn to visit his brother Hodge Drake and Hodge's family.*
—Photo: J. F. Drake Memorial Learning Resources Center, Alabama A&M University

▶ *All-American halfback Jimmy Hitchcock (left) and end Porter Grant sported varsity A sweaters in front of the Sigma Nu house in this shot in about 1932. Both became assistant football coaches at API. Later, Hitchcock served on the Alabama Public Service Commission. Grant became an Army brigadier general. Hitchcock, a premier runner, punter, and passer, was Auburn's first player named to the National Football Foundation Hall of Fame. The 165-pounder led undefeated Auburn to nine victories and a 20-20 tie with South Carolina in 1932. He scored touchdowns on runs of sixty-three and sixty yards as Auburn dealt Tulane its first Southern Conference loss in four seasons. Duke Coach Wallace Wade said after losing to Auburn 18-7, "I have never seen a finer all-around back play against one of my teams."*
—Photo: Mrs. Jimmy Hitchcock

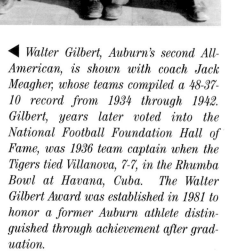

◀ *Walter Gilbert, Auburn's second All-American, is shown with coach Jack Meagher, whose teams compiled a 48-37-10 record from 1934 through 1942. Gilbert, years later voted into the National Football Foundation Hall of Fame, was 1936 team captain when the Tigers tied Villanova, 7-7, in the Rhumba Bowl at Havana, Cuba. The Walter Gilbert Award was established in 1981 to honor a former Auburn athlete distinguished through achievement after graduation.*
—Photo: AU Athletic Department

◀ *Ralph Jordan was a steady center as a junior in 1930, when this picture was taken. The next year he played sixty minutes in Auburn's first football victory over Georgia Tech in twelve seasons. He also led the basketball team that reached the semifinals of the conference tournament, then hit a home run and pitched in the baseball championship victory over Florida. Neil O. Davis was a freshman in 1931 when Jordan was a senior. Nearly fifty years later, after Jordan's death, Davis recalled in the* Auburn Bulletin: *"My freshman view of the campus 'wheel' saw him as football-basketball-baseball hero*

who, despite his 'star' status, had the common touch. He was a warm, friendly fellow who hadn't let prominence in athletics and election to major campus honor societies go to his head." Davis ended: "Shug Jordan was Auburn through and through. He loved the place. He never lost that touch of friendliness that attracted to him so many died-in-the-wool, loyal friends. He hated to lose. But he was a gracious winner. In victory and defeat he maintained his equilibrium. That is hard to do in these days of pressure-packed, big-time football. Auburn will miss him."
—Photo: AU Special Collections

▶ A fountain pen and memo pad probably helped save the life of Auburn Police Chief George Franklin "G. F." Hawkins in 1937. They partially deflected a bullet that hit him in the vest pocket and wounded him slightly. Hawkins was trying to arrest an armed man, who had been charged with disorderly conduct in Opelika. The suspect had overpowered an Opelika policeman and had taken his pistol. He shot Hawkins with it. "If it had not been for my fountain pen and memorandum book, I guess I'd be a dead man now," the chief said. The suspect, a groundskeeper of API athletic fields, surrendered to Hawkins and officer F. M. Henry right after the shooting. Hawkins, a railroad man, had turned to police work during the Depression. The Hawkins family lived for three or four years in a house on North College Street up the hill southeast of the Tichenor intersection. The town's one-room jail was near today's city parking deck.

—Photo: Bill Hawkins

▲ This 1939 pep rally in Langdon Hall was typical: standing room only. Down front facing left are members of the API band, who usually led the procession into the hall or came in by the fire stairs at the sides. In all probability, team captain Milton "Hatch" Howell and "Dynamite" Dick McGowen were on the stage along with Coach Jack Meagher or one of his assistants to tell the crowd: "We're going to win this one." Langdon had been modernized and had propeller fans suspended from the ceiling. Even with a magnifying glass, the authors could find only four coeds in this picture.

—Photo: AU Archives

▲ This picture of Professor J. A. Parrish appeared in the first volume of the Lee County High School yearbook, the Tiger, dedicated to him in 1944. 'Fessor, as he was called, had been principal since 1915-16, the second year the school had been in Auburn. At the start, there were seventy students. In 1940, 'Fessor's twenty-fifth year, the Lee County Bulletin reported that he had the longest continuous service as principal at the same high school of anyone in the state. Parrish was "always on the right side of every question for the good of his town, country, state, and nation," the article said. He retired in August 1946.

—Photo: the Tiger

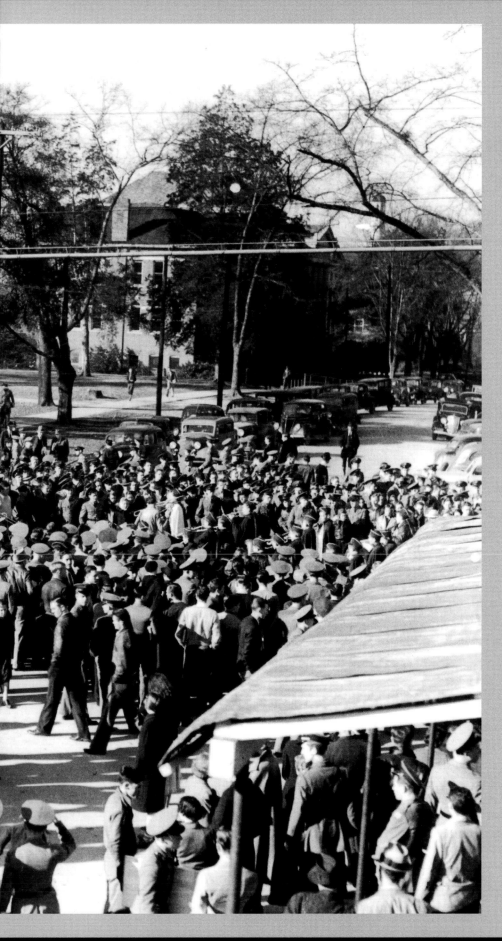

◀ *Band-led celebrants at Toomer's Corner savored Auburn's 6-0 victory over Michigan State in the 1938 Orange Bowl football game. Auburn held the Spartans to two first downs and sixty-five yards total offense. Guard Ralph "Happy" Sivell, tackle Bo Russell, and linebacker Boots Antley led the defense. Ralph O'Gwynne scored the touchdown. Note the space between the Main Gate and Broun Hall, where Biggin Hall later was built.*

—Photo:
AU Photographic Services

▲ Auburn High School's first band in 1936 was all-male, and many old Auburn families were represented. Left to right, front row: John C. Ball, Seddon Lee, Frank Wilmore, Jim Flanagan, James Allgood, Joe Hare, W. J. Isbell, Billy Tamblyn, Harold Blackburn, Lan Lipscomb, Fred Allison, David Winters, Clark Hudson. Middle row: Director Lawrence Barnett, Jack Hill, John Scott, Ferrell Williamson, Charles Hixon, Shel Toomer, Albert Thomas, Homer Wright, Rene Bidez, Redding Sugg, Principal J. A. Parrish. Back Row: John Turner Hudson, Spillman Fitzpatrick, J. B. Wilson, John Bruce Martin.

—Photo: Carolyn Ellis Lipscomb

▲ Mrs. Bessie Bailey, a widow, sold her forty-acre farm and came to Auburn in 1938 determined that her son Wilford be educated in veterinary medicine. She first operated a boardinghouse, mostly for veterinary students, and then became API's chief telephone operator. She is shown at the switchboard in 1947. In 1958, after twenty years in Auburn, "She not only has a veterinary son, but two veterinary sons-in-law and eight veterinary-minded grandchildren," a college press release said. Her older daughter, Freda, became secretary to Dean R. S. Sugg of what became the College of Veterinary Medicine. Her son became not only a Vet School department head, but also interim president—the title later changed by the trustees to president—of Auburn University.

—Photo: AU Archives

▲ Lee County High School was built on Samford Avenue at Payne Street in 1931 and more than six decades later still served the community. For many years, it housed all students from first through twelfth grades. It became the middle school after the high school was built on Samford at Dean Road in the mid-1960s, and later became Auburn Junior High School.

—Photo: AU Archives

▶ Auburn was a village when Dr. Cecil S. Yarbrough (standing at left) became a resident in about 1900. Many credited him with working for the town's progress as a private physician; as a multi-term council member; as mayor in 1918, 1922-28, and 1936-44; as a state senator; and as the college physician during World War II. He bought the antebellum Scott House at the end of East Magnolia Avenue in 1912 for his family home, and he lived there until his death in 1946. He is shown at a clinic, circa 1938.

—Photo: AU Archives

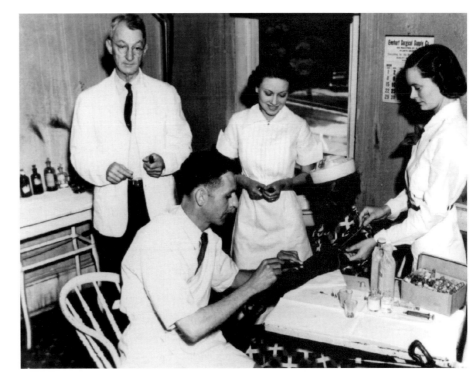

▶ Olin L. Hill (right) had been in business in Auburn for sixty-eight years in 1996, the longest of any local merchant. After moving to Auburn from Notasulga in 1928, he began selling tailored-to-measure suits off a big table in J. B. Richards' barbershop, paying Richards rental of one or two dollars per suit sold. Hill opened a men's clothing store in 1936 on West Magnolia Avenue and later operated it at eleven different locations, ten on College Street. Known as "the man with the tape," he offered in the early days "a free suit of clothes" to anyone who caught him downtown without his tape measure. He was caught a time or two when he went for a Coke, other College Street merchants recalled. They also remembered his sneaking down the alley behind the stores to avoid detection. Whether he actually gave up a suit without charge is Hill's secret, but since the late 1940s, a Coke has been the prize for catching him without his tape. Hill estimated in 1979 he had been caught twenty-five times since opening his first store. He is shown with Harold Richardson, an employee in his store, circa 1939.

—Photo: Olin L. Hill

◀ *Tiger Theatre was a happening from its opening on College Street in 1928. Ad libs from the audience and crowd reaction—laughing, crying, booing, applauding—immediately became part of the show. The Tiger's 715 seats were inadequate for Saturday midnight shows and frequently for all four Sunday shows during the 1940s. Patrons lined up on College Street to Magnolia Avenue many times for tickets. Manager Gus Coats brought* Gone With the Wind *to the Tiger in 1940, and his successor, Donnie Stone, in 1977 brought* Star Wars *to the Tiger, its two greatest attactions in its first fifty-three years.*

—Photo: Leonard W. Thomas and H. C. Morgan, Jr.

▲ *C. R. "Red" Meagher opened The Doll House on East Glenn Avenue, just off College Street in 1939, featuring barbecue, hot dogs, and hamburgers. Red, seated, posed at the grand opening with his wife, Luckie, standing second from left, and employees. Years later, The Doll House became Sani-Freeze, a popular dairy bar. AmSouth Bank acquired the property and in 1995 demolished the old wooden structure and replaced it with a red brick branch office. Luckie Meagher was the premier kindergarten teacher in Auburn for more than three decades.*

—Photo: Mrs. Luckie Meagher

▶ *Auburn's polo team in the 1930s defeated such national powers as Ohio State and Missouri, thanks to the coaching of Army Captains T. S. Gunby and W. J. Klepinger and the riding and mallet swinging of team members. The mounts were field artillery horses, and the home team provided the mounts. Guess which team usually had the advantage?*
—Photo: Emily Hixon Gunter

▲ *The Samford Tower bell that used to sound reveille and summon students to chapel had been silent for many years when in 1939 President L. N. Duncan climbed the steep belfrey stairs, pulled the rope, and signaled the start of a Greater Auburn Day and a $1.5-million building program. The coed with Dr. Duncan is unidentified. An estimated three-thousand people, including Governor and Mrs. Frank M. Dixon, attended the ceremonies. They saw approximately fifteen-hundred cadets parade briskly to the music of the Auburn band. Some two-thousand visitors ate barbecue at Bibb Graves Centre, and Coach Jack Meagher's Blues beat his Orange team 19-2 in a wintry football game.*
—Photo: AU Archives

◀ *The Beaux Arts Ball traditionally marked the approaching end of an exhausting year of labs, projects, and late-night toil for students of architecture and the fine arts. So it was in 1939, with the ball in Langdon Hall basement.*

—Photo: AU Archives

▲ *The Auburn Lions Club and guests met at the Thomas Hotel in the late 1930s. Left to right, front row: Hugh Cottle, George Hargreaves, a child whose medical care was paid for by the club, Mildred Moore (a social worker), A. F. Nickel, Keith Reeves, Kirtley Brown. Second row: Jimmy Seale, W. T. Ingram, Charles W. Edwards, Joe Roop, Leslie Wright, N. J. Peddy, L. S. Blake, B. Lowe. Third row: Ralph Jordan, Harry Dearing, Pattie Haney, Robert G. Pitts, Charline Baughman, Willie Tucker, W. J. Klepinger. Back row: Buddy McCollum, Cecil Ward, R. E. "Bob" Smith, Ottis Ward.*

—Photo: Robert G. Pitts.

The graduation line wended its way into the Graves Centre dining hall-auditorium in May 1939.
—Photo: AU Archives

▶ An attentive class heard Charles R. Hixon, professor of mechanical engineering, in about 1939. Hixon was also a magician, an inventor, an alligator-catcher, a photographer, and, in his younger years, chief of the volunteer fire department. He invented "a very useful attachment for cameras and a decarbonizer for automobiles," the Plainsman reported. He saw Auburn advance from fighting fires with a two-wheel hose reel that students pushed to fires to buying a secondhand fire truck. But sometimes the truck was hard to start, and the old reel beat it to the fire, the Alumnews said.
—Photo: AU Archives; Glomerata

▶ *API President L. N. Duncan welcomed FDR with a handshake as the visitor's Cadillac stopped behind the Quad Dorms. President Roosevelt got a booming ovation from the crowd occupying special bleachers when he started his speech with the familiar, "My friends." In his address he urged Auburn students to work toward helping the South become self-sufficient. He also said he had been strictly neutral about the Auburn-Georgia football game, noting that he was a part-time resident of Warm Springs, Georgia, but added: "Perhaps (next fall) I shall lean a little bit more toward Auburn." Auburn beat Georgia 7-0 in Columbus eight months later.*

—Photo: Ann B. Pearson

▼ *A twenty-four-hour gullywasher stopped in time on March 30, 1939, for a smiling, waving Franklin Delano Roosevelt to ride onto campus in his top-down Cadillac.* The Lee County Bulletin *said it looked like all of east Alabama had shown up for the first talk ever given at Auburn by a United States president. FDR waved his hat in passing the AAA Building, later named Extension Hall, and the crowd waved back as Secret Service agents rode the running boards. "Wild cheers went up from the thousands gathered on Bullard Field,"* wrote Henrietta W. Davis in the Auburn Alumnus, *"as the presidential cavalcade, including Governor Frank M. Dixon, Senator Lister Hill, and Congressman Henry Steagall, rounded the bend at Bibb Graves Centre."*

—Photo: Gladys Steadham Stewart

◀ *In September 1939, Auburn welcomed another visitor from the White House. Coeds Virginia Adams, left, and Amy Drake greeted Eleanor Roosevelt at the Social Center after her brief address to an estimated 5,000 people at Bullard Field. "I am glad to see this remarkable institution," she said, "and to observe the federal government's work on campus." She referred to a $1.5-million Public Works construction program. Mrs. Roosevelt stopped briefly at President L. N. Duncan's home, one of the Public Works projects, before making her talk.*
—Photo: Ann B. Pearson

▲ *ROTC students are shown leaving Bullard Field after completing drill in 1940. At left is Duncan Hall. This field was dedicated in 1930 in honor of General Robert Lee Bullard, World War I hero and Auburn alumnus. In 1952, women's dormitories 5 through 9 were built on the field. ROTC drills were moved to Max Morris Field at Wire Road and Thach and West Magnolia avenues. Morris, an outstanding API student and football player, was killed in action during the Korean War.*

—Photo: AU Archives

Chapter 6

WAR
AND
PEACE

or the second time in twenty-five years, a world war disrupted college life at Auburn in the early 1940s. Most male students left for the armed forces. Regular enrollment dwindled from 3,640 in the fall of 1942 to 1,710 in the fall of 1943. "In the fall quarter of 1944, there were for the first time at Auburn more women (904) than men (864) enrolled, although the addition of some 3,152 males participating in the Army Specialized Training Program (ASTP) and the Naval Radio and Aviation Training kept the ratio of men on campus high," historian Leah Atkins wrote. Coeds moved into empty fraternity houses in 1943, and male military trainees took their places in the Quad dorms.

Women students also moved into Auburn Hall, which had been a men's dorm. For sixteen months, Alumni Hall housed naval trainees, who called it the *USS Enterprise*. Stepping up the campus pace after Pearl Harbor, the college shifted from the semester to the quarter system in 1942. This enabled year-round students to graduate a year early.

API didn't field a football team in 1943, but held a pep rally in the stadium anyway—"giving yells for a phantom team and a phantom student body which today is scattered all over the world," wrote Executive Secretary Ralph B. Draughon in a "Christmas Letter to the Boys, 1943." Draughon reported that Private Monk Gafford, a hero in the previous year's upset of Rose

Bowl-bound Georgia, had finished basic training and was back in Auburn awaiting orders for Officer Candidate School. Auburn men and women carried their school spirit with them into war service. One alumnus, who may have gone too far, even claimed to have carved the storied battle cry "War Eagle" on the cheek of a sphinx in Egypt before serving in the North African campaign.

Another AU alumnus, Major Robert Kelley Posey, directed the discovery and preservation of "fabulous art treasures," from, in Posey's words, "'the breakthrough at St. Lo until the end of the combat in Czechoslovakia and Austria,'" the *Auburn Alumnews* and *Plainsman* reported. Altogether, more than 300

▶ *Auburn's Shag Hawkins stretched for a basket in a packed Alumni Gym in 1941. The six-foot-two center led SEC scorers that season and was second to teammate Frank Manci (No. 30 in picture) the next year. Hawkins scored 644 points in three seasons during the era of low-scoring basketball. "Shag was a helluva perimeter man, and his drive for the basket was awesome," his coach, Ralph Jordan, recalled nearly forty years later. Hawkins was Jordan's only scholarship basketball player at API. The profits from a nickel-a-drink Coke machine at the gym went to Shag.*

—Photo: AU Archives

► *Benson's Drug Store, a few doors north of the Auburn Grille, remained open late on Friday and Saturday nights to catch the hungry during intermission of college dances. Virtually all of the customers in this picture hurried to Benson's during the break in a 1940 midterm dance. Note the metal shakers on the table. The milk shakes they contained cost a dime. Sandwiches, unless you wanted something fancy, were fifteen cents. The ham and cheese was twenty cents and the club a quarter.*

—Photo: AU Archives

▲ *While the Auburn Knights were booked in at the Village Barn on Virginia Beach for the summer of 1941, Frank Sinatra sometimes dropped by to join them. Others from the Tommy Dorsey Band, including Dorsey, Buddy Rich, and Ziggy Elman, and musicians with Glenn Miller frequently joined the Knights for after-hours jam sessions that went on till daybreak.*

—Photo: Auburn Knights Collection; AU Archives

▲ *The thumb was a mighty important appendage to hundreds of male students at API from the late 1930s through the 1940s and into the 1950s. Few students had cars, and on weekends, during holidays, and at the semester or quarter break, many went home, went to see girl friends, or just went. They got there and back by hitchhiking.*

Motorists in Alabama and neighboring states came to recognize the Auburn ROTC hat and the orange and blue "rat cap," and thumbing frequently was a more rapid means of transportation than train or bus. Thousands thumbed to Auburn football games in Birmingham,

Atlanta, Montgomery, and Columbus, and few missed a kickoff. The hitchhikers in this picture were at the Main Gate, hoping to get a ride down U.S. 29 to Montgomery or points beyond. At the same moment, others probably were lined up at Opelika Corner, north of the railroad track on Gay Street at Mitcham Avenue, seeking rides to Columbus, Atlanta, or other points east. Some heading toward Birmingham thought it best to start on Opelika Corner, and some tried their luck by thumbing on College Street north of the track toward The Bottle.

—Photo: AU Archives.

repositories containing cultural treasures stolen by Nazi leaders were uncovered. The hoard at the Alt Aussee salt mines in Austria included "the early Michelangelo 'Madonna and Child' in marble" and "da Vinci's bas-relief of David and Goliath." At a church, according to *Art News Magazine*, "Noticing traces of color under the damp plaster on the side walls, Major Posey counted seven separate skin-coats of paint and

thin plaster coatings. They were loose enough to brush off easily. On the righthand wall, the Annunciation was quickly uncovered—a fresh, lovely faint ghost from an early epoch of North Gothic painting."

Brigadier General Robert D. Knapp, who grew up in Auburn, earned the Distinguished Flying Cross, the Silver Star, Bronze Star, and other medals for his

exploits in combat. As a wing commander in 1944, he led B-25 bombers in "a daring attack against an enemy convoy in the Mediterranean." The *Lee County Bulletin* reported, "Six of the planes assigned to hit the convoy were forced to return because of bad weather, but General Knapp led his formation to the convoy and bombed it from 5,000 feet, sinking a large ship." Future Auburn journalism Professor Paul C. Burnett was cited in a national magazine for his resourcefulness as a navigator on a bombing raid. Burnett had been shot through the leg by a machine-gun bullet; his charts were out of reach; his radio wasn't working; and it was foggy. Yet, relying on memory, he guided the crippled Flying Fortress from France to a safe landing in the first field on the England side of the English Channel.

The API faculty earned national prestige in 1943 when soldiers in Term 2 of the Army Specialized Training Program at Auburn took standard examinations also given at thirty or more other institutions, including Yale, Princeton, and Purdue. Auburn's trainees ranked first in chemistry, physics, geography, and English, second in history, and third in mathematics.

Away from the classroom, many ASTP students enjoyed Auburn hospitality, especially jitterbugging and waltzing with coeds to jukebox music at the Student Center in the Langdon Hall basement. Some ASTPs later sent their children to Auburn. For the duration, though, townspeople, faculty members, and students made the best of shortages, rationing, and a

few practice blackouts, ever alert for news of loved ones in service and for signs the war would end.

The radio announcements in August 1945 that the Japanese had agreed to surrender touched off "ringing bells, shrieking whistles, and an excited group of people on the streets and front porches," the *Lee County Bulletin* reported. An hour later about three thousand townspeople, faculty members, and students united in a service of prayer and rejoicing at the stadium. Students also lit a bonfire and held an impromptu pep rally outside the stadium.

Soon the servicemen and women came marching back to the classrooms, using the GI Bill for college education. Auburn's enrollment jumped 241 percent in one year—to 6,290 in the fall of 1946. Of that number, two-thirds were military veterans. These included 900 or so men who at first were turned down by API because of a shortage of both teachers and space for instruction. After the vets packed Langdon Hall inside and out, clamoring to go to school, President Duncan ordered them admitted. "Even if they had a watered-down education, it was better than none at all," W. T. Ingram, AU treasurer emeritus, recalled many years later. Most veterans took their studies seriously and, after about a quarter of adjusting to academic life, outdid the younger students in the classroom.

The record enrollment in 1946 made housing as scarce as gasoline had been during the war. Married students, mostly the 1,446 married veterans with their wives and 607 children, lived in apartments and trail-

▲ *Jim Washington drove this ice wagon to homes throughout Auburn for the Auburn Ice and Coal Company in 1941. The company also operated a large lumber yard on Bragg Avenue where E. L. Spencer Lumber Company was located later. "You could buy a nice square piece of ice for a dime, and a bigger piece that would last three or four days for a quarter," Mrs. Susie Giddens recalled. After trucks replaced wagons, they taught Washington how to drive and he continued delivering ice. Ice deliveries ceased after refrigerators became too plentiful, but the water tank that fed the ice plant from a well remained standing at Spencer's in 1996. Starting in 1932, E. L. Spencer had owned and operated lumber yards in three other locations at Auburn before buying the Auburn Ice and Coal property in 1965.*

—Photo: Leland Long

▲ *Monk Wright took his children Spud and Ann to Chewacla Park on this cold winter's afternoon in 1940 to check out a report that the lake was frozen over. They found the area from shoreline past the diving tower frozen solid. But on out toward the middle it wasn't. This picture shows the chidren standing on ice a few yards from shore. Spud was G. H. Wright, Jr., who had an illustrious career as a Lee County district attorney and circuit court judge. The man standing near the diving tower is unidentified. The Weather Bureau listed January 1940 as the coldest month on record throughout Alabama up to that time. The high at Auburn for the last sixteen days of January never got above freezing, and the daily lows for that period ranged from the teens down to seven degrees on January 27.*

—Photo: John M. Wright

ers. Single men stayed in old military barracks, tugboat cabins, trailers, boardinghouses, fraternities, and what had been a prisoner of war camp in Opelika. Coeds moved back into the Quad Dorms. Many new professors and their families and some of the more fortunate married students and wives lived in war-surplus housing on West Samford Avenue near where the Architecture and Fine Arts complex is now.

Soon the student body returned to a traditional enrollment pattern. In the fall of 1946, male students outnumbered females once again, nearly 5 to 1. Although the men were free to come and go as they pleased at the new Magnolia Hall dormitory in 1948, the college continued regulating the lives of women students. On weekdays, there was a 7:15 p.m. curfew for first-quarter freshmen, a 9 p.m. curfew for freshmen who had made satisfactory grades and for sophomores, and an 11 p.m. curfew for juniors and seniors. On weekends it was midnight, but 12:30 a.m. for those attending formal dances at Graves Center Auditorium or Alumni Gym and, in later years, the Student Activities Building. Dress rules prohibited coeds from walking across campus in just their gym suits. Most wore raincoats over their blue shorts and blouses while going to and from physical education classes.

Academically qualified Negro servicemen returning to civilian life could not attend API. Racial segregation barred the door. Yet, the war caused "a lot of people to start thinking," J. C. Woodall, a black citizen, recalled in 1996. Woodall said blacks thought, "If I was good enough to die for my country, why am I not good enough to sit anywhere on a bus when I have paid the fare?" But years of segregation in schools, restaurants, transportation, and other public places lay ahead for Auburn and other Southern blacks.

Both town and gown grew in number during the

◄ *Auburn Ford dealer Anderson Blackburn (holding hat) walks with famed Tuskegee Institute (now University) scientist Dr. George Washington Carver (wearing overcoat), Carver's friend Henry Ford (at Carver's left), and Carver's assistant, Austin Curtis, at Tuskegee on March 11, 1941. Ford completed his first car in 1896. Ford told Blackburn he, as reporter Kirtley Brown worded it, "had a particularly warm feeling for the people of the South because of the fine support they gave him when he first began marketing cars many years ago." Ford toured the library, saw firsthand the results of Carver's research, and listened raptly to a private concert of timeless spirituals, such as "Swing Low, Sweet Chariot" and "Deep River."*

—Photo: Chris Danner

▲ *These six men had a total of 191 years of service at API—almost thirty-two years each—when they retired in 1959. This picture caught them together in Ross Square. All except P. O. Davis, top left, director of the Extension Service, seemed to be peering into the future. Next to Davis is General James B. Crawford, mathematics. Middle row: Dean Lynn S. Blake, School of Pharmacy; and P. P. Powell, professor of chemistry. Front row: Dr. Armin A. Leibold, head of Veterinary Medicine's department of bacteriology, parasitology, and pathology; and Dr. Charles L. Isbell, professor of horticulture.*

—Photo: Lee County Bulletin

1940s, Auburn's non-student population increasing from 4,652 to 6,298, and the API enrollment from that low of 1,710 in 1943-44 to more than 7,600 in 1948 before slipping to 5,757 in 1951. More residents meant more regulations. Despite heated resistance, the City Council approved Auburn's first zoning ordinance in 1946.

Auburn's Community Chest, a predecessor of United Way, dates to at least the 1930s. In 1940, the Inter-Club Council led a drive for $2,550 with which to fund twelve projects. Among these were library help for white and Negro schools, lunches for needy school children, books for school children, additional help for Negro and white schools, Christmas fund for the needy, emergency medical care for the needy, transient relief, Boy Scouts, and Girl Scouts. In 1988, Auburn and Opelika United Ways merged into the United Way of Lee County, Inc. Its budget in 1996 was $706,000, funding forty-two charitable agencies, said Jude Peterson, executive director for twenty years. The high level of "caring and responsibility" of the citizens is demonstrated through this community-based, volunteer organization, Mrs. Peterson said. "There is a great outpouring of love and affection."

A major political fight erupted in 1947 over new Governor Jim Folsom's four appointees to fill vacancies on Auburn's Board of Trustees. Folsom had campaigned against "the Big Mule power structure that included the Agricultural Extension Service and the

Farm Bureau Federation (now ALFA)," professors Carl Grafton and Anne Permaloff of Auburn University-Montgomery wrote nearly fifty years later in an article published in the *Birmingham News*. To help break this clique, Folsom wanted to remove the Extension Service from politics. One of his nominees, Folsom's speech writer, Gould Beech, edited "the *Southern Farmer*, a newspaper that represented tenant and family farmers. Its publishers and Beech's friends, Marshall Field and Aubrey Williams, were widely viewed as radicals or worse," Grafton and Permaloff wrote. Beech's nomination sparked reaction against the Folsom nominees by "Extension Service officials, Farm Bureau executives, and other agribusiness leaders." Folsom responded in a talk to about 6,000 students and faculty members: "Auburn has got to be one institution. The college, the Experiment Station and the Extension Service are part of one institution. . . . It gets its money from one place. The people . . . The Extension Service has got to get out of politics and stay out of politics. And I mean all kinds of politics. Local politics. State politics . . . Government politics and farm organization politics . . ." Incumbent trustees and Folsom's nominees were unanimously critical of the Extension Service, but Extension and its Big Mule allies managed to keep the four unwanted trustees off the board.

Dr. Duncan's death in 1947 brought the college new but familiar leadership in Ralph B. Draughon, the third Auburn graduate to be named API president. Dr. Draughon had taught history at Auburn, had been Duncan's executive secretary, and had been director of instruction. Draughon served for more than a year as acting president before being inaugurated at age forty-nine. He led the Topsy-like growth in buildings, enrollment, and course offerings after World War II. "Draughon's most significant and defining contribution to this university was to get the Extension Service

out of politics," a retired journalist said in 1996. In 1962, Draughon dismissed the former associate director of Extension and forced him to retire because of his "political activity." Draughon said he had evidence the man had been actively promoting a candidate in the governor's race. Draughon said the trustees in 1959 had reprimanded the same man and warned him not to take part in political activity. At that time, he also was reassigned. A former Extension insider in 1996 credited "changing times" with removing the service from politics. Not all Extension people, of course, had engaged in partisan politics while serving the state's rural population. Meanwhile, early in the Draughon years, Auburn alumni and students served in yet another war, this time in Korea. A few months before that conflict ended, a natural disaster struck the city.

The Great Tornado of 1953, as writer Ann Pearson named it years later, arrived at 4:10 p.m. on a sultry Saturday in April. "Thunder without a letup" and pitch darkness signaled its descent onto homes west of Ridge Grove Road. The tornado smashed through north Auburn, demolishing 49 homes, damaging 519 others, flattening several businesses, and leaving behind a "no-man's-land" of twisted and broken trees, many seventy-five years old. The storm so heavily damaged the antebellum Cauthen House on East Drake Avenue that repair was not feasible. It had been built in the 1850s by Simeon Perry, the surveyor who originally laid out the town. The twister injured twenty persons, five seriously, but no deaths were reported.

Telfair B. Peet, head of the Department of Theatre, suffered a heart attack at his home on Sanders Street shortly before the tornado struck. Despite danger to herself, Mrs. Peet waded in knee-deep water past fallen trees and "electric wires everywhere" to a drugstore uptown and got the medicine a physician had prescribed for her husband. Workers that night cut a lane for an ambulance to take Peet to the hospital. He

◄ For several decades during summer school, a weekly event was the community sing in the evening at Langdon Hall steps. This one was held in the early 1940s.

—Photo: AU Archives

◄ Coach Jack Meagher (fifth from left) brought in Jimmy Conzelman, coach of the professional Chicago Cardinals, during 1941 spring pactice to help hone the T Formation. Players, left to right, are: end Jim Samford, halfback Monk Gafford, center Tex Williams, fullback uncertain (perhaps starting halfback Clarence Harkins, filling in for picture purposes), quarterback Lloyd Cheatham, end Clarence Grimmett, and Ty Irby, a halfback later converted to fullback.

Note the dog at left. Until the stadium was enclosed, dogs showed up regularly for practice and sometimes wandered onto the field during games. No ROTC parade at Auburn has ever been complete without a dog or two as participants.

—Photo: AU Archives

◄ This pep rally on College Street in 1940 must have been on drill day, judging from the number of ROTC uniforms. It was held in the morning as the football team departed for Texas and the SMU game. Note the shadows of band members and their instruments on the pavement. The cheerleaders, left to right, were: Joe Gandy, Dottie Norman, David Gammage, Margaret McCain, and Dick Peck. Dottie Norman married Bill Sherling, and both had long teaching careers at the University.

—Photo: AU Archives

▲ *A festive Homecoming crowd of 15,000—largest ever assembled for a football game at Auburn—roared in approval as Coach Jack Meagher's Plainsmen whipped Clemson, 28-7, on November 29, 1941. Eight days later the nation was at war, and many of the young men in this picture shortly became members of the military. Elements of the cadet corps are shown assembled behind the Field House (Petrie Hall) and on the baseball diamond (upper right) before marching onto the football field.*

The Auburn skyline consisted of Samford Hall, the water tower behind Toomer Drugstore, and the college smokestack. Just to the right and northeast of the Field House is Tichenor Hall, completed in 1940 and known as "new building" for more than a decade before being named for Auburn's third president. The Quadrangle at upper right, completed just in time for 1940 fall occupancy, housed 404 of the 700 women students that semester.

—Photo: 1942 Glomerata

recovered and later returned to his API duties.

The next year Auburn sweated through its worst drought on record. Less than half the normal amount of rain fell in the first ten months of 1954. The city had lowered the level of its main reservoir, Lake Ogletree, that winter to install new equipment that would have doubled the pumping capacity—but the spring rains to refill the lake did not come. The women's dormitories and campus cafeterias went without water for up to sixty hours before the college closed on October 28 for two class days and the weekend. Students left town so the water tanks could fill and pressure rebuild.

Despite a hastily laid second line from Opelika, and other emergency measures, water remained scarce enough for even bathing to become suspect. One group proposed that townspeople bathe on Tuesdays, Thursdays, and Saturdays while students shower on Mondays, Wednesdays, and Fridays. Everyone was relieved when winter rains finally made water plentiful again.

The sports high-water mark of the college's first 101 years came in 1957 when Auburn won the national football championship. It was the Tigers' first unbeaten, untied football season since 1913, part of a school-record 24 games without a loss and with only one tie. After seven lean years, through 1950, Auburn had turned to alumnus Ralph Jordan to restore its football credibility. Jordan, his assistant coaches, and players posted 21 winning seasons and won 176 games, lost 83, tied 6, and won the national title. Auburn played in 12 bowl games under Jordan and would have played in more except for serving probations after being convicted by the NCAA of recruiting violations.

Halfback Pat Meagher, son of former API coach Jack Meagher, and Pat's Class of '53 teammates led the Lee County High School football team to an undefeated, once-tied season in the fall of 1952 under coach R. L. Beaird. The school (later named Auburn High) had many strong football teams in the next forty-three years, but none went undefeated. In fact, no other Auburn High team had finished unbeaten as far back

These Royal Air Force cadets were much more familiar with British rugby, and although the thumbs-up in this photo could have been a sign of approval of the Auburn-Clemson football game, this perhaps was just the British way of saying, "Keep Smiling!" Thumbs-up later gave way to a great extent to the "V" for victory signal made popular by British Prime Minister Winston Churchill. These cadets attended the game while on holiday from training at Maxwell Air Force Base in Montgomery. Within a few months, they were directly involved in Great Britain's grim battle for survival.
—Photo: AU Archives

as 1937 when the *Lee County Bulletin* began publishing. Beaird's 1948 team went 8-1. Another high point for Beaird in his twenty-one years as coach was defeating Opelika from 1961 through 1963. It marked the first time either school had beaten the other three consecutive years and retired a rotating trophy that had been offered since 1938. Of the tough Beaird, a former Birmingham Southern football captain, one of his ends said: "He is not *of* the old school; he *is* the old school." Across town, coach Stewart Bennett's Lee County Training School teams were undefeated in 1958 and 1959, and one year gave up only six points in ten games. Bennett's teams at the Training School and later at Drake High school never had a losing season in sixteen years, and as best the coach could recount to the *Auburn Bulletin*, won 125 games, lost 32, and tied two. Nineteen team members played college football. Bennett had been a 275-pound tackle at Knoxville College in Tennessee.

The same month that the API football team won the national championship, the departments of electrical and mechanical engineering lost their accreditation. The Legislature hadn't appropriated enough money to Auburn and other institutions to keep pace with the growing number of students. To meet the crisis, President Draughon urged the Alumni Association to raise $250,000. Instead, it collected a half million dollars in money and equipment, and the two departments were reaccredited in 1961.

Despite its financial problems, API grew in range and quality. During the ten years ending in 1955, the college awarded more degrees than it had from 1859 until 1945. One example shows the value of its academic research in that decade. Dr. S. Allen Edgar, poultry pathologist, and his graduate students developed a highly effective vaccine for immunizing chickens against cecal coccidiosis. Twenty million birds were inoculated in less than a year after the vaccine's 1952 release to growers. This meant a savings of $3 million to the poultrymen involved.

In 1956, the college celebrated its centennial anniversary and moved toward becoming a university in name as well as deed. It had seven doctoral and thirty-six masters programs, and major expansion of graduate and undergraduate work would follow. For thirty-five years, instruction within the so-called cultural areas had been gaining increasing recognition with the technical and professional schools on campus. As of 1960, even engineering students delved into such classics as Plato's *Republic* and Dante's *Inferno* before receiving diplomas. Enrollment figures told a significant story in 1956. About 25 percent of the course registrations were in the applied sciences related to agriculture and engineering, and 15 percent were in other professional curricula, such as Architecture, Business Administration, Home Economics, Pharmacy, and Veterinary Medicine.

The remaining 60 percent, however, "were in subjects peculiar to the College of Liberal Arts—that is, in the pure sciences, the humanities, and the social sciences," Dr. Eugene Current-Garcia, professor of English, wrote in the *Alumnews* in 1959. Current-

◀ *Most of those pictured here were API students waiting at the ever-familiar depot for a train, this time to take them to Atlanta and ROTC summer camp at Fort McPherson in 1942 or 1943. A keen eye or magnifying glass can pick out All-American halfback Monk Gafford, standing at the curb facing the camera and wearing a dark letter sweater with an "A" on it.*

—Photo: AU Archives

◀ *Halfback Monk Gafford (25) and his teammates shocked the football world in November 1942 by thrashing Rose Bowl-bound Georgia, 27-13, at Memorial Stadium in Columbus. Tackle Joe Eddins (18) and fullback Jim Reynolds, trailing the play, are the other Auburn players in the picture. Trying to catch Monk is end George Poschner (41), and that could be All-American Frankie Sinkwich on the ground. Gafford ran for 119 yards on 20 carries and returned three punts for 92 yards.*

—Photo: 1943 Glomerata

Garcia, later the first recipient of the Phi Kappa Phi National Scholar's Award, added: "Thus, well before the end of the 1950s, the Alabama Polytechnic Institute had obviously burst through the confining limitations of a typical polytechnic institute, implicit in its name, to become in fact a university in the modern American sense of the term." The Legislature agreed and changed the name to Auburn University, effective January 1, 1960.

Women had served on the City Council since Bessie Williamson was appointed by Alabama Governor James E. Folsom in 1955. She and Sarah Spencer Roy were elected to four-year terms the next year, and Mrs. Roy became the first woman to serve as council president.

Mary Brooks became the city's first black council member in 1972 and served three consecutive terms, a total of ten years. Jan Dempsey became the first woman mayor in 1980 and was to complete a record eighteen consecutive years in that office in 1998. ◞

▲ The Japanese bombing of Pearl Harbor stunned Auburn along with the rest of the nation. The next day classes were dismissed and solemn students and faculty members gathered at Langdon Hall to hear over loudspeakers President Franklin D. Roosevelt tell Congress: "Yesterday, December seventh, 1941—a date which will live in infamy—the United States of America was suddenly and deliberately attacked by naval and air forces of the Empire of Japan." The president told Congress, "Hostilities exist…our people, our territory, and our interests are in grave danger," and promised, "We shall not settle for less than total victory." Congress agreed. America was at war. So was Auburn. "Prominent Auburn leaders urged students to guard against war hysteria and remain in classes until the government called upon them to serve," the AU Report recalled. "Auburn students heeded their message and adopted a 'How can I help?' philosophy." Students enlisted in the armed forces in great numbers, and Auburn enrollment of 3,640 in the fall of 1942 dropped to 1,710 in 1943.

—Photo: AU Archives

◀ After Captain Louie James and his bride, Meriam, were married in September 1942, they took the traditional Caisson Ride for field artillery newlyweds, through town to a party at the home of Colonel John J. Waterman, on Mell Street. Some couples rode on caissons like those headed north on Gay Street. Some rode in a wagon like the one turning onto Gay from Thach Avenue. At left was Mrs. Fortner's boardinghouse. In its basement, fronting on Thach, was Jake's Joint, with the strongest black coffee in Auburn. The original Wittel Dorm, later Auburn Hall, is seen through a break in the trees, and "new" Wittel Dorm is at right. James served two terms as Auburn mayor in the 1950s and 1960s.

—Photo: AU Archives

◀ Auburn fans celebrated the 1942 conquest of Georgia by tearing down the goal posts at Memorial Stadium in Columbus. One section of the wooden posts, autographed by players, was on display later in a barbershop on College Street. This was the greatest victory in Coach Jack Meagher's nine seasons at API, and it was sweet revenge for the heartbreaking 7-0 loss to the Bulldogs in 1941, when on the final play Frankie Sinkwich uncorked a bomb from his own 35-yard line that Lamar Davis caught and ran in for a touchdown. Meagher's teams beat Georgia five times, lost three times, and played to a scoreless tie in 1937.
—Photo: AU Archives

▶ Colonel John J. Waterman, commandant of the Army ROTC unit, found an attentive audience for his remarks about this artillery piece at the gun shed west of Bullard Field in 1943. Pete Turnham, second from right, became an Auburn businessman and a half century later the senior member of the Alabama House of Representatives. Edwin R. Goode, Jr., fifth from right, became a prominent veterinarian with the federal government and returned to Auburn with his wife, the former Betty Ware, upon retirement in the late 1970s.

—Photo: AU Archives

◀ Military trainees and coeds assembled on the steps of the Westminister House for a picnic during World War II.
—Photo: First Presbyterian Church

CHRISTMAS LETTER TO THE BOYS, 1943

Dear Fellows:

This brings good wishes and good cheer from us at Auburn to you — wherever you are. Below are things we think might interest you, and which may express our genuine appreciation of the work you are doing. May make you laugh a little, and even shed a tear. The main theme, however, is to give you a word from home.

Auburn is beautiful now with all the glorious colors of a long dry fall. Leaves are flying this evening in the cool North breeze, and here and there some wise citizen has on an overcoat as he hastens home for supper.

Auburn men will add to the scroll of illustrious men who have departed the names of Deans Wilmore and Biggin who so long gave of their lives and substance to the building of a fine tradition at Auburn.

There are now 1700 regular college students — about evenly divided between boys and girls — and all seeming much younger than the average used to be. Your scribe can say with truth — there's never been such a wonderful looking collection of sweater girls! One looks across the campus on the hour when classes change and sees them in little clusters of bright and lovely colors, chattering like birds — sweaters, sweaters, sweaters!

The year has brought about 1000 soldiers to the campus in the Army Specialist Training Program. Fine, bright lads who start to class at 8 A.M. on Mondays and get no liberty until 2 P.M. on Saturdays. They are here from almost every state, and they have a terrific load to carry in classes. Most of them are getting the Auburn Spirit about as you did when you were freshmen.

There is no football this year — but we are having an old-time pep meeting, band, cheerleaders and all — out in the stadium this week — giving yells for a phantom team and a phantom student body which today is scattered all over the world. For you guys! And may you hear their cheers, as the poet said it, "like the horns of Elfland faintly blowing" — wherever you may be, and be heartened thereby.

Private Monk Gafford — All-American left half — the guy who just about a year ago made Sinkwich look like a fiddle-footed sandlotter, has finished his basic training and is back in Auburn in school awaiting his orders for OCS. As modest as ever, Monk is wrestlin' mightily with Math and physics which the Army prescribes for men in his category.

Miss Allie Glenn has been ill for sometime but is now back at the old stand — hugging and kissing the "old boys" who can get enough extra gas for a visit to the campus, and dispensing the Auburn Spirit to all. Miss Allie is the original Miss Auburn and her only regret is that she can't be young again and join the sweater girls, for her spirit is forever young.

Merry Christmas
and a
Happy New Year
to you all.

Ralph B. Draughon

Governor Sparks delivered the commencement address at the end of the Fall Quarter, November 26, and promised us a new auditorium. Graduation now four times a year. About 177 graduates. All of the males who can walk going right into the armed services.

November 26 was also Homecoming Day — for the few who could gather. A strange Homecoming with no game in the stadium. There was a military review for the Governor and Alumni. We are trying to keep things together for the greatest day in Auburn's history — the first big Homecoming after the war! I've heard of plans for that day from North Africa to the Solomons and all way-stations. When we pick up all the pieces, classes will resume as usual!

Doctor Petrie, hale and hearty again, and full of fun and laughter, enjoys the luxury of going without a shave occasionally, just for the heck of it, after 55 years of routine. He has just written a creed for Auburn students that is a gem.

Dean Funchess, on the job but not feeling so well, still fumes when the fish in Lake Auburn won't bite like he wants 'em to.

Doctor Duncan is here and there quietly working to make Auburn bigger,

better and stronger, and — along with all of us — looking forward to the days when you'll all be home again.

The dogs still come to classes and attend drill and Physical Ed formations. Like everyone else they've gone Army or Navy and hang around the various mess halls. The only thing about it is — they've gotten to the point that they growl at all civilians, and one actually bit a Professor on the leg the other day!

Dean Hare still enjoys limericks, and will appreciate any you may send to him that will pass the censor. In that connection, someone should make a collection of the various versions of "Gertie."

Life in Auburn is different — very considerably different — in these times, but no college in the country is making a finer contribution to the Nation. The halt and the lame and all of us museumpieces who are left on the staff are doing our best to do the kind of job at home that you are doing in the armed forces. We are inordinately proud of the records that you are making — and we wouldn't ever want you to be ashamed of the job we are trying to do.

Auburn is more fortunate than most colleges in that we have kept Colonel Waterman, our beloved Commandant. No better soldier or finer gentleman ever served here.

Every week or so, the campus breaks out in a perfect rash of Second Lieutenants, Ensigns, etc., as the various officer's schools close. Every new officer that can make it gets back for a day or two, and its rare fun to hear some friend of his who is a private in the army here, awaiting orders for O.C.S., kid the pants off him with extremely precise salutes, "Sirs," and military courtesy.

Hodge Drake is bemoaning the fact that we have no football team this season, but greets all the "old boys" that come back in true "Doctor Snort" manner. Hodge knows more about military rank than most of us, and often elevates a Captain to a "Majah" and picks up an honest two-bits thereby.

Whatever this war is doing to those of us who are left here — and some of us are looking drawn and harassed — most of you who come by to see us look well and strong and young and tough and good. And that recalls Colonel Boozer Pitts and his famous version of "Private John Allen" — and we'd like to swap all of our past accomplishments for a part of your future!

The Auburn Creed

I believe that this is a practical world and that I can count only on what I earn. Therefore, I believe in work, hard work. I believe in education, which gives me the knowledge to work wisely and trains my mind and my hands to work skillfully. I believe in honesty and truthfulness, without which I cannot win the respect and confidence of my fellow men. I believe in a sound mind in a sound body and a spirit that is not afraid, and in clean sports that develop these qualities. I believe in obedience to law because it protects the rights of all. I believe in the human touch, which cultivates sympathy with my fellow men and mutual helpfulness and brings happiness for all. I believe in my country, because it is a land of freedom and because it is my own home, and that I can best serve that country by "doing justly, loving mercy, and walking humbly with my God."

And because Auburn men & women believe in these things, I believe in Auburn and love it.

George Petrie
November 12, 1943

Auburn started experimenting in 1927 with planting pine trees to control erosion. The "before" picture was taken in 1926, with Otto Brown of the Extension Service surveying a washed-out field within a ten-minute walk of the main campus. The "after" picture was taken seventeen or eighteen years later at the same general location. When the trees got large enough to provide privacy, the roads through the "Forestry Plots" became a popular parking place for male students with cars and dates.
—Photo: Auburn Alumnews; AU Department of Forestry

◀ *Japan's surrender in the summer of 1945 brought this reaction from API students Starr Prolsdorfer of Mobile and Marilyn Sheffield of Pine Hill, pictured in Toomer Drugstore.*
—Photo: 1946 Glomerata

► *Continuing a campus tradition that began in the World War I era, these Auburn players helped present the comedy* Papa is All *in 1944. The bearded Papa was better known to his Shakespeare classes as English Professor Theodore C. Hoepfner. Called the Footlights in their opening season of 1914, the Players produced a comedy that year. Through the years, the mostly student casts have performed on campus in Langdon Hall, Graves Amphitheatre, the old Y-Hut, and the modern Telfair B. Peet Theatre. During the 1920s, the Players created a little theater in the attic of Samford Hall, rehearsing and presenting short plays there. The bell tower served as a dressing room. Finally, the Attic Theater was condemned because theatrical remodeling had weakened the roof.*

—Photo: AU Archives

▲ *Soldiers lived in the Women's Quadrangle in 1943-44, receiving instruction at Auburn under the Army Specialized Training Program. Naval trainees occupied Alumni Hall and called the dormitory a "ship," its floors "decks," and its walls "bulkheads." They also "went ashore" and "reported aboard." Displaced female students moved into fraternity houses, where occupancy had been sharply reduced by the call to military service, and the remaining frat members found lodging elsewhere. Coeds also moved into Auburn Hall, formerly a men's dorm.*

—Photo: AU Archives

▲ Japan's surrender and the end of World War II touched off a celebration at Toomer's Corner in August 1945. Bells and whistles greeted the first radio news of victory. Three-thousand people shared services of prayer and rejoicing at the stadium. Most businesses took a one-day holiday.

—Photo: 1946 Glomerata

▲ Allie Glenn, college treasurer for approximately forty-seven years, welcomed visits from former Auburn students, such as Marine Major General Franklin A. Hart. In her earlier years, many of the boys deposited money to cover their year's expenses with her. She kept individual accounts, cashing checks as they needed money and sending a monthly statement to each student's parents.

Hart, later a lieutenant general, starred as a light but fighting halfback on two undefeated Auburn football teams before graduating in 1915. He also competed in track and soccer. Hart served in both World Wars and received the Navy Cross for heroism on a beach in the Marshall Islands in 1944. Auburn bestowed an LL.D. degree on him in 1953.

—Photo: AU Archives

▲ The first twelve presidents of the Woman's Club posed for a photograph in 1944. Left to right, seated: Mrs. John Ivey, Mrs. Zebulon Judd (the first president in 1919), Mrs. Charles Cary, Mrs. Mollie Hollifield Jones, Mrs. P. O. Davis, Mrs. J. T. Williamson. Standing: Mrs. J. C. Grimes, Mrs. Cleburne Basore, Mrs. Sheldon Toomer, Mrs. Walter Schreiber, Mrs. Fred Allison, Mrs. Benjamin Showalter.

—Photo: the Woman's Club

► *Street dances in Ross Square behind Samford Hall were a Saturday night fixture at Auburn during the summer in the early and mid-1940s. Auburn High School senior-to-be Gene Hurt and Hugh Williams, left, a first-quarter API freshman from Auburn, are shown cuttin' a rug en route to winning the jitterbug contest at this dance of August 4, 1945. Gene graduated from the University in 1950 and married attorney C. C. "Bo" Torbert, Jr., Class of '51, who became chief justice of the Alabama Supreme Court. Hugh had a distinguished career as a professor of art and watercolor painter at Auburn after graduating in 1949. Music for the street dances usually was recorded, but Zombie Lauderdale's Auburn Collegians and vocalist LaHolme McClendon performed for this one.*

—*Photo: AU Archives*

▲ *Here's what World War II veterans faced when they enrolled in API in 1946. Seated with his back to the camera is P. M. Norton, college coordinator of veterans affairs. He and his assistants registered more than 4,300 returning veterans during the fall and winter quarters.*

—*Photo: Auburn Alumnews*

◀ *The Hitchcock brothers got together for this picture during a family reunion in the 1940s. Left to right were Walter B. "Bully," principal and coach at Demopolis High School; William C. "Billy," a major league baseball player and manager and president of the Southern Association, after starring at Auburn in football and baseball; James F. "Jimmy," Auburn's first football All-American and later a member of the Alabama Public Service Commission; and J. G. "Jake," Auburn businessman, city commissioner, and postmaster.*
—Photo: Bert Hitchcock

◀ *A bugler set the solemn tone as Auburn Daughters of the American Revolution honored "the boys who were killed in World War II" in a ceremony south of Samford Hall in April 1946. Soldiers stood at present arms, and a sergeant saluted near the tree planted in memory of the dead. Within the nearby chain enclosure, a bronze plaque placed in 1919 already memorialized Auburn men who gave their lives in World War I. A tree from the Argonne Forest also had been planted there in 1919, but it died. The event in 1946 was part of the fiftieth anniversary celebration of the founding of the Light Horse Harry Lee Chapter in 1896 by Mrs. P. H. Mell. Identifiable are DAR Regent Mollie Hollifield Jones, second from left; Lieutenant Colonel John E. "Boozer" Pitts, in khaki uniform with hand over heart; and API President L. N. Duncan, nearest bugler. As a young lieutenant, Pitts also had taken part in the 1919 tree planting.*
—Photo: AU Archives

◀ *Marine General H. M. "Howling Mad" Smith, a 1901 Auburn graduate, reviewed API's Navy ROTC unit in 1945. Known as "the father of modern amphibious warfare," he helped plan and personally directed Marine campaigns from Tarawa through Iwo Jima during World War II. He attributed his nickname to a mispronunciation of his first name, Holland, but others suspected it came from his impatience with inefficiency that might cost lives. At his retirement in 1946, Smith became the third Marine officer to obtain the rank of full general. He died in 1967, leaving a bequest of $100,000 to Auburn University.*
—Photo: AU Archives

▲ Navy veteran Herschel C. Duke built this house in three weeks for his wife and himself on Ross Street during the critical post-World War II housing shortage in Auburn. The house cost about $650. It was built in early 1946 on land rented for $1 per year for four years. Mrs. Duke, pictured in the doorway, described the house in Woman's Home Companion. The Dukes lived in the house until his graduation in 1948.

—Photo: AU Archives

▼ In 1946, forty-nine years after formation of the first cadet band on campus, five coeds became the first API drum majorettes. They were, left to right: Zilpha Ann Draper, Danny Sue Gibson, head majorette Kelda M. Ward, Nancy Young, and Joann "Bunny" Bennett. David A. Herbert became assistant to Paul R. "Bedie" Bidez, longtime director, and developed dramatically different routines for the band's halftime performances at football games. Two years later, majorettes were at the fore when the Auburn band passed in review in Washington, D. C., at the inauguration parade of President Harry S Truman.

—Photo: AU Archives

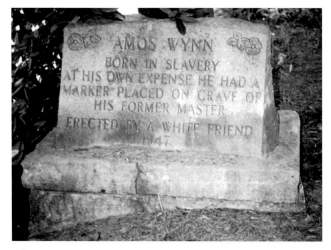

▲ Young Jeff Wynn was killed in a hunting accident. He was "a member of one of the original settlement party families," Ann Pearson wrote, but his relatives, "caught in the whirlwind of [the Civil] war, never put a marker on the young boy's grave." Jeff's former slave, Amos Wynn, a well digger, saved for about sixty years and placed a marker for Jeff in Pine Hill Cemetery. Nearly twenty years after Amos died, "a white friend," Dr. Charles Glenn, put a gravestone for Amos in Baptist Hill Cemetery in 1947. Glenn was a member of a family closely linked to the college and for whom Glenn Avenue was named.

◀ *Travis Tidwell came out of the Navy in time to become Auburn's starting quarterback in 1946. He ran or passed the ball 339 times that season and led the nation in total offense with 1,715 yards. Auburn sports information director Frank Sego dubbed him "Travelin' Trav" by the third game. An Associated Press sports writer said in 1981, "I've never seen in forty-five years of watching football a better freshman player than Travis. He could do everything—run, pass, punt, play defense." Other than panty raids, Travelin' Trav was the most exciting thing at API during his four years. He broke an ankle sliding into second in a baseball game before his sophomore season and after that ran with a noticable limp. Tidwell's teams won only 9 of 38 games, but one was a 14-13 victory over Alabama in 1949, after the Tide had drubbed Auburn 55-0 the previous year. Tidwell became an insurance agent and financial consultant in Birmingham after a back injury ended his brief professional football career with the New York Giants.*

—Photo: AU Athletic Department

▼ *Why does George S. Patton's Jeep have "War Eagle!" written on it? There are several possible answers. "General Patton was stationed at Fort Benning and apparently liked Auburn football," said alumnus Pete Turnham, who served under Patton during World War II. "I have been told that he said he wanted his troops to fight like those fighting Auburn Tigers." Turnham "also heard that one of Patton's aides was an Auburn man, and he sold the general on Auburn." Another theory is that Patton's driver was an Auburn fan. Still another is that Patton was simply using a subordinate's vehicle while he inspected units of the 301st Combat Team at Strakonice, Czechoslovakia, soon after Germany surrendered in 1945. If so, that commander might have been an Auburn man. Perhaps the explanation is as simple as coincidence.*

—Photo:
Auburn Alumnews

▲ *Clyde B. Ellis, above, became an Auburn policeman-fireman in 1937 for eighty dollars a month. He became police chief a few years later and after retiring in the early 1960s said, "In all my time, I never had to pull my pistol out of its holster." He was remembered as the friendliest man around Toomer's Corner to all who passed his way. Auburn's next police chief, Fred Hammock, also maintained a good relationship with University students. "We went for crime prevention, not*

for raising revenue," Hammock said. He and his twelve officers worked twelve-hour shifts, six days a week. Hammock never shot at anyone or got shot, but he had to disarm a number of persons "who had guns in their hands." The most sensational case Hammock helped investigate was the triple murder committed in 1967 by Edward A. Seibold. Chief Millard Dawson headed the campus security unit from 1951 to 1981.

—Photo: Glomerata

Military veterans at API, unwilling to pay local food prices, formed a cooperative grocery store in 1946. Their wives saved an average of 30 percent on food bills by shopping at the co-op, the *Alumnews* reported. Confirming what the veterans had thought about the town's prices, a nationwide survey found that Auburn had the second highest cost of living in the United States. Washington, D.C., was number one, the *Plainsman* reported.

—Photo: Auburn *Alumnews*

182

◀ Auburn must have held the world record in the 1940s for per capita consumption of Cokes, limeades, and milk shakes. All six drugstores did a booming soda fountain business, and for several years most offered curb service. Toomer's, Benson's, Lipscomb's, and Wright's were within about a hundred yards of each other on the east side of College Street toward the railroad track from Toomer's Corner. Bayne's was across the street, next to the Tiger Theatre. Markle's, shown here in 1946, was on East Magnolia, across from the Pitts Hotel. Lynwood Story of Auburn is behind the counter. Carroll Keller of Birmingham, a member of the wrestling team, is drinking coffee in the foreground. Soda fountain prices were competitive: Coke and root beer a nickel, limeades a dime, and milkshakes fifteen cents. Markle's featured a foot-long hot dog for a dime.

—Photo: C. C. Markle

▲ *A trailer village helped fill the housing needs of about fifty married veterans and their families. Two of these war surplus trailers were equipped as bathhouses for those living in the village. The trailers stood behind Cary Hall and on the parking lot behind what was then Magnolia Dorm. Downhill from the trailers was Drake Infirmary, part of which is visible behind the man holding the baby at right. Magnolia Dorm was replaced by the $15 million Lowder Building, which became the home of the College of Business in mid-1992.*

—Photo: Auburn Alumnews

▲ *A beer joint that got its name from the huge blades out front was a popular hangout on U.S. Highway 29 a few hundred yards from Dean Road. The Windmill was off-limits to coeds, but offered male students and other customers cold beer and the warmth of an old stove. Veterans liked to hoist a few and tell war stories there. One former patron recalled observing "whooping and hollering" but no fighting at the Windmill in the late 1940s. However, a decade earlier, the operator was indicted by a grand jury on charges of running a "disorderly house," the* Lee County Bulletin *reported.*

—Photo: AU Archives

◀ *Tugboat deckhouses on campus? That's right—ninety-three of 'em. Two male students lived in each one during the post-World War II housing crisis. They bunked upstairs, studied downstairs, and showered in a nearby bathhouse.* Life *magazine featured Auburn's war-surplus deckhouses to show how colleges were coping with the shortage of living quarters. The cabins were light blue-gray, 17 feet long, 7 feet wide, 7 feet high, and with a 7x7 pilot house for the upstairs. These stood on West Samford Avenue, across Donahue Drive from the USDA Tillage Lab and at about the same spot where the Educational TV complex later was built. In 1949, the university sold them to a businessman for a total of $1,860.*

—Photo: AU Photographic Services

◀ *Auburn didn't have nearly enough classrooms to accommodate enrollment after World War II. Almost overnight, temporary buildings shipped in from military bases dotted the campus. They made hot classrooms in summer and were drafty in winter, but helped API get through the enrollment crunch.*

—Photo: AU Archives

Freshmen women apparently were learning to render an appropriate "War Eagle" on Rat Activities Day in 1946. The coed at left holding the doll is Anna Jean Franklin of Birmingham, who later served as president of the Women's Student Government Association.

—Photo: AU Archives

▲ A fire caused a commotion in a men's barracks in 1949 off West Samford Avenue. No one was injured, and damage was confined to a couple of mattresses and a small portion of the building. Perhaps miraculously, there were no serious fires in the barracks, classrooms, or apartments—all of wood and all tinder dry—that had been brought to Auburn as war surplus material in 1946-47. The hill dorms for women were built on this site during the 1960s.

—Photo: AU Photographic Services

▲ Roland "Chief" Shine (pointing), owner of Chief's U-Drive-It and service station at College Street and Glenn Avenue, continued a tradition that went back at least as far as Police Chief Ben Smith and the early 1900s. Both men offered transportation for students.

Smith had rented horses and carriages; Shine rented cars in the 1940s, to API varsity athletic teams as well as individuals. In addition, Shine operated a bus service to and from Chewacla Park during gas rationing in World War II.

—Photo: 1948 Glomerata

▲ Auburn played baseball in the 1940s on what is now the site of Haley Center and its lower parking lot.
—Photo: AU Photographic Services

▶ Spring-fed Prather's Lake, off East Glenn Avenue, was a popular place during the 1940s, especially when gas rationing cut down even on trips to Chewacla Park. Hundreds of 4-H Club members attending the annual state convention in Auburn went swimming there. The lake was closed to the public in the 1960s and later rented out to individuals.
—Photo: Mrs. O. C. Prather, Sr.

◀ This 1949 aerial shows the southwest portion of the campus when housing was at its tightest. At upper right are barracks used from 1947 to 1952 that at one time housed 570 male students. On the other side of Samford Avenue are the prefab apartments for faculty and married students. West of the barracks at extreme right are the ninety-three tugboat deckhouses. Just across Wire Road in the foreground is the USDA Regional Parasite Research Laboratory complex, swapped years later to the University for property adjoining the College of Veterinary Medicine which by then had been established about a mile farther out Wire Road.
—Photo: Mrs. B. T. Simms

▲ The registration line was a way of life for Auburn students until the discovery of computers. Some of the more than 7,284 students enrolled for fall quarter 1949 are shown waiting to register. The line sometimes extended from the main gate, and some students waited as long as four hours to complete registration. Auburn's highest pre-war enrollment had been 3,728 in the fall of 1940.

—Photo: Auburn Alumnews

▶ Travis Tidwell (11) led Auburn to a 14-13 upset victory over Alabama, a three-touchdown favorite at Legion Field in 1949. How sweet it was for Auburn fans who the year before had watched the Tide swamp the Tigers, 55-0, in the first football game between the two universities in forty-one years. Many Auburn players contributed to that upset of Alabama, but it was Tidwell, and not Coach Earl Brown, who team members carried off the field when the game ended. During his four years, Travelin' Trav gained 3,820 yards passing and rushing. Going into the 1996 season—47 years after he left the field, Tidwell still ranked seventh among Auburn's all-time yardage leaders.

David Housel, long-time sports information director, was asked in 1995 after becoming athletic director, "Could Travis play today with these 240-pound linebackers, 300-pound defensive linemen, and all of these tall, fast defensive backs?" Housel's response: "Travis says he could play, and I believe him 100 percent!"

—Photo: 1950 Glomerata

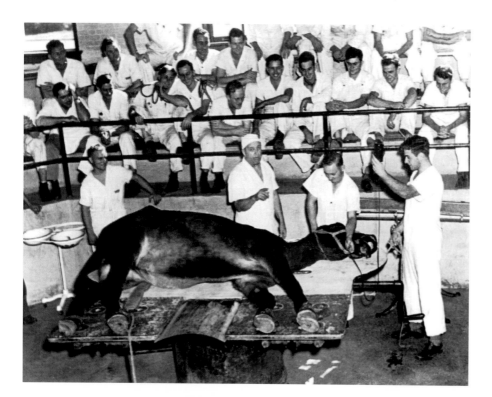

Dr. F. P. Woolf had this class of veterinary students laughing during an examination of a mule. Assisting him, left to right, were R. W. Porter, C. J. Young, and Jim Schuler. The vet school had quotas on enrollment of students from other Southern states during the 1940s. Freshman class enrollment was limited to sixty.

—Photo:
Dr. and Mrs. Harold W. Nance

A new $400,000 home was in the making for the School of Education in 1950. The foundation of Thach Hall had been poured, and the building was occupied the next year. Directly uphill on Thach Avenue stood Tichenor Hall, known as "new building" for many years after its completion in 1940. Peeking out to the right of Tichenor is one of the many temporary classroom buildings on campus at that time. To the left rear of Tichenor, is Alumni Gym. The tower of Samford Hall, of course, stood tall in the distance.
—Photo: Auburn Alumnews

▼ Street dances behind Samford Hall highlighted the entertainment in the summer of 1950.
—Photo: Auburn Alumnews

◀ API President L. N. Duncan's funeral took place in July 1947 in a pine-shaded amphitheatre that had been part of a dream come true in his lifetime. As Extension Service director, he had wanted to build a camp site for farmers and 4-H youths among the beautiful trees southwest of Duncan Hall. As college president in 1935, he saw twenty-five cottages built there with Public Works money. The Graves Amphitheatre, named for Governor Bibb Graves, five additional cottages, and a dining hall that doubled as an auditorium were built later. Through the years not only farm and 4-H conferences, but other events ranging from plays and pep rallies to community church services were held there. Eventually, athletes were housed and fed in Graves Centre until the completion of the athletic dormitory, Sewell Hall, in 1962. Most of the cottages and the dining hall had been removed for the Physical Science Center and the new architecture building. The last three cottages were removed in the 1990s. The amphitheatre became a part of the Fine Arts complex.
—Photo: AU Archives

▲ *Auburn fans showed their true colors at this pep rally in 1950. Despite five straight losses, they lined the College-Magnolia intersection in hopes of a victory that did not come against Tulane the next Saturday. Biggin Hall, about to become the new home of Architecture and the Fine Arts, was under construction.* Betty Hutton *was appearing in* Annie Get Your Gun *at the War Eagle Theatre.*
—Photo: W. N. Manning

◄ *In January 1951, newly appointed Athletic Director Jeff Beard contacted his friend Ralph Jordan, basketball coach and football line coach at Georgia. At Beard's insistence, Jordan wrote this one-sentence letter to the API selection committee: "I hearby apply for the head football coaching job at Auburn." Jordan was offered and turned down a three-year contract, but later signed a five-year contract, effective March 15, 1951. At the signing were, left to right: Jordan, President Ralph Draughon, Beard, and Business Manager W. T. Ingram.*
—Photo: AU Photographic Services

Alabama Governor James E. Folsom (left) installed Dr. Ralph B. Draughon as Auburn's tenth president in May 1949. The trustees had named Draughon acting president after Dr. L. N. Duncan's death and named him president in October 1948. At the installation ceremony, Trustee Frank P. Samford, Sr., sat at the viewer's far left. Dr. Frank B. Davis, at right, grand marshal at commencements for many years, wore saddle oxfords. Construction was proceeding on the stadium's east stands. Draughon, third alumnus to serve as president, guided Auburn in the growth-packed years after World War II from being API to being Auburn University. In Draughon's seventeen years as president, Auburn awarded 11,153 more degrees (including its first doctorates) than in its previous ninety years. This president engaged in an unending struggle for funds needed to take care of growing enrollment.
—Photo: AU Archives

▲ John Gazes, at the cash register in the early 1950s, and his brother Lucas operated the Auburn Grille from its opening near Toomer's Corner in 1936 until 1965. They had been little boys on the Greek-speaking Isle of Patmos before their father, Emmanuel Gazes, decided to quit the uncertain life of a sea captain and move to Auburn. He founded the Auburn Cafe in 1907 and ran it until about 1921 on College Street, about one hundred yards north of Toomer's Corner. His sons later operated a soda fountain in Auburn and restaurants in other towns before opening the Grille. The Auburn Cafe had one of the town's earliest refrigerators, and the Grille was the first air-conditioned restaurant in Lee County.
—Photo: John Gazes

▲ The rear guard in Kappa Alpha fraternity's secession parade moved past an old home on Mell Street toward Thach Avenue and Toomer's Corner in 1950. Life magazine covered the KA party weekend that year from the secession proclamation to the last dance of the Old South Ball. For most Southern white readers of that day, Life probably painted a generally pleasant picture of the weekend for the KAs and their dates, but the magazine noted that the Confederate uniforms worn "had to be rented from a firm in the arch-Yankee city of Philadelphia . . ." During the parade, George Pierce, with sideburns, sits in the back seat of the Jeep behind the driver. Pierce made the cannon barrel from a sewer pipe, the wagon axle from a water pipe, and the wagon wheels came from an old hay rake.
—Photo: George Pierce

◀ *This familiar bridge leads uphill to the gravel pit of Lake Chewacla. In earlier days, covered bridges stood here. Even earlier, a bridge crossed upstream near Wright's grist mill. J. Peavy Wright said that the bridge collapsed in about 1903 or 1904 just after his brother had finished driving some cows across it.*
—Photo: AU University Relations

▲ *Chewacla State Park has been a recreation center for Auburn townspeople and students since its completion in 1939 by the Civilian Conservation Corps. It features a twenty-six-acre lake for swimming, diving, and boating, and 696 acres of hilly-to-rugged grounds for picnicking and hiking. "Some of the oldest known rocks in eastern North America are exposed at Chewacla and elsewhere in [Lee] County," AU geologist Mark Steltenpohl told a newspaper. They are part of the southern end of the Appalachian Mountain system. Overlooking the lake, at the end of a scenic drive, is a picturesque peak. Indian hunters—perhaps even one named Chewacla—used to look down on that valley.*
—Photo: AU Archives

▼ *Tennis courts replaced the baseball diamond north of Drake Field in the early 1950s when baseball moved to Plainsman Park, and in 1969, Haley Center and its parking lot were built on the site.*
—Photo: Auburn Alumnews

▶ *Howard Hill, an Auburn football end in the early 1920s, later became one of the world's best archers. From 1936 to 1952, he won 196 field tournaments. "Not only has Hill, with bow and arrow, shot an apple off a man's head," the* Alumnews *reported, "but he did it three times, and then shot a prune off the same noggin." He killed this elephant in Africa. Hill produced thirty-two motion picture shorts for Warner Brothers and three for Paramount and doubled for Errol Flynn in the film,* Robin Hood. *Hill loved Auburn and the friends he made there. "The Auburn spirit . . .cannot be duplicated anywhere in the world," he said.*
—Photo: Auburn Alumnews

▲ *Auburn coed Leah Marie Rawls won national championships on water skiis and honors in the classroom during the 1950s. She became the first woman inducted into the Alabama Sports Hall of Fame and the first recipient of an Auburn Ph.D. in history. She married George Atkins, an outstanding guard of the early fifties on the Auburn football team who later became an associate director of the Office of Alumni and Development. After teaching at Auburn, University of Alabama-Birmingham, and Samford University, Dr. Atkins became the first director of the Auburn Center for the Arts and Humanities. She still enjoyed water skiing at Lake Martin after she and her husband retired in 1995.*
—Photo: AU Athletic Department

▼ *A photographer caught these four Marine Corps officers rendering a mighty "War Eagle" during a get-together at Auburn in the early 1950s. Lieutenant General Franklin A. Hart, API '15, second from left, commanding general, Fleet Maine Force, Pacific, and retired Marine General Holland M. "Howling Mad" Smith, API '01, with cigar, are flanked by Colonel George B. Bell, left, professor of Naval Science and Tactics at Auburn, and Major R. H. McCormick of the Naval ROTC faculty. Another illustration of Auburn's considerable contribution to America's military leadership.*
—Photo: AU Archives

▲ The vacated college supply store building, camouflaged by untrimmed privet, stood next to Mary Martin Hall long after its business was transferred to the new Union Building. The store had operated in one of many surplus military buildings erected on campus soon after World War II ended. They helped meet the needs of an enrollment swelled by thousands of veterans attending Auburn on the GI Bill of Rights. Similar frame structures served as temporary classrooms in several locations on campus, including where Draughon Library was later built.
—Photo: AU Photographic Services

◀ Spring dresses and hats blossomed like dogwoods after a Sunday morning service at the Methodist Church in 1952. This building had first become part of Auburn's religious heritage with the laying of its cornerstone in 1850. It was restructured near the turn of the century, and its stained-glass windows, flared roof lines, and arches, became a landmark at Gay Street and Magnolia Avenue. To serve a growing congregation, a larger sanctuary was built nearby in the 1950s, and the old structure became the church's Fellowship Hall.
—Photo: Auburn Alumnews

▲ The legendary Pop Raines Beverage Shack, 2.6 miles south of Toomer's Corner on U.S. Highway 29, provided beer and atmosphere for about two decades to a contingent of male students and others from the 1940s into the sixties. University rules prohibited coeds from frequenting such establishments. The Shack sat on a knoll off the road a bit, and during much of its existence patrons had to go through a gate and up a washed-out gravel road to reach the old wooden structure. Many customers got their beer to go. But those faithful who whiled away the hours there dubbed it The Cornfield Country Club. Cardboard beer cartons served as wallpaper and insulation. The cracks in the board floor were wide enough in places to see the ground below. The furniture consisted of a few tables and several crude chairs. The bar was placed at an angle in a corner with a small sign above it stating: "No Profanity Allowed." Mounted on the wall back of the bar within easy reach of the bartender was a pistol. Paul Martin, an ROTC teacher at Auburn in 1951-62, remembered years later for an Auburn Alumnews story that behind the Shack was the biggest pile of beer cans he had ever seen. "It would be no exaggeration to say that the stack was four feet high and a hundred feet long," he said. "They would just take the beer cans and throw them out back."
—Photo: Dr. Russell Skinner '56; AU Archives

▲ The Great Tornado of April 18, 1953, gave the area north of Drake Avenue "the appearance of having been bombarded by a field artillery barrage," the Lee County Bulletin reported. This scene is in Cary Woods, a block from the Donahue Drive entrance. The Joseph B. Sarver home is to the right of the car, and the A. A. Liebolds lived to the left. Winds estimated at 150 miles per hour ripped the area after first attacking along Opelika Road and flattening the Auburn Gin and Warehouse, heavily damaging the Drake Motor Company building, and damaging Brittain Drake's grocery store. Forty-nine homes were reported destroyed and 519 damaged. Twenty people were injured, five seriously, but no deaths occurred. Local historian Ann Pearson later called the tornado "the worst calamity ever to hit the City of Auburn."
—Photo: AU Photographic Services

▲ The 1953 tornado took the roof and top floor off the old William W. Wright home at Drake Avenue and Gay Street. Wright's family had lived in the last quarter of the nineteenth century at Wright's Mill, later a part of Chewacla Park.

Wright, who owned a grist mill where many picnics and social events took place, was born in Georgia in 1825 and died in this house in 1905.
—Photo: W. N. Manning

▲ *In 1917, the Presbyterians built this church with two identical entrances, one facing Thach Avenue and the other facing Gay Street. It was replaced in 1953 by a larger sanctuary. To the left on Thach was the manse, the home of ministers and* *their families for almost four decades. Dr. Sam Burney Hay and family lived there for twenty-two years and Dr. John H. Leith and family for eleven years. The Leith Lecture series, established in the mid-1950s in the minister's name, brings* *to Auburn each year a theologian of national or international stature to present a Sunday morning sermon and three evening lectures.*

—Photo: Leonard W. Thomas and H. C. Morgan, Jr.

◀ *Auburn's main water source, Lake Ogletree, looked like a narrow creek in places during the drought of 1954, the driest year on record in the city. Less than half the normal rainfall fell from January through October, leaving the lake with less than 4 percent of its normal volume of water. The shortage caused the college to close on Thursday for a long weekend in late October. Emergency steps were taken to replenish and conserve the water supply until winter rains ended the drought.*

—Photo: AU Photographic Services

▶ Coach Arnold W. "Swede" Umbach is shown with Dan McNair, Auburn's first national champion wrestler. McNair won the heavyweight title in 1953 and at 196 pounds was the lightest ever to win in that weight division. Umbach, who produced powerful teams during many of his twenty-nine years at Auburn, retired in 1973. The University dropped the sport in July 1981 as an economy move.

—Photo: Dan McNair

▼ Nearly a quarter of a century before Fob James made his first run for public office—and became Alabama governor—he ran 11 yards for this touchdown against Georgia in 1954. Other Auburn men at work included Frank D'Agostino (77), Bob Scarbrough (60) and Joe Childress (35). The Tigers won 35-0. They had become a powerhouse after abandoning the X and Y system that had been losing after succeeding so well the year before. Coach Ralph Jordan later credited James, quarterback Bobby Freeman, and other players with recommending that he put all of the best players on one unit rather than spreading them over two teams.

—Photo: Ralph Jordan

▶ Auburn discus thrower Jim Dillion, a two-time NCAA champion, was dubbed "One in a Million Dillion" by AP writer Vernon Butler in 1951. The next year he finished third in the Olympic Games at Helsinki, Finland. He won the discus throw three times at Southeastern Conference meets and in 1954 also won the shot put. Perhaps most significant, his discus throw of 180 feet, 8 inches in 1954 was still an Auburn school record more than 42 years later.

—Photo: AU Athletic Department

▲ *Lee County Training School's first Student Council was elected during the 1953-54 year. Members shown during a meeting in the school library were, left to right, Willie Wright, vice president; Betty Williams, parliamentarian; Nell Hill, recording secretary; Curtis Harper, president; Sarah Slaughter, corresponding secretary; and Jimmy Smith, treasurer.*

Harper later received a B.S. degree in chemistry from Tuskegee Institute, an M.S. in organic chemistry from Iowa State, and an M.S. and Ph.D. in biochemistry from University of Missouri. For many years, he has been a professor at the University of North Carolina Medical School in Chapel Hill.
—*Photo:* Lee County Bulletin

▶ *Auburn's football team got a big welcome home after beating Georgia Tech 14-12 in 1955 to end a string of thirteen straight losses to the Engineers. Trains, pep rallies, and the Young's Laundry sign in the background formed a typical Auburn scene for many years.*
—*Photo: AU Photographic Services*

▲ Lillian Carter, mother of U.S. President Jimmy Carter, served as Kappa Alpha housemother from 1956 through 1962. "Those seven years in Auburn were the happiest of my life," she told the Plainsman in 1976. Miss Lillian recalled that all her boys were good boys; it was the girls who needed watching. The flag in the background later became a major source of controversy on campus.

—Photo: AU University Relations

▲ An honor guard from Fort Benning led the funeral procession of Lieutenant General Lewis A. Pick down Gay Street in December 1956. Pick commanded the Allied Forces that built the Ledo Road, connecting India and China during World War II. While assigned to duty in Auburn in 1924, he met and later married Alice Cary, daughter of Auburn Veterinary School Dean and Mrs. C. A. Cary. After retirement in 1953, the Picks made their home in Auburn. Alice Cary Pick Gibson, in 1996 at age ninety-two, was living at 360 North College Street in the antebellum home of her birth. She still slept in the bedroom and bed in which she was born.

—Photo:
Mrs. Alice Cary Pick Gibson

▲ All-American Jimmy Phillips caught this touchdown pass from Lloyd Nix that beat Georgia 6-0 in 1957. Auburn now needed victories over only Florida State and Alabama for a perfect season and a shot at a national championship. College football has seldom seen the equal of Phillips and Jerry Wilson as a pair of defensive ends. On offense, Phillips held most of the school's receiving records until another fleet redhead, Terry Beasley, broke nearly all of them. However, Jimmy's career 19.5 yards per catch was tops for 23 years, until Byron Franklin finished his four years in 1980 with an average of 21.3 yards per reception.

—Photo: AU Photographic Services

▲ The Auburn All-Stars, paced by future Atlanta Braves pitcher Arnold Umbach, finished third in the 1955 Little League World Series at Williamsport, Pennsylvania. Regulation in Little League games is six innings, and Umbach struck out fifteen in Auburn's 4-1 victory over San Diego. In its second game, Auburn held a 4-3 lead with two outs in the top of the sixth, only to lose to New Jersey, 6-4. Umbach struck out thirteen in six innings of the seven-inning 1-0 conso- lation game victory over Massachusetts. Catcher Ted Wilson hit two home runs at Williamsport, and Umbach and George Salter each hit one. The trip included a stop in Washington, D.C., where the play- ers met Ted Williams and former Auburn pitcher Willard Nixon, both of the Boston Red Sox. About one thousand fans and the Auburn High School Band turned out when the team returned home on Sunday, August 27. Players, left to right: O'Neal Whitman, Tom Flint, Jim Neal, John Whatley, Wilson, Stan Weldon, Buddy Hollis, Charlie Dowdell, Lewis Cherry, Flem Wilson, Berner Chesnutt, Allen Tapley, Arnold Umbach, Frank Salter, George Salter. Manager Horace Smith, Assistant Manager Verl Emrick, and Auburn Little League President Henry Summer accompanied the team. Dowdell, Chesnutt, Flint and the Salter brothers also played in the 1956 Little League World Series, when Auburn was eliminat- ed in the opening game.

—Photo: Ted Wilson

▶ Citizens helped recreate history at Langdon Hall on November 9, 1956, as API celebrated its one hundredth birth- day. This scene dramatized the 1857 lay- ing of the cornerstone for the main build- ing at East Alabama Male College, fore- runner of API. Portraying members of the Auburn Masonic Lodge were, left to right: Henry A. Young, F. R. Attleberger, and F. Gordon Bush. Others on stage included, from left, Molly Brasfield Sarver, P. O. Davis, B. Conn Anderson, P. R. "Bedie" Bidez, Elizabeth Glenn Smith Wilder, James E. Greene, and Eleanor Wright McGowen.

—Photo: AU Photographic Services

▶ *Leading the celebration at Toomer's Corner after Auburn won the national football championship in 1957 was Hodge Freeman Drake, a landmark on North College Street and a familiar figure at Tiger football games. He dispensed "shoe shines and Auburn spirit from his Varsity Barbershop station for forty years," Graham McTeer wrote in an obituary for the fifty-nine-year-old "Doc" Hodge in the* Lee County Bulletin *in 1961.*
    —Photo: AU Photographic Services

▼ *Eleven good men savored the rainy opening victory at Knoxville in 1957 that put Auburn on the road to a national football championship. Their reactions ranged from unabridged joy to silent resolution in this classic photograph by Ed Jones of the* Birmingham News. *The players were, left to right: Dan Presley, Red Phillips, Bobby Hoppe (top), Zeke Smith (61), James Warren, Tim Baker, Jackie Burkett, Jerry Wilson, Lloyd Nix, Tommy Lorino, and Billy Atkins.*
    —Photo: Ralph Draughon

▲ *All-American guard Zeke Smith may have saved a national championship when he recovered this Georgia fumble near the Auburn goal in 1957. Auburn's stonewall defense shut out the Bulldogs, 6-0, and five other opponents, including Alabama, 40-0. Nobody scored more than one touchdown on the Tigers.*
    —Photo: Ralph Jordan

▲ *The business that brought this august group together in the 1950s has been lost, but it must have been important. Outside, left to right, were: Marshall Conner, Mutt Gregory, Yetta Samford, Jr., Ralph Draughon, Charlie Rush, Ira Weissinger, Joe Sarver, Bill Ham, Neil Davis, Pete Turnham. Inside, left to right: Tommy Edwards, unidentified, C. H. "Babe" McGehee, Ed Lee Spencer, Milligan Earnest, J. C. Grimes, Mac Lipscomb, Bobby Blake.*

—Photo: Lee County Bulletin

◀ *Auburn's first council-woman, four other council members, and a new mayor took office in 1955 after voters approved a change from commission to council government. Appointed by Governor James E. Folsom to serve sixteen-month terms were, left to right: Dr. James E. Greene, W. T. Ingram, Mayor Louie W. James, Bessie Williamson, McAdory Lipscomb and C. R. "Red" Meagher. City Attorney Knox McMillan (right) swore them in. At the election the next year, Mrs. Williamson and Sarah Spencer Roy became the first council-women chosen by the voters.*

—Photo: AU Archives

Ralph Jordan showed how it felt to be No. 1 in college football, hugging the Associated Press national championship trophy of 1957 for his team, for his assistants, and for Auburn people everywhere. The Tigers hadn't had a winning season since 1942 when the former Auburn player and assistant coach took over the football program in 1951. Things changed. During Jordan's twenty-five years as head coach, the Tigers won 176 games—including five straight over Alabama in the 1950s—lost 83, and tied 6. They played in twelve bowl games. From the last four games of 1956 through 1958, Auburn went a school record of 24 games without a loss. Jordan produced 22 all-Americans and 67 all-Southeastern Conference players, including 19 all-SEC repeaters. He was chosen national coach of the year in 1957 by the prestigious Washington Touchdown Club. Pat Sullivan, Auburn quarterback 1969-71, said, "Winning the Heisman Trophy was the second highest honor of my life. The first was playing for Coach Jordan."

▲ Governor John Patterson (seated) signed a bill on October 30, 1959, changing the name of the Alabama Polytechnic Institute to Auburn University. The change became effective on January 1, 1960. Auburn President Ralph B. Draughon (left) and Trustee Paul S. Haley witnessed the signing.

—Photo: Montgomery Advertiser

▶ Mrs. Mollie Hollifield Jones is shown breaking ground in September 1959 for construction of the city's first library building. Mrs. A. L. Thomas and Mrs. Benjamin F. Showalter spearheaded a drive to get a city library established, and it was first located in a room on Magnolia Avenue across from Toomer Drugstore. For the first building, Miss Mollie donated to the city a lot next to her home on Gay Street, just north of Auburn National Bank. With 1,500 square feet of usable space, the structure served as the library more than twenty-seven years— until September 1987, when the library building in the City Hall Complex on North Ross Street was opened. Mrs. Margie Huffman, in her twen- ty-fifth year as city librarian, commented in 1996: "The old building would fit inside the main reading room of the building we have now. We went from 1,500 to about 14,000 square feet of space, and now the present building is too small."

Pictured with Miss Mollie in 1959 were, left to right, Billy Joe Kirkley, contractor; E. B. Lancaster, architect; Mayor G. H. "Monk" Wright; and Francis J. Marshall, Library Board chairman. The librarian at that time was Mrs. Frances Woodall. Four others served as librarian at the Gay Street building, Mrs. Carol Blanton, Mrs. Carol Anthony, Miss Janell Baker, and Mrs. Huffman.

—Photo: AU Archives.

◀ *The athletic connection with the University of Georgia couldn't have been much stronger than among the 1958 Tiger football coaching staff. Eight played college football at Auburn and three at Georgia. Ralph Jordan '32, kneeling, served as an assistant coach at Georgia for four seasons before returning to Auburn as head coach for twenty-five years. Others on the front row, left to right: Shot Senn '33, an Auburn assistant for twenty-three years; Hal Herring '48, who got his doctorate at Georgia in 1971 and became dean of students at DeKalb College in Decatur, Georgia; Gene Lorendo, a 1949 Georgia graduate and Auburn assistant twenty-five years; Buck Bradberry, 1949 Georgia graduate and for thirty-four years associated with Auburn, first as an assistant football coach and then as associate director and later as executive secretary of the Auburn Alumni Association. Back row: Vince Dooley '54,*

Georgia head football coach from 1964 through 1988 and in his seventeenth year as Bulldogs' athletic director in 1996; Joel Eaves '37, Georgia athletic director for sixteen years after serving as Auburn's head basketball coach in 1949-63 and as a football assistant; Joe Connally, a 1949 Georgia graduate who served as an Auburn football assistant twenty-eight years, as assistant Coliseum manager ten years until retirement and then a part-timer for several years; Dick McGowen '41; Erk Russell '49, defensive coach at Georgia in 1964-80 and then head coach at Georgia Southern; and George Atkins '55, later associate director of Alumni and Development at Auburn. Russell joined the Auburn staff in July 1958. The other ten made up the coaching staff of the national championship team of 1957 that went 10-0. In 1958, Auburn won nine and tied one.

—*Photo:* Auburn Alumnews

▲ *When the Sports Arena was put together on campus in 1948, students quickly and affectionately dubbed it "The Barn." Arriving early to ensure getting a seat for varsity basketball games became a ritual extending over two decades. Back then, penny loafers, bobby sox, and flat tops or crew cuts, were a part of student identity. Note: not a Nike or Reebok shoe in sight. The 2,000 or so who crowded into this war surplus gymnasium on game nights usually left smiling. From the 1950-51 season through 1967-68, Auburn won 140 home games and lost only 35 in the friendly confines of "The Barn," which rival coaches sometimes referred to as a snakepit.*

—Photo: AU Photographic Services

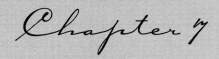

Chapter 7

THE
BOOM YEARS

he biggest news of the 1960s was the desegregation of the University and the local public schools. Negroes had worked on campus as janitors, mail clerks, maids, cooks, laborers, and handymen for many years, but none of their race had ever attended the University until January 4, 1964, when Auburn, under federal court order, with "dignity and restraint" admitted the first black student in its 107-year history. President Draughon had made it clear that disruption and violence would not be tolerated, and security measures were planned. Harold L. Franklin, thirty-one, of Talladega, who held an A.B. degree from Alabama State College in Montgomery, enrolled at Auburn as a graduate student in history and began classes without serious incident. He did not, however, complete the requirements for the master's degree. The first black student to graduate from Auburn was Josetta B. Matthews, awarded a master's in education in August 1966. Five years later, she became an instructor, the History Department's first black teacher.

◀ *Any definition of The Auburn Spirit would of necessity include these blithe characters, Katharine C. Cater and James E. Foy, shown pedaling on campus in 1967 after the University bought a few bicycles-built-for-two for student recreation. Deans Cater and Foy were among the most popular faculty members with students during their long tenures. She served as dean of women from 1946 to 1976, then almost four years as dean of student life and social director. Dean Cater became one of the few University employees to have a building named in her honor when in 1980, a few months before her death, she attended ceremonies during which the Social Center became Katharine Cooper Cater Hall.*

Foy served as dean of student affairs from 1950 until his retirement in 1978. The Student Union promptly was renamed James E. Foy Union. Two years after going to Montgomery to serve in Governor Fob James' administration, Foy and his wife, Emmalu, were back in Auburn, engaged in affairs of Phi Eta Sigma national freshman scholastic honor society. Foy served as national secretary or national secretary-treasurer from 1953 through 1992. Mrs. Foy served as local office manager. Foy's father, Erle, majored in electrical and mechanical engineering at Auburn in 1896-1900. As a senior, Erle Foy was editor-in-chief of the Orange and Blue *and captained API's baseball team. A right-handed pitcher, he beat Alabama twice in two days. His catcher told Jim Foy years later that Erle's curve ball "curved all the way from third base."*

—Photo: Emmalu Foy

◀ *President and Mrs. Ralph B. Draughon fish at Lake Martin on July 4, 1960.*
—Photo: Caroline Draughon

Auburn's first black professor, Dr. C. G. Gomillion, visiting part-time lecturer, taught foundations of education and was a consultant on desegregation problems in 1968. At Tuskegee, he taught sociology after serving as dean of education, dean of students, and dean of the College of Arts and Sciences. He was a civil rights leader. When letter writers questioned Gomillion's loyalty to the United States, Auburn President Harry M. Philpott defended him and praised his work at Auburn. Professor Robert D. Reid joined the History Department fulltime in 1972 after extensive service as a faculty member and administrator at Tuskegee Institute and Alabama State University. In addition to teaching American Negro History at Auburn, he was "an easy, jovial colleague of great human wisdom and graciousness," Dr. Robert R. Rea wrote in *History at Auburn*.

Jimmy Fibbe sank two free throws against Kentucky in the last five seconds at the Sports Arena in 1960 to give Auburn a 61-60 victory and keep the Tigers on a tightrope toward their first SEC basketball championship. Auburn players watching Fibbe's second shot were, left to right, John Helmlinger, Porter Gilbert (12), Ray Groover (22), and Captain Henry Hart. Groover later hit the layup that beat Alabama in overtime at Montgomery for the title. Only two starters were as tall as six feet three, and the team was dubbed Coach Joel Eaves' "Seven Dwarfs."
—Photo: AU Photographic Services

In sports, Henry Harris of Boligee was the University's first black varsity athlete when he became a starting forward in basketball as a sophomore in 1969-70. He was team captain his senior year. James Owens of Fairfield followed as the first black football player, lettering in 1970-71-72. Owens is remembered as a blocking back for Terry Henley in the 10-1, "Punt-Bama-Punt" season of 1972. Harvey Glance became one of Auburn's most memorable black athletes by winning a gold medal in the 400-meter relays at the 1976 Olympic Games in Montreal. Seventeen years after Harold Franklin had broken the racial barrier, all of Auburn's basketball starters and many of its football players were black. Yet, in the fall of 1980, black students made up less than 3 percent of the main campus enrollment— 482 of 18,603 students.

Auburn public schools began integrating in 1965 under court order. This historic change wasn't easy, but it was less disruptive than in numerous other Southern towns. It took the efforts of many parents, teachers, and students—black and white. Coping with fears, suspicions, racial prejudice, and educational disparities, they integrated all the schools by late 1970, from the first grade through the twelfth. School board members and administrators helped. Teachers were trained to provide individualized instruction to the extent that class sizes and available adult assistants would make possible, recalled Dr. Wayne Teague, city school superintendent in 1969-75. Black senior high students moved from Drake to the new Auburn High School, and all sixth-graders attended Drake. The black junior high students from Drake joined the whites at the Samford Avenue school. The fourth- and fifth-graders were taught at Boykin Street Elementary School, a former black grade school. First through third-graders went to Cary Woods, Dean Road, and Wrights Mill Road elementary schools. Only "a very few" students transferred from Auburn schools

at the time, said Teague, who later served a record 19 1/2 years as state superintendent of education. Acknowledging that his objectivity could be questioned, Teague rated the Auburn system in the early 1970s one of the four or five best of 125 public-school systems in the state. And it continued among the best, he said. By 1980, about 61 percent of the 3,286 public school students were white and about 39 percent were black.

A number of white students from Auburn, Opelika, elsewhere in Lee County, and surrounding counties attended the new Lee Academy in 1967. The private school offered the first grade through the sixth in the old Drake-Samford House on North Gay Street. In two years, the academy had a kindergarten and eight grades. After the Christian school moved to about sixteen acres on East Glenn Avenue in 1969-70, it grew to offer college-preparatory instruction through the twelfth grade. In 1981, the school united with Scott Preparatory to form Lee-Scott Academy, "committed to excellence."

In 1972, two teachers and twelve children, grades two through six, began another alternative school, the Village School on East Drake Avenue. A decade later, the nondiscriminatory school continued to have small, flexible classes, special projects, "high academic standards," and instruction "tailored to a child's ability."

Ralph Draughon stepped down as Auburn University president in 1965 after eighteen years. From his Samford Hall window, he could see the last of the central campus "temporary buildings" that had arrived in 1947 being hauled away in a truck, Trudy Cargile of University Relations wrote. World War II veterans had attended classes in those hastily erected white frame buildings. The Draughon years had seen their share of brick and mortar, including the con-

struction of more than twenty major buildings, such as Thach Hall, Funchess Hall, the first phase of Foy Union, and Draughon Library. The School of Veterinary Medicine moved out Wire Road to McAdory Hall and Sugg Laboratory. The stadium's seating capacity had been increased from about 7,500 to 44,500. But "building a strong staff and faculty" were the president's strong points, a veteran trustee said.

Draughon turned over the reins as president to Dr. Harry M. Philpott, who was one week short of his forty-ninth birthday when installed in May 1966. Philpott, a Yale graduate, Baptist minister, and former executive vice president of the University of Florida, was the first Auburn president to have an earned Ph. D., according to the AU Archives. He continued Draughon's effort to develop a coordinated legislative budget for educational institutions in Alabama. This leadership helped yield a 170 percent increase in state appropriations to Auburn in the 1960s. Within Philpott's first five years as president, Auburn had opened Auburn University at Montgomery, had added the 12,500-seat Memorial Coliseum, and had completed the

largest building on campus, Haley Center. This ten-story structure was named for Paul Shields Haley, believed to have missed only one or two meetings in fifty-one years as a member of the Auburn Board of Trustees.

Enrollment went up from 8,829 students in 1960 to 14,229 in 1970, and tuition jumped from $60 per quarter to $150. The city's total population rose during the decade from 16,261 to 22,767.

Gardner Drive seemed the safest of places in early September, 1967, much like the rest of Auburn in the between-quarters quiet. Then late one night at the Sinclair home, calm turned to terror. Sarah Elizabeth Sinclair, eighteen, Mary Lynn Sinclair, nine, and Mary Matherly Durant, eight, who was spending the night in the Sinclair home, were murdered. Auburn residents experienced a tension unknown to them until Edward A. Seibold, twenty-one, was apprehended in Florida. He was a former Auburn resident and had attended the University. At his trial, Seibold pleaded not guilty and not guilty by reason of insanity. He received two death sentences, but the law providing for the death penalty later was rescinded. He was serving a term of

For more than a century, the Lane House occupied this corner at Thach Avenue and College Street. It was built before the Civil War on land once assigned to the Creek Indian, Lostiyoholo. Former Confederate General James H. Lane, a professor of civil engineering and drawing, bought the house and its grounds in 1884 for $1,200. Lane's daughter, Kate Lane, deeded the property to the University in 1960 for $150,000. The house was to be torn down to make way for a new library, but the Woman's Club of Auburn bought it and had it moved to Sanders Street.

The structure was moved in three sections down College Street to its new location in Cary Woods. Along the way, the house passed such once-familiar downtown sights as Barney's Cub Cafe, Elmore's 5 and 10, and Wright's Drugstore. It was redesigned for future use when being put together again. Besides saving the historic landmark, the club completed a quest that had begun almost from its founding in 1919 for a permanent building.

—Photos: Paul Kennedy, Sr.; AU Photographic Services

life in prison in 1996, but with a chance for parole.

As the 1960s wound down, the Vietnam War claimed new attention at Auburn, but the students avoided the riots and violent demonstrations that jolted other campuses. Anti-war and pro-war advocates made their feelings known peacefully at such events as the Vietnam Moratorium Day of 1968 and the Strike Day of 1970, but most students didn't get involved in the protests.

The anti-war mood among many Americans helped sound taps for a ninety-eight-year-old tradition in the summer of 1970 as Auburn ended compulsory ROTC for underclassmen. A new voluntary program attracted less than half the previous numbers, but Auburn continued to graduate many able officers for the armed forces, as it had done since becoming a land-grant college in 1872. From 1872 until about 1977, forty-two alumni had risen to the rank of general or admiral.

Another tradition died in 1970 when the Crescent Limited made its last run through Auburn. For the first time

since Federal raiders burned the depot and ripped up the track during the Civil War, the city was without passenger train service. In the heyday of the route between Atlanta and Montgomery, twelve trains a day had steamed through Auburn—six each way, *Trails in History* says. One could still hear that lonesome whistle both day and night in Auburn a quarter century later, but only from freight trains.

The 1970s also brought the end of special campus housing rules for women, such as dormitory curfews, which had been in effect since Smith Hall became the first women's dorm in 1921. Student complaints resulted in concessions in the late 1960s and early 1970s. In 1976, the University discontinued regulations that might be in violation of federal guidelines against discrimination based on sex. The changes included eliminating the office of Dean of Women, which became Student Life, expanding the Athletic Department to add an assistant director of women's athletics, and offering additional scholarships in women's sports. In 1975, after 119 years, a woman began serving on

▲ Businessmen Louie W. James (left) and G. H. "Monk" Wright ran against each other for mayor three times, with Wright winning twice and James once. They are shown in 1964 when Wright unseated incumbent James. Despite their strong political rivalry, James said later that there was no personal antagonism between them. In fact, James credited Wright with introducing him to his pretty wife-to-be. All told, Wright served nineteen years as mayor, beginning his first term in 1944. Besides his elected term, James served sixteen months as Governor James E. Folsom's appointee when Auburn changed from commission to council government in 1955.
—Photo: AU Archives

▲ Leila A. Terrell, an Auburn boardinghouse operator for many years, was 103 years old when the University dedicated Terrell Dining Hall in 1969. She is shown after the ceremonies being assisted by Polly Philpott, left, wife of Auburn President Harry Philpott, and by Margaret Varner.

Mrs. Terrell was born the year after the Civil War ended. She "lived to be 104," Editor Neil O. Davis wrote. "She was probably known by more Auburn students than any other resident of this college community."
—Photo: Harry M. Philpott

the Board of Trustees. A businesswoman working toward a doctorate in education when Governor George C. Wallace appointed her, Sue Fincher of Wedowee also may have been the first student to serve on the board.

The Toomer Building changed owners in 1974. For the first time in nearly seventy years, it no longer belonged to the family for whom it was named. But this landmark, the site of an apothecary even before the Civil War, continued to dispense the "Auburn Spirit" in lemonade and remained a favorite location for pep rallies. Mac Lipscomb, who bought the drugstore in 1952, became new owner of the two-story building, which also housed The Auburn Grille and a hardware store. Acknowledging the tradition that had been growing since Sheldon L. Toomer had become a druggist there, Lipscomb told the *Auburn Bulletin*, "I feel the purchase was more like a transfer of custodianship than a hard business deal."

The Auburn Bicentennial Committee, headed by William A. McMillan, helped celebrate the nation's two-hundredth anniversary by sponsoring exhibits in Samford Park in the spring, a fair at the Student Activities Building,

and other events. Claude Layfield got a California firm to strike five hundred silver and three thousand bronze commemorative coins, which were sold to help finance committee activities. To climax the celebration, the Samford clock peeled two hundred times beginning at 1 p.m. on Sunday, July 4, 1976. At precisely that hour, a fierce electrical storm hit Auburn and knocked out power in much of the city. At the First Baptist Church, Dr. John H. Jeffers conducted the bicentennial wedding of Jane Moon Simms and Thomas Alan Love totally by candlelight.

The biggest explosion in the city's 142 years didn't injure anyone, but it left a historic Auburn corner looking like the London blitz on January 15, 1978. The blast at 8:13 a.m. missed the Sunday school traffic by about half an hour. It turned the now legendary Kopper Kettle restaurant on the northwest corner of Magnolia Avenue at Gay Street and next-door businesses into rubble. The force also smashed the stained-glass windows in the Methodist church built in about 1850 and rebuilt in about 1900, bombarded Auburn National Bank, and heavily damaged Parker's Department Store. The explosion was traced to a

▲ *Auburn's first black student walks near Samford Hall after enrolling for graduate study in history under court order in January 1964. Thirty-one-year-old Harold Franklin left Auburn after one year without completing work toward the degree. In the 1980s, he told a newspaper reporter he left because he was "getting the runaround" about his thesis. His major professor told the reporter that Franklin's thesis committee was extremely fair to him. Franklin received a master's degree in international studies from the University of Denver in 1976. He later taught history at Tuskegee University and Talladega College, where he also headed the Upward Bound Program. In 1996, Franklin, sixty-three, was managing a mortuary.*

—*Photo: AU Photographic Services*

Comer Hall was gutted in 1920 and Smith Hall was heavily damaged in 1933. A hidden spark started the Hargis fire during its remodeling for office use. The "glow and smoke" were seen as far away as Waverly. The building's exterior survived, but the interior had to be rebuilt.

Both the University and the city grew in numbers—and traffic problems—from 1950 to 1980. The main campus enrollment nearly tripled—from 6,641 in the fall of 1950 to 18,603 three decades later. The ratio of male to female students dropped from a little more than 4 to 1 in 1950 to 7 to 5.5 in 1980. During the same years, the city's population, which included all students except those commuting from other communities, more than doubled—from 12,939 to 28,471.

Building permits were issued for enough new houses in Auburn from the fiscal years 1965-66 through 1979-80 to have sheltered more people than had lived in the entire city during any one year of the 1930s. All told, 1,715 houses were built. The 119 houses begun in 1965-66 cost an average of $14,803. Fourteen years later inflation and recession were at work. Eighty-seven new houses in 1979-80 cost an average of $63,422, a 328 percent increase in per-house expenditure but nearly a 27 percent decrease in the number of houses built. Reflecting the number of students living off campus, building permits were issued for 1,964 apartment units during this period. The construction also included more than 330 new commercial buildings, the largest the $4.8 million Village Mall shopping center. In the 1960s and seventies, the city paved miles of dirt road and installed badly needed water and sewer lines. Property owners were assessed for some improvements, and federal revenue sharing money was used at times. In 1996 only two of 122 miles of city streets were unpaved.

The city bought land in the early 1970s for a second industrial park west of town. The property quickly attracted light industry, and the city developed this area beyond Webster Road off Highway 14 before the end of the decade. One of the biggest and most controversial city government projects was the new City Hall-Library-Police Department complex built on the old Beasley's pasture recreation grounds on Ross Street.

The University completed such major construction during the Philpott years as the Architecture and Fine Arts Complex, the Pharmacy Building, Caroline Draughon Village Extension, and, at the School of Veterinary Medicine, the Basic Sciences Building, to become James E. Greene Hall, and the Small Animal Clinic, renamed for Benjamin Franklin Hoerlein. Construction also included Beard-Eaves-Memorial Coliseum, several Hill Dorms, and Homer Scott Swingle Hall for fisheries and aquaculture.

While Auburn was developing from API into a comprehensive land-grant university under Draughon and Philpott, some alumni and professors believed that engineering needed more attention. A consultant agreed. "The very serious

gas leak under one of the stores. The corner had been important in Auburn life at least as far back as 1887 when the famous N. T. Lupton Conversation Club was founded there. The Kettle's faithful held an annual memorial breakfast—with improved cuisine—for ten years, meeting eight of those years in the lobby of Magnolia Plaza, next door to the site of the explosion.

About eleven months after the Kettle explosion, a fire consumed the inside and cupola of one of the oldest buildings on campus, Hargis Hall, remembered as the Music Building for several years after World War II. It had been built in 1888 for chemistry instruction after another fire had leveled the administration and classroom building called Old Main. The Hargis fire was the worst on campus since

▲ Seven persons who had a building or an area named for them during the 1960s were, left to right: Dr. Paul S. Haley, an Auburn trustee for fifty-one years; Zoe Dobbs, former dean of women and professor of English and education; Berta Dunn, retired secretary to four Auburn presidents; Leila A. Terrell, former boardinghouse operator; President Emeritus Ralph B. Draughon and his wife, Caroline Draughon; and Dr. Fred Allison, physicist and graduate dean emeritus.

—Photo: AU Photographic Services

needs of the School (now College) of Engineering were brought to light in a study by a private planning consultant in 1979," said R. G. Millman in the *Auburn University Walking Tour Guide*. "According to the consultant, existing facilities were 'about half that required to support the present curriculum.'" To meet engineering and other University needs, a campaign was begun in 1982 to raise $61.7 million.

Philpott in 1972 refused to allow football coach Ralph Jordan to also become athletic director when Jeff Beard retired as AD. Philpott said Jordan could be either football coach or athletic director, but not both. This denied Jordan the authority and prestige that Bear Bryant had as football coach and AD at the University of Alabama. Some alumni held that Jordan needed both positions to compete on equal footing with Bryant. Philpott said he wanted an athletic director who was not tied to one sport and who would emphasize all sports. Jordan was displeased, and insiders believed this influenced decisions that put him at odds with Philpott while Jordan served as a trustee from 1976 until his death in 1980. But, in a 1983 newspaper interview, Philpott said he "couldn't say we had hard feelings." In a letter in 1979 informing the trustees of his resignation, Philpott said, "The decision is a personal one made without pressure from anyone in the Auburn family." An energetic and able raiser of private gifts for the University, Philpott offered his services in the approaching campaign.

Auburn won its first Southeastern Conference All-Sports Trophy in 1977-78. One of Jordan's former football captains, Lee Hayley, was athletic director. Jordan's successor as head coach, Doug Barfield, had been a talented assistant coach, was considered "a good man," and won more games than he lost. But he couldn't beat Alabama and departed after the 1980 season.

Dr. Philpott in 1980 ended a presidency dedicated to academic quality and quantity. Soon after his inauguration, Auburn established alumni professorships to retain and attract well-qualified faculty members. Over the Philpott years, rising state appropriations led to a 140 percent increase in faculty salaries. The schools of business and nursing were formed. The number of degree offerings rose from 63 fields of study to more than 140.

Philpott presented 55 percent of all degrees that Auburn awarded in its first 124 years. The president, alumni, and others helped raise money to increase Auburn's endowment and similar funds by 475 percent—from $4 million to about $23 million. Philpott himself served as president of the National Association of State Universities and Land-Grant Colleges. Yet, Philpott's finest hours may have been spent puffing on a pipe and chatting with students in rap sessions in Samford Park or elsewhere, with topics ranging from rules for women students to the Vietnam War. ◑

▲ *"The Ugliest Man on Campus" contest was no contest at all in winter 1965. Shown this picture thirty years later, a close friend of the winning contestant said, "He's ugly, all right, but I haven't a clue as to who that could be." Tucker Frederickson, the contest winner, was a consensus All-American football player a few months earlier. Kappa Alpha and Pi Beta Phi endorsed his candidacy as Ugliest. He easily outdistanced seven other candidates in the Alpha Phi Omega contest. A vote cost a penny, and A Phi O collected $3,123 for its campus projects. Tucker's personal winnings included shirts from three stores; a windbreaker; gift certificates of $4, $5, and $7 toward clothing; after-shave lotion from four stores; meals from six restaurants; six free games from Bowl-O-Matic; one music record; complimentary dry cleaning from two firms; and a free car wash and wax.*
　　　　　　—Photo: AU Photographic Services

▶ *The Sani-Freeze, alias "the Flush," began serving ice cream, hot dogs, and other treats in 1962 through a window in this small building on Glenn Avenue, just east of College Street. Students and townspeople from 1939 through the 1950s sat in booths or at the bar and ate hamburgers, hot dogs and barbecue sandwiches in the same building when it was The Doll House. AmSouth Bank demolished the structure in 1995 and replaced it with a red brick branch office, despite student protests led by the Auburn Plainsman. Sani-Freeze had a drive-up window at another location for a few months, then ceased to exist.*
　　　　　　—Photo: Vickey Hunt Williams

◀ *An Auburn landmark since being erected behind Toomer Drugstore in 1908, this water tank was taken down in 1967 to make room for a parking lot. Nobody knows how many students climbed its narrow ladder to paint football scores, "Wreck Tech," class numerals, and Greek letters on the tank. One of the daring lads had been Ralph Brown Draughon, later Auburn's tenth president. As a freshman in 1918-19, he had painted his class numerals on the tank, where only senior numerals were permitted. Many years later he told of receiving "quite a hazing" from the seniors.*
　　　　　　—Photo: Auburn Alumnews

▲ "Christ is the answer to the world's ills," Billy Graham told an estimated 17,000 people in Cliff Hare Stadium in April 1965. It was the largest crowd ever assembled for a religious meeting in Auburn. President Ralph B. Draughon welcomed the evangelist to campus.

Although he did not refer directly to integration of Alabama's public schools in his twenty-five-minute talk, Graham later predicted that the state would solve its racial problems and that it might well set the pace for the rest of the nation.
—Photo: AU Archives

▲ Coach Ralph Jordan described Tucker Frederickson in 1964 as "the most complete football player I have seen." He was a consensus All-American fullback that fall and the first player selected in the NFL draft. He played seven seasons with the New York Giants. In addition to being a powerful runner, at Auburn he was a two-time winner of the Jacobs Blocking Trophy, awarded annually to the player selected as best blocking back in the South. Fans in 1992 selected him as a first-team defensive back on the "Auburn Team of the Century." They also selected him as the "Auburn Player of the Century." Frederickson became one of the University's first four inducted into the National Football Foundation Hall of Fame. Footnote: Frederickson's father was the veterinarian for eccentric oil heiress Eleanor Ritchey's dogs. He gave her a vet school brochure that led to her leaving her estate to the school.
—Photo: AU Athletic Department

▲ The Greenhouse, home of API physician J. H. Drake and later a popular boardinghouse, was torn down in 1965 and for a decade was the site of Jack's Hamburgers at North College Street and Thach Avenue across from the Draughon Library grounds. The Auburn Plainsman led the opposition to placing Jack's so close to campus, saying it would "by its very nature be a loud and unsightly building." The Drama Department feared that noise from Jack's would interfere with performances at the theatre (now University Chapel). In the early 1980s, Varsity Inn restaurant occupied the building briefly, and then it served as a Domino's Pizza parlor for seven years. In the 1990s, the corner became a landscaped parking lot for tenants of The Commons, a residence hall around the corner on Gay Street.
—Photo: Auburn Alumnews

▶ *Governor George C. Wallace installed a beaming Harry Melvin Philpott as Auburn's eleventh president in 1966. Wallace was governor and ex officio president of Auburn's Board of Trustees during most of Philpott's time as University president. Wallace attended only one trustee meeting, Philpott recalled during interviews with Archivist Dwayne Cox in the early 1990s. Philpott said Wallace "did not interfere" at Auburn during Philpott's years as president. For instance, Wallace "did not raise a question about the employment of black faculty [or] about the admission of black students." Auburn had admitted its first black student before Philpott became president, and Wallace had not stood in the schoolhouse door then, as he had done at Tuscaloosa in his "segregation forever" mode. Auburn signed a black athlete to a scholarship for the first time after Philpott arrived. Philpott said Alabama's Bear Bryant did not sign a black player until Auburn had done so.*
—Photo: AU Photographic Services

▲ *The Auburn Alumni Association began its Annual Giving Program in 1965, partly to initiate Alumni Professorships. A survey requested by President Harry M. Philpott had shown "how low Auburn salaries were," the* Alumnews *reported. "After a sizeable raise, they remained 10 percent below the average of Southern state and land-grant colleges." For Auburn "to become [as Philpott wanted] the 'raider and not the raided,' something had to be done to retain good faculty who were leaving for better salaries elsewhere." A partial answer was Alumni Professorships. Philpott is shown with the first recipients. Seated with him are Dr. John Lovell of educational administration and Dr. H. Hanly Funderburk of botany and plant pathology. Standing, left to right, are Dr. William S. Smith of speech, Dr. B. F. Horlein of small animal surgery and medicine, Dr. R. I. Vachon of mechanical engineering, and Dr. Robert R. Rea of history.*
—Photo: the Auburn Alumnews

▶ *Turning out at Auburn Union (later Foy Union) in 1960 for an organizational meeting of the Auburn Development Fund were these community leaders: (front, left to right) Zebulon Judd, L. M. Ware, J. D. "Duck" Samford, E. L. Spencer, (back) Alonco "Lonnie" Meadows, J. C. Grimes, W. L. Long, Martin L. Beck, Dr. B. F. Thomas, Sr., and E. W. Camp.*

—Photo:
Lee County Bulletin

▼ *Auburn's Jose Rocha is caught upside down at the 1987 NCAA Diving Championships in Austin, Texas, where he won the one-meter title. Southeastern Conference coaches voted him SEC Diver of the Year in both 1986 and 1987. He won the SEC one-meter title three times and the three-meter title twice.*

—Photo: AU Athletic Department

▲ *Governor George C. Wallace made a rainy-day campaign speech in 1966 for his wife, seated at left, from a platform across Magnolia Avenue from Saint Dunstan's Episcopal Chapel. Lurleen B. Wallace carried Auburn in both the Democratic primary and general election. However, her husband didn't fare well with Auburn voters in primary or run-off elections. He lost five straight before winning the 1974 primary.*

—Photo: Wink Blackmon

▲ A future U.S. president, Georgia Governor Jimmy Carter, attended the Auburn-Georgia football game in 1970. Rosalynn Carter and Auburn President Harry M. Philpott were among the 60,000 people at Cliff Hare Stadium. Auburn lost, 31-17, but two weeks later beat Alabama, 33-28.

—Photo: AU Archives

▲ Eleanor Ritchey of Fort Lauderdale, Florida, loved dogs and took in every stray that came along. She knew about Auburn's research on canine cardiovascular disease, although no one at Auburn was aware she existed. When she died in 1968, Miss Ritchey, an oil heiress, left $4.2 million to take care of her 150 dogs for as long as they should live and to support research on canine diseases at the AU School of Veterinary Medicine. Her will stated that the University would receive earnings from the estate until the last dog died, then get the principal. Musketeer, the final survivor, died in 1984 and Auburn University realized a total of almost $12 million from Mrs. Ritchey's will.

The Scott-Ritchey Center at the College of Veterinary Medicine, an outgrowth of the generosity of Kenneth A. Scott and Miss Ritchey, is the world's only partly endowed research and research training center for inherited diseases of companion animals. Scott, a shipping magnate, entered his pointers in field trials in Alabama, and the dogs received shots and treatment at the AU Small Animal Clinic. At the suggestion of Dr. B. F. Hoerlein, Scott started matching privately endowed funds for canine research at Auburn.

—Photo: AU University Relations

▲ The inaugural game in Memorial Coliseum came January 11, 1969, and Auburn's Wally Tinker (33) sank the first field goal attempted as Bill Lynn's Tigers defeated LSU 90-71 before 11,166 fans. The other Auburn player was John Mengelt (15), who the next year scored a Coliseum record 60 points in a victory over Alabama. He set the team's single-season scoring record in 1971 with 738 points, eclipsed during the next quarter century only by Chuck Person with 747 points in 1985. Barely visible behind Mengelt was LSU's Pete Maravich, who scored 46 points in the Coliseum opener.

—Photo: AU Athletic Department

▲ What logo should the football helmets have? This was the question coach Shug Jordan and Bill Beckwith, sports information director, were discussing in 1967 in the coach's office. Jordan recommended putting a tiger on the helmets; Beckwith favored using an eagle. Entering the room, Athletic Director Jeff Beard suggested working the University's initials into the logo. "They didn't think much of my idea," Beard, with a grin, told Pete Pepinsky, director of University Relations, years later. Unswayed, Beard did a rough stenciling of "AU." For "grace and artistry," he went to C. H. "Babe" McGehee's National Screen Printers (NSP Corporate Graphics in 1996) in Auburn. McGehee, of course, was the first Auburn player to score a touchdown in Jordan-Hare Stadium. Beard and McGehee soon had a winner. "Jeff was the artist," McGehee said. "All the NSP artists did was to clean it up and make it presentable." The McGehees' daughter Susan is admiring Beard's and NSP's handiwork.

—Photo: Pete Pepinsky

▲ Oscar winning actress Susan Hayward came to Auburn in June 1969 for the graduation of her son, Gregory Barker, who received a degree as doctor of veterinary medicine. She is shown in Samford Hall with Veterinary Dean James E. Greene, left, and Barker. Gregory's twin brother Timothy attended Auburn briefly before enlisting in the Army. Their father was motion picture actor Jess Barker. Gregory practiced veterinary medicine in Jacksonville and Neptune Beach, Florida, before moving to Valley Head, Alabama, in retirement.

—Photo: AU Archives

◀ Bob Hope and War Eagle IV matched beaks at the half of Auburn's 31-7 victory over Georgia Tech at Cliff Hare Stadium in 1970. Presented a framed eagle's feather as a memento, Hope quipped, "It looks like a Houston job to me," referring to Auburn's Bluebonnet Bowl loss to the Cougars.

—Photo: Montgomery Advertiser and Alabama Journal

► *Three members of Drake High School's last football team received instructions from coach Frank Tolbert in 1969. The next year black and white players all played for Auburn High School with hardly any racial problems, Tolbert said. Tolbert's Auburn High basketball teams later twice made the finals of the state 6-A basketball tournament. Shown assisting Tolbert at Drake was John Dunn, an Auburn police officer for about twenty-five years. Lieutenant Dunn led the department in collecting toys for needy children at Christmas for most of his career. The players are Chris Neloms (21), Joe Devance (34), and Cody Blackmon (43).*

—Photo: AU Archives

► *Auburn, and particularly its School of Engineering, played an important role in the nation's space program on a continuing basis, starting in the 1950s. During more than thirteen years ending in 1980, Auburn received about $6 million in research contracts from the National Aeronautics and Space Administration. Thirteen years later, in 1993 alone, NASA funding to Auburn had risen to more than $4.1 million. Here, NASA's head, Wernher von Braun (center) visits a National 4-H Club meeting at Huntsville. Others include Hanchey Logue of Auburn, Alabama 4-H leader (left), and U.S. Senator John Sparkman (lower right). Logue explained why several in the picture were laughing or smiling. A little 4-H boy*

had asked, "Dr. von Braun, why are you walking with a stick?" The scientist replied, "Son, yesterday I started upstairs and was reading this sign [that said] 'Watch your step!' I slipped and sprained my ankle."

Madison Jones, whose novel An Exile *was the basis for the motion picture* I walk the Line, *posed in front of the War Eagle Theatre at the Alabama premiere in October 1970. Jones retired in 1987 and became English professor and University writer-in-residence emeritus. He published his ninth novel,* To the Winds, *in 1996 and had completed a tenth. Allen Tate, distinguished poet and literary critic, once called Jones "our southern Thomas Hardy; his small town and backwoods characters are Everyman and Everywoman." Novelists James Dickey and Robert Penn Warren also have praised Jones' work.*

—*Photo:* Auburn Alumnews

▲ James G. "Jim" Smith was a familiar figure at the steering wheel of the Auburn president's limousine during the administrations of L. N. Duncan, Ralph B. Draughon, and Harry M. Philpott. He also served in the homes of these presidents from 1940 until his death in 1971. A Tiger football fan, he used to rub his "good luck" buckeye during the games.

—Photo: Veola B. Smith

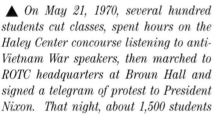

▲ On May 21, 1970, several hundred students cut classes, spent hours on the Haley Center concourse listening to anti-Vietnam War speakers, then marched to ROTC headquarters at Broun Hall and signed a telegram of protest to President Nixon. That night, about 1,500 students demonstrated for women's rights. The quest for fewer dormitory restrictions on coeds continued. In 1976, the Board of Trustees abolished all curfews at women's dorms and authorized a plan for male visitations.

—Photo: AU Photographic Services

◀ St. Michael's Catholic Church moved its services from the old church at left to the new building at right in 1966. St. Michael's later closed its black mission in Auburn and incorporated those members into this church on East Magnolia Avenue. The pastor, Father Joseph F. Konen, is shown with a group of children. They are, left to right: Tom Saunders, Michael Brooks, Bernard Card, Richard Peterson, and Meleia White.

—Photo: St. Michael's Church

◀ The Auburn Knights Orchestra has graduated many excellent musicians since 1930. One of their star singers, Toni Tennille, went on to a successful career in television and as a recording artist. So did another member of this 1959-60 band, saxophonist Dave Edwards (second from Toni's left), who played with Lawrence Welk's orchestra. Another Knights alumnus, Urbie Green, was the only sideman featured on camera in the movie, The Benny Goodman Story. Gerald Yelverton was ranked in the top ten of the nation's great jazz clarinetists. Incidentally, Toni Tennille's father, Frank Tennille, sang with the first Knights Orchestra.

—Photo: Auburn Knights Collection at the AU Archives

◀ The clock face on the west side of Samford Tower was transformed into a Mickey Mouse Watch the night of May 18, 1977. Some thought it the work of a fraternity and speculated on how much rope or scaffolding had been used. Two years later, AU graduates Jim Dunaway and Scott Farr told Plainsman reporter Winkie Williams they and a third student, Jesse Evans, staged the prank. The three learned the previous night that the door to the Samford attic had been left unlocked. Jesse painted a Mickey Mouse portrait on a white sheet and cut hands out of cardboard, painting them yellow and outlining them in black. The three took the sheet and hands up to the attic, then climbed a ladder to the room inside the clock faces. The number 12 on the clock face was designed to swing out like a door, making a two-foot hole. Dunaway's shoulders could just fit through the square. The three had to wait till 10 p.m., when both hands of the clock were in Dunaway's reach. Then he attached the cardboard hands with masking tape and positioned the sheet with thumbtacks. They recalled that Mickey Mouse's face remained on the clock for several days and that several newspapers carried a picture of it. The students said they were just looking for something better to do than putting Tide in the Haley Center Fountain or Jello on a sidewalk, and, "This was just a good, clean prank."

—Photo: AU Photographic Services

◀ An 8.5-inch snowfall—Auburn's greatest in at least half a century—covered the town and campus overnight in February 1973. Classes were canceled for the day and students built snowmen, sledded and threw snowballs.

—Photo: AU University Relations

▲ *Pat Sullivan gave credit to his family, coaches, teammates, and others in accepting the 1971 Heisman Trophy as the best college football player in the land. The presentation was made in New York City. As Sullivan responded, Auburn President Harry M. Philpott, movie actor John Wayne, and Coach Ralph Jordan sat to his right. Teammate Terry Beasley also was at the head table, at Sullivan's far left. More than seventy years earlier, John W. Heisman, the man for whom the trophy was named, had coached at Auburn. One of Sullivan's best compliments came after he had led the Tigers to a 33-28 comeback victory over Alabama in 1970. "He does more things to beat you than any quarterback I've ever seen," the Tide's Bear Bryant said.*
—Photo: AU Photographic Services

◄ *Ralph "Shug" Jordan commiserated with Paul "Bear" Bryant when they met after the 1972 game. Auburn's 17-16 victory made Jordan one of the few ever to defeat modern football's winningest coach three times in four years. However, Bryant held the upper hand, beating Auburn thirteen times and losing only five during the Jordan years. Jordan's record of 176 victories, 83 losses, and 6 ties earned him a place in the National Football Foundation Hall of Fame alongside Bryant and others. Years earlier, during World War II, Jordan set a record few, if any, other coaches could match: participating in U.S. Army invasions in North Africa, Sicily, France, and Okinawa.*

—Photo: Ralph Jordan

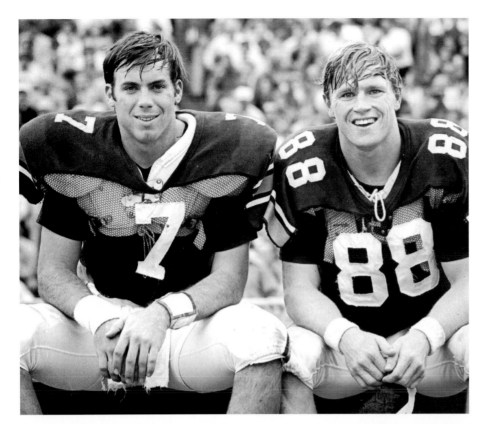

Auburn's candidates for college football's greatest passing combination: quarterback Pat Sullivan (7) and split end Terry Beasley (88). Sullivan threw 53 touchdown passes and Beasley caught 30 in three varsity seasons. Both were consensus All-Americans as seniors in 1971 when the Tigers won their first nine games, then lost to Alabama 31-7 and in the Sugar Bowl to Oklahoma, 40-22. They are remembered on The Plain as "Bama Beaters," winning three of four from The Tide. The Auburn freshman team in 1968 fell behind Bama 27-0, but fought back to win, 36-27. Two years later, with the varsity Tigers trailing Alabama, 7-17, Sullivan reminded Beasley of the earlier rally. "Come on Bease," he said. "We're going to beat 'em just like we did when we were freshmen." And so Auburn did, 33-28.

—Photo: AU Photographic Services

This play before a Legion Field crowd of 72,386 enabled Auburn to defeat Alabama 17-16 on December 2, 1972, and score one of its greatest football victories. The favored Tide led 16-0 until Gardner Jett kicked a 42-yard field goal with 9:15 remaining. With 5:30 left, Bill Newton blocked Greg Gantt's punt at midfield, and David Langner grabbed the ball and raced for a touchdown. On the ninth play after the kickoff, Gantt again was in punt formation, this time at fourth and nine from the Bama 43. Again Bill Newton blocked the kick, and again the ball bounced into the arms of Langner (28) who raced untouched into the end zone. Jett's second conversion with 1:34 remaining gave Auburn its one-point victory. Bill Newton's head is barely visible between Roger Mitchell (25) and the punter. Other Auburn players include Benny Sivley with arms raised, and Bob Newton (76).

—Photo: AU Photographic Services

T. K. "Ken" Mattingly and Henry W. "Hank" Hartsfield made in 1982 what has been called "the 'Auburn Flight'—the first time in NASA history two astronauts from the same university flew together" in space, Janet McCoy wrote in Auburn Magazine. The Mattingly and Hartsfield mission of the shuttle Columbia was met by President and Mrs. Ronald Reagan as it landed on the nation's 206th birthday. "You've given America a Fourth of July present to remember," Reagan told the duo, calling them "two sons of Auburn." ∾ ∾ ∾

◀ Hartsfield is seen in 1972 with a former teacher and colleague, Dr. Fred Allison. The astronaut was working that year on development of the space shuttle's entry flight-control systems. Allison, head professor of physics at Auburn from 1922 to 1953, became internationally known for his magneto-optical method. He and co-workers claimed the discoveries of chemical elements 85 and 87, and also heavy isotope of hydrogen. Allison served as graduate dean in 1949-53. After retiring at age seventy, he taught at two other colleges and continued his Auburn research. He died in 1974 at ninety-two. One of Allison's successors as physics head, Howard Carr, helped inspire Hartsfield. "Dr. Carr encouraged me at the critical point in my career," Hartsfield recalled. "I was very depressed, but he convinced me not to lose faith. And he was right. Fate smiled on me."

—*Photo:* Auburn Alumnews

▶ Mattingly (right) is shown in 1972 presenting to President Philpott a framed display that included the Auburn University flag he took with him as module command pilot of the Apollo 16 flight, a 250,000-mile voyage into space. Inscribed under the flag were Mattingly's words: "This flag was flown to the moon as a symbol of that enduring force, 'The Auburn Spirit,' which transforms dreams into reality. It is returned as a tribute to those War Eagles, past, present and future, who represent the essence of that spirit." The presentation was made during halftime of the Georgia Tech football game, won by Auburn 24-14. In 1970, Mattingly had been kept from making the ill-fated Apollo 13 mission because he had been exposed to measles. He "became the expert on the ground with the most knowledge of the crippled spaceship and its crew as NASA fought twenty-five years ago to bring three astronauts home to earth," Janet McCoy wrote. Mattingly's role in the massive team rescue was dramatized in the 1995 hit movie Apollo 13. Mattingly graduated in 1958 in aeronautical engineering and was president of the Student Government Association his senior year.

—*Photo:* AU Archives

◄ *Millard Dawson served as the University's police chief for thirty years, from 1951 to 1981, and at retirement received the Algernon Sydney Sullivan Award "in recognition of his friendliness, thoughtfulness, sincerity, acts of kindness, and deep regard for others." In 1969, Alpha Phi Omega named him an honorary member because of his service to the students. The Board of Trustees directed in 1993 that the AU police building be renamed the Millard Edwin Dawson Building.*

—Photo: AU Archives

▼ *Bold Ruler, world's leading thoroughbred sire in the 1960s, is shown with Lawrence Robinson, a Claiborne Farm's groom, who brought him to Auburn in 1970 for cobalt treatment of a malignant tumor. After returning to Kentucky, Bold Ruler sired twenty-nine more foals before his death. He won the Preakness Stakes and a total of $784,204 in purses. His offsprings won more than 800 races and more than $13 million. One of his great-grandsons, Seattle Slew, won the triple crown in 1977. Dr. Jim Hill, a veterinarian (Auburn '64) and his wife, Sally Jones Hill (Auburn '63), went into partnership with another couple and bought Slew as a yearling for the bargain price of $17,500.*

—Photo: Nuclear Science Center

231

◄ *Consumer advocate Ralph Nader gave Lee Cannon and her educational television audience tips on getting the most for their money in an interview during the 1970s. Mrs. Cannon produced and directed the Auburn station's first program, "Today's Home," on August 5, 1955, about two years after the Alabama Legislature established the first state ETV network in the nation. Edward Wegener was Auburn's first station manager, Jack Dunlop its first program manager, and George Murphy its first engineer.*
—Photo: Will Dickey

▼ *Freshman Mike Mitchell shoots over a Georgia defender in a 1975 game in Memorial Coliseum as sophomore Eddie Johnson (22) looks on. The Tigers, coached by Bob Davis, were undefeated at home that season, but it was downhill after that. Mitchell became Auburn's career scoring leader with 2,123 points in four seasons before joining the Cleveland Cavaliers. And Johnson,*

Stan Piet-kiewicz, and Miles Patrick from that team eventually played in the National Basketball Association, Johnson making the All-Star Team. But Auburn's record fell off, and Davis was replaced in 1978 by Sonny Smith.
—Photo: Dan Doughtie

▲ *Football Coach Ralph Jordan, left, and trainer Kenny Howard watch practice in the early 1970s. They were such close friends that Jordan told Howard two years in advance that he planned to retire after the 1975 season. Of Jordan, Howard said in 1996, "The biggest thing I remember about him was his approach to athletics. He placed a high priority on winning, but a lot more important to him than winning games were the individual person, how he conducted himself, and the academic world." During his AU career, Howard "was a friend and confidant to Auburn coaches. To Auburn athletes in all sports, he was a father, a friend, a big brother, a favorite uncle, whatever was needed," David Housel wrote in his collection of Auburn stories. Howard served twenty-eight years as Auburn's head athletic trainer, three years as a student trainer, and four years as assistant athletic director. He was named to the National Athletic Trainers Association Hall of Fame and served as trainer for swimmers in the 1976 Olympics and trainer for track and field in the 1952 Olympics. After he retired from AU, he became director of sports relations for the Hughston Sports Medicine Foundation, Inc.*

◀ Joe Beckwith displays an intensity that resulted in his pitching a record 20 complete games for the University in 1974-77. The Auburn High School product also had a 1.92 earned run average for 338 innings pitched, and was selected all-SEC in both his junior and senior years. Three of his record six shutouts came in 1976, a year Auburn played in the College World Series. In seven major league seasons with Los Angeles and the Kansas City A's, Beckwith appeared in 229 games, all but five as a reliefer. He shut out St. Louis for two innings for the A's in the 1985 World Series, allowing one hit and striking out three. Beckwith's father, Bill, was AU sports information director nine years and athletic ticket manager 34 years before retiring in 1992.

Another of Auburn's best pitchers was Q. V. Lowe, with a career winning percentage of 88.5 and twenty-three victories against three losses in 1966 and 1967. Included were fifteen victories with the '67 team that finished third in the College World Series. John Powell, who helped take Auburn to the 1994 World Series, set an NCAA record of 602 career strikeouts. His 477 innings pitched and 43 victories also were Auburn records. Lowe posted the top career earned run average of 1.69, and Paul Susce had the best one-season ERA, 0.99 in 1954. Greg Olson set the Tigers' career saves record at 20 in 1986-88. Olson became the youngest player in major league baseball history to record a hundred saves. He was twenty-five and in his fifth season with the Baltimore Orioles when he reached that milestone.

—Photo: AU Athletic Department

▶ Elvis Presley became in 1974 the first rock star to sell out all 13,329 seats in Memorial Coliseum. Before the show began, the audience was asked not to take pictures. But when "the King" came on stage, it seemed as if thousands of flash bulbs went off all at once. Startled by the sudden brightness, one Coliseum employee wondered for a moment whether the lighting system had exploded. Singer John Denver, appearing in 1976 near the height of his popularity, drew a crowd of 10,578.

—Photo: AU Special Collections

This Sky Crane-54, the world's largest helicopter of its day, was flown by National Guardsmen from Birmingham in August 1974 to be used to replace a burned-out 3,000-pound air conditioner on top of ten-story Haley Center. The SC-54's 77-foot-long rotors created a severe dust storm upon liftoff from the parking lot of Haley. But the assignment was a piece of cake for the 'chopper and its twin 4,500-horsepower jet engines. Haley Center, with 142 classrooms on the first three floors, and faculty offices on the next six, has been the largest building at the University since its completion in 1969. For years, it housed most units of the College of Education and virtually all faculty and staff members of the College of Liberal Arts. In the early nineties, however, to alleviate a severe shortage of office space in Haley, the departments of communication, geography, history, journalism, and psychology moved across the street to Thach and Tichenor halls.

—Photo: AU Archives

These Auburn businessmen met in September 1974 at The Omelet Shoppe on West Glenn Avenue in Auburn with Frank James, Omelet Shoppe district manager, second from left, to finalize plans for the grand opening of a shoppe in Opelika. Each played a role in Auburn business and industrial development. Left to right were Ted Wilson, president, Auburn Bank & Trust Company; James; K. M. Varner, president, First National Bank of Auburn; Bobby Blake, president, Auburn National Bank; Andy Gentry, Auburn attorney and general counsel and board member, Omelet Shoppe; and Vandy Harper, contractor. The three banks helped finance the venture. Gentry owned the property, and Harper's firm built the shoppe.

—Photo: AU Archives

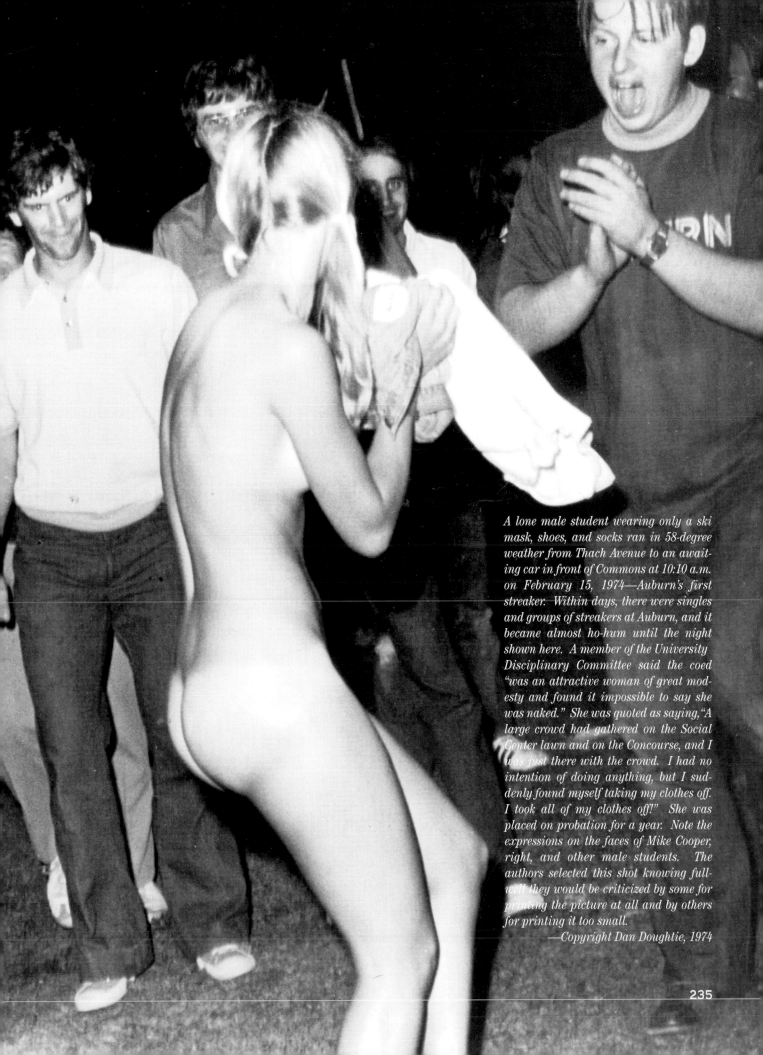

A lone male student wearing only a ski mask, shoes, and socks ran in 58-degree weather from Thach Avenue to an awaiting car in front of Commons at 10:10 a.m. on February 15, 1974—Auburn's first streaker. Within days, there were singles and groups of streakers at Auburn, and it became almost ho-hum until the night shown here. A member of the University Disciplinary Committee said the coed "was an attractive woman of great modesty and found it impossible to say she was naked." She was quoted as saying, "A large crowd had gathered on the Social Center lawn and on the Concourse, and I was just there with the crowd. I had no intention of doing anything, but I suddenly found myself taking my clothes off. I took all of my clothes off!" She was placed on probation for a year. Note the expressions on the faces of Mike Cooper, right, and other male students. The authors selected this shot knowing full-well they would be criticized by some for printing the picture at all and by others for printing it too small.

—Copyright Dan Doughtie, 1974

235

▲ *The University Chapel is the oldest building still in use on campus. Since its construction in 1850-51 of slave-made bricks, it has been a Presbyterian Church, Confederate hospital, classroom, YMCA center, Players Theatre, and chapel. Some contend it has even been inhabited by a ghost. The building's conversion from theatre to chapel was completed in 1976, with AU Professor Nicholas Davis as architect.*

A "lich" was placed outside to keep people from seeing the hamburger place then across the street, former President Harry Philpott said. The shed-like structure is used in Scotland to exhibit a corpse before a funeral. North of the chapel and its courtyards on College Street are Smith and Ingram (formerly Alumni) halls.
—Photo: Paul Kennedy, Sr.

AUBURN CHURCHES

Twenty-three Auburn churches provided the years in which they were founded. So did Congregation Beth Shalom (the Jewish Community of East Alabama), founded in 1989. The churches were: Auburn Church of Christ, 1935; Auburn First Assembly of God, 1964; Auburn United Methodist Church, 1837; Believers Church, 1985; Bell Missionary Baptist Church, 1926; Covenant Presbyterian Church, 1965; Ebenezer Missionary Baptist Church, 1865; First Baptist Church of Auburn, 1838; First Presbyterian Church of Auburn, 1850; Grace United Methodist Church, 1958; Holy Trinity Episcopal Church, 1957; Lakeview Baptist Church, 1959; Mount Vernon Missionary Baptist Church, 1866; Mt. Moriah Baptist Church, 1907; North College Street Church of Christ, 1965; Parkway Baptist Church, 1970; St. Dunstan's Episcopal Student Center, 1857; St. Luke Christian Methodist Episcopal Church, 1872; St. Michael's Catholic Church, 1912; Unitarian Universal Church, 1962; Village Christian Church, 1957; West Auburn Baptist Church, 1986; White Street Baptist Church, 1938.

~~~

◀ *Mary E. Brooks, left, a vocational counselor with the Lee County school system, became the first black member of the Auburn City Council in 1972. She served ten years. Shown with Mrs. Brooks at City Hall are Donald E. Hayhurst, AU political science professor who served as Auburn mayor 1976-80, and Mrs. Vida Greenleaf. Mrs. Brooks worked to desegregate city schools in the 1960s and to see that black children were treated fairly in the classroom.*
—Photo: AU Archives

▲ The Auburn community was over-joyed when the general election of 1978 put into office Auburn graduates Fob James as governor, George McMillan, Jr., as lieutenant governor, and C. C. "Bo" Torbert as chief justice of the Alabama Supreme Court. The Auburn faculty soon found itself at odds with James over the controversial hiring of H. Hanly Funderburk as University president, han-dling of the search for a football coach, and James' views on state appropriations for the University.

—Photo: Opelkia-Auburn News

◄ Auburn National Bank opened a drive-up across Gay Street in 1979. One of the oldest business firms in the city, the Bank of Auburn opened its doors in 1907 on the northwest side of Toomer's Corner, with its founding directors including S. L. Toomer, C. A. Cary, Bennett Battle Ross, Thomas Bragg, Dr. Oliver M. Steadham, W. Pierce Zuber, and Thomas O. Wright. It became Auburn National Bank in 1964 when it moved to the northeast side of Gay Street at Magnolia Avenue. And AuburnBank—one word—became its name in 1995 when it again became a state bank. It had long been the only inde-pendent bank in the community.

The drive-up facility was named The Super Six because it could accommodate six customers at a time. At groundbreak-ing were, left to right: Denson Lipscomb, Linda Fucci, Jerry Holley, Rowe Fesperman (front), unidentified, Lan Lipscomb, Clark Hudson, Spud Wright, H. R. Hubbard, Bobby Blake, B. F. Thomas, Sr., Martha Jones, E. L. Spencer, Bob Haley, Ed Lee Spencer, J. A. Kassler. All were employees or board members of the bank except Fesperman and Kassler, who represented the contractor.

—Photo: AU Archives

▶ *Tailgating has long been about as essential as the game itself for thousands who flock to the campus on Auburn football Saturdays. Visiting and looking for old acquaintances take high priority. This group arrived early enough in 1978 to park in the lot just west of the stadium. Out came the card table, and on it were placed a tablecloth, flowers, candelabra, silver goblets, and bone china, then sandwiches and snacks. Left to right are Frances Coxwell, Monroeville; Ray Gay, Wadley; Jay Crowder, Wadley, and later Auburn; Buster, Jay, and Sue Fincher, Wedowee; Toni Gay, Wadley; Alyce Benefield, Wedowee; and Margaret Crowder, Wadley. Mrs. Fincher was on the AU Board of Trustees at the time, the first woman appointee.*

—Photo: AU Archives

◀ *The Kopper Kettle seemed destined to go on serving beef stew, hot chili, and chocolate pie forever at Magnolia Avenue and Gay Street when a picture was taken in 1973. But its days, as well as those of adjacent stores and offices, were numbered. After the explosion of January 15, 1978, patron Billy Jack Jones wrote that the Kettle had been the forerunner of Auburn's fast-food restaurants. It was "the only place in those days that stayed open all night." He recalled the ten-cent Kettleburgers of the late 1950s; the late-night mixture of drunks, students, and just-hungry people; and the early-morning ketchup battles that ended in the late sixties when a retired military policeman took over. Another patron, Ann Pearson, wrote of losing the "two decades of grease-splattered atmosphere" that had been shared at the Kettle. She, Jones, and other Kopper Kettle faithful kept alive "the memory of twenty years of egg eating at that local institution" with annual reunions held near the site in the eighties.*

A gas leak touched off the explosion. Miraculously no one was injured when the blast shook the community at 8:13 o'clock that Sunday morning. Blown away were the Kettle, the Brownfield Building, and the Whelchel Building. Many other places were heavily damaged.

—Photos: AU Archives; Montgomery Advertiser

Sculptor Jean Woodham, an Auburn art graduate and 1946 Glomerata *editor, earned an international reputation for her welded art pieces. One of Woodham's sculptures, an eighteen-foot work of bronze and brass from the late 1970s called "Monody," is pictured below. The work was funded by James W. and Virginia Goodwin and stands near the Goodwin Music and Band Complex on West Samford Avenue. "Monody," Woodham said, is "the sculptor's effort to express and to communicate, through form, the feeling that music rises from the earth, soars to the heavens and elevates the human spirit."*
—Photo: AU University Relations

◄ *Fire gutted ninety-year-old Hargis Hall in Samford Park on December 22, 1978, while it was being renovated. A fire which destroyed Old Main in 1887 had led to the building of Hargis for chemistry instruction. Later, pharmacy, architecture, and music classes were taught there. "In late 1979, the contractor began again to create a new Hargis Hall inside the shell of the 1880s building," R. G. Millman wrote in* The Auburn University Walking Tour Guide. *"Ironically, the new plans included a sprinkler system and a fire alarm wired directly to the Auburn fire station."*
—Photo: Rick Helmke

▲ *Marianne Merritt averaged 20.1 points and 10 rebounds a game during four seasons with the Auburn women's basketball team. The only AU players to best her total of 1,951 points when her career ended in 1979 were two from the men's teams, Mike Mitchell (2,123) and Eddie Johnson (1,988). Marianne still held the AU women's season and individual game rebounding records going into 1996. The five-foot-eight star was twice voted to the coaches Top 20 team in the South and after graduation was drafted by the Chicago Hustle in the Women's Professional Basketball League.*

—Photo:
Harold Blackwood, copyright 1978

"Before 1959 all Lee County [Auburn area] cotton was picked by hand; ten to twelve persons would pick a bale a day," Lee County and Her Forebears *reported.* "By 1976, virtually all cotton was harvested mechanically." This one-row machine being operated by Bill Nunn of Auburn will pick as much as sixty-to-one-hundred workers could. A two-row machine will keep up with 75 to 140 pickers.
—Photos: AU Archives;
Agricultural Experiment Station

► *President H. Hanly Funderburk con-gratulated Auburn's 100,000th graduate, Jackie Lee Holley, a sociology major from Montgomery, in the 1980 spring com-mencement exercises on the Montgomery campus. Holley earlier had majored in fashion merchandising at the Auburn campus. Of being the 100,000th, she said, "I cracked up. It reminded me of Laverne and Shirley on TV when they went to the grocery store and lights flashed because they were the millionth customers." The* Auburn Bulletin *reported she "was awed to learn" that it had taken the institution nearly 125 years to award 100,000 degrees and that she had received the his-toric one. Chartered as the East Alabama Male College in 1856, Auburn had award-ed diplomas to its first five graduates in 1860. It reached the 50,000 mark in 1968, and added another 50,000 graduates in the next twelve years.*

—*Photo: Will Dickey*

► *Alma Smith Stoves stands arm-in-arm with high school and college class-mates G. H. "Monk" Wright, left, and George Alfonso Wright during a reunion of Golden Eagles at the University in 1980. The three were graduates of Auburn High School in 1915 and API in 1919. Alma and Monk were virtually lifelong residents of Auburn, and they and Alfonso were lifelong friends.*

—*Photo: AU Archives*

► *Harvey Glance became a household name in Alabama in 1976 by winning the NCAA 60-, 100-, and 200-meter dash championships and a gold medal in the Olympic Games 400-meter relay at Montreal. Glance won the 100-meter dash every time he ran it on the Auburn track, including this last time against Alabama's James Mallard in 1979. He won the 100 in the U.S. Olympic trials and finished fourth at Montreal in that event, then won the NCAA 100 again in 1977. Glance was one of five black ath-letes on Coach Mel Rosen's teams of 1974 through 1980 who won a total of eleven NCAA championship races. Others were James Walker (3), Willie Smith (2), Clifford Outlin (1), and Stanley Floyd (1). Glance was an NCAA all-American an amazing fifteen times. Walker was so honored eleven times and Smith nine.*

—*Photo: Mark Almond*

◄ *Rowdy Gaines is shown at the 1980 AAU Swimming Championships in Austin, Texas, the moment he learned he had set a world record in the 200-meter freestyle. Gaines also held the world record in the 100-meter freestyle. Swimming World magazine named him World Swimmer of the Year, and he was elected Southeastern Conference Athlete of the Year for 1981, an honor that had gone to Auburn track star Harvey Glance in 1976. Gaines appeared a likely multiple winner in the 1980 Moscow Olympics, but the United States boycotted the Games. Four years later in Los Angeles, he won gold medals in the 100 freestyle and two relay races. Auburn finished second in the NCAA Swimming Championships under Coach Eddie Reese when Gaines was a freshman, and sixth, fifth, and fifth under Coach Richard Quick the next three years.*

—Photo:
Austin American-Statesman

► *Catcher Tommy Morton, Coach Paul Nix, and third baseman Richie Howard showed 'em who was No. 1 after Auburn won the 1976 SEC baseball title. The team later won the NCAA South Region title and made its second appearance at the World Series in Omaha, Nebraska. Nix retired in 1984 after 22 years as Auburn baseball coach. His teams won four Southeastern Conference championships.*

—Photo: AU Athletic Department

▲ These aerials show the changing face of the campus in the 1970s. Just to the north-west of Haley Center is the Pharmacy Building completed in 1975. The dormitories at extreme top right were torn down after being deemed unfit for housing. That area became a parking lot when the Lowder Building was completed in 1992 on Magnolia Avenue as the new home of the College of Business.

—Photo: AU Archives

▶ Across Samford Avenue from the hill dorms stand Goodwin Music Hall and Annex, built in 1973-74, and Telfair B. Peet Theatre, dedicated in 1973. The new Architecture Building (not shown) went up behind Goodwin Hall in the late 1970s. Before the Auburn-Alabama football game in 1972, alumnus James Goodwin promised President Harry Philpott that he would pay for Phase II of the Music Building if Auburn won. With three minutes to play and Alabama leading 16-10, Philpott told Goodwin, "'I hope we get the building, but I don't believe we will,'" Philpott recalled years later. "Lo and behold they blocked the second punt. When I saw him that night after the game, he said, 'OK, you've got a million dollars for Phase II,' which we built. . . ." Philpott called it "the blocked-punt building."

—Photo: AU Archives

◀ After more than thirty-two years out on Highway 29 South, the radio station moved to uptown Auburn in July 1980. Would city living spoil WAUD? Listeners were relieved to hear that Bob Sanders (standing at the doorway) sixteen years later still welcomed the Coffee Slurpers, the Hog Sloppers, the Brown Book Openers, The Choir, the Helicopter Crew, and B-24 fans. Founder and former owner Elmer Salter kept firing guest editorial zingers through the eighties, and the staff continued serving news, sports, and music to the community from WAUD's new home—a couple of doors west of the Kopper Kettle Corner.
—Photo: Rick Helmke

◀ Katharine Cater is shown with her familiar silver service in the Social Center in 1980, a few weeks before the building was renamed for her and fewer than five months before her death.
—Photo: Donna Wiggins

▼ From the opening of Haley Center in 1969, the place to be between classes, unless raining or unbearably cold, has been Haley Concourse. An increasing number of students used bikes to get to campus in the late seventies, and many riders parked them in racks set up on the Concourse.

—Photo: Auburn Plainsman

▲ Take any decent day on the Auburn campus in the 1970s and you'd find a number of students throwing frisbees—a fad that didn't go away. More than two decades later, frisbee participants were still at it. And dogs were still putting the humans to shame as catchers.
—Photo: Dan Doughtie

▲ The greatest pair of backs to run "Between the Hedges" on a single afternoon since the days of Sinkwich and Trippi left Sanford Stadium in Athens smiling after Auburn's 33-13 victory over Georgia in 1979. James Brooks, left, gained 200 yards and Joe Cribbs 166, and each scored two touchdowns. Each rushed for more than 1,000 yards that season, the first time two runners from the same SEC team had done so. In 1978, Auburn's running backs were Brooks, Cribbs, and William Andrews. All three played in the National Football League.
—Photo: Mark Almond

◄ Doug Barfield, an assistant at Auburn for four seasons, succeeded Ralph Jordan as head football coach in 1976. His teams won 29, lost 25, and tied one game in five seasons. Barfield resigned under pressure at the end of the 1980 season, after the Tigers lost all six SEC games. He is shown in 1979, sending end Mark Robbins in with a play.
—Photo: Auburn Plainsman

Neil O. Davis (center), co-founder of the Lee County Bulletin in 1937 and its editor and publisher for thirty-eight years, got together with long-time staff members after his last edition came off the press in June 1975. The paper had become the Auburn Bulletin several years before he sold it to the Boone Group. Pictured with Davis were, left to right: J. C. Woodall, production supervisor; Alma Shaffer, women's editor; Henrietta Davis, associate editor; and Graham McTeer, managing editor. Owen Davis, inset right, worked at the paper from age six through high school, then returned several years later as sports editor. In 1996, he was deputy sports editor of the Detroit Free Press. Under Neil Davis, the Bulletin won many honors, including a national Herrick Memorial Award for editorials on human rights, and several General Excellence first places from the Alabama Press Association. "We figured we had only one role—to be a community newspaper," he once said. "That means informing the public, dealing with issues and providing some informed basis for discussion." Partly on the recommendation of Neil Davis, McTeer, who died in 1975, was named to the Press Association Hall of Honor at AU in 1993. A city park also was named for McTeer. "He had the best feel for the role of news in a community such as this of anyone I've seen," Neil Davis told writer Carmel Thomaston. "He was unusual because he was an excellent reporter, writer and also handled several major advertising accounts." Neil Davis was a leader in founding the Presbyterian Community Ministry and remained its treasurer in 1996. Auburn lawyer Andy Gentry bought the paper in 1980, a few years after acquiring Radio Station WAUD. Paul Davis, also an award-winning journalist but not related to Neil, became publisher and then owner before selling the paper to Thomson Newspapers in 1995.

—Photos: Henrietta and Neil O. Davis

The initial rolling of Toomer's Corner by students after a football victory may be lost in history, but it probably was in 1962 or 1963. This was the studied opinion of Pharmacist Mac Lipscomb, who operated the drugstore on the Corner from the early fifties into the mid-eighties. Pictured is a 1985 celebration, probably after Auburn's 17-14 victory over Georgia Tech in Atlanta. For several years, rollings occurred only after an away-game victory, but in the 1990s many home-game victories also rated a rolling.

—*Photo:* Auburn Plainsman

▲ Jan Dempsey became Auburn's first woman mayor in elections of July 1980. Denson Lipscomb, youngest city councilman in the community's history when elected in 1976 at age twenty-three, became the youngest City Council president in 1980. They are shown in front of the City Hall complex, completed in 1976 at a cost of $1.8 million. In 1991, Publisher Paul Davis wrote of Mayor Dempsey: "She has been supported by the overwhelming majority because 99 percent of the things she has sought to accomplish have been good for the city and its residents." She would have served a record eighteen consecutive years as mayor in 1998 with the end of her four-year term.

—Photo: Will Dickey

▶ Dr. Dorothy DiOrio, who had climbed the Matterhorn, played the violin in orchestras on two continents, and skin-dived in Sardinia, became Auburn's first female department head outside home economics in 1972. A specialist in French, German, Italian and Latin, Dr. DiOrio served as Auburn's Castanoli Professor of Italic Languages. She headed the Foreign Languages Department for seven years until choosing to return to full-time teaching in 1979. She retired in 1993.

—Photo: Auburn Alumnews

AUBURN • A PICTORIAL HISTORY OF THE LOVELIEST VILLAGE

▼ *The Auburn Heritage Association undertook in spring 1979 to restore the antebellum Scott-Yarbrough Home at the end of East Magnolia. Participating in ground-breaking were, left to right: Wilella Plant Ingalls, Danny Sue Gibson Conner, Nancy Ann Nipper (granddaughter of Nancy and Forrest Shivers), Vera* *Blackburn, A. M. Pearson, Mary George Lamar, Ruth Speake, Hoyt Warren, Alice Cary Pick Gibson, K. M. Varner, Louie James, Andy Gentry, Denson Lipscomb, Fran Pick, Andy Pick, and Grace Jones. An anticipated grant to help finance the work failed to materialize, and in August 1981, after restoration had been complet-* *ed, financial problems plagued the association. Auburn National Bank acquired the property to satisfy a loan and in the mid-1980s gave the house and grounds, appraised at $208,000, to the University. It shortly became the home of the AU Center for the Arts and Humanities.*
—Photo: Auburn Heritage Association.

▲ *Residents hung around Toomer's Corner after the parade of April 25, 1986, to be in this picture commemorating Auburn's 150th birthday. A Columbus, Georgia, station televised the parade and also this scene, and a copy of the "World's Largest Living Birthday Card" was sent to the "Today" show. The shadow in the foreground is that of the TV crew on a tower atop a truck in the middle of the intersection.*

—Photo: AU Archives

Chapter 8

POLITICS, PRORATION AND PROBATION

*T*he Board of Trustees split over selection of a successor to President Philpott in 1980. Half favored Dr. Rex K. Rainer, head of civil engineering at Auburn, and half favored Dr. Steven Sample, executive vice president of Academic Affairs at the University of Nebraska. Fob James, who as governor also served as president of the AU Board of Trustees, asked, "Why do we need to get an outsider? We have plenty of qualified candidates right here in Alabama?" The governor put off a formal vote.

Finally a Rainer backer announced he was switching his support to Dr. H. Hanly Funderburk. To block Sample, others favoring Rainer also switched, thus creating a Funderburk-Sample deadlock. Shortly thereafter, Sample withdrew his candidacy. In April 1980, more than three months after the governor first delayed a vote, board members elected Funderburk as president. He became the fourth Auburn alumnus to serve as the University's chief executive. Funderburk, forty-eight, had been chancellor of Auburn University-Montgomery, where he had helped convert an old cotton field into a campus with seven major buildings, a $16 million budget, and 4,700 students.

▲ Coach Al Martincic led an exercise class for students, professors, and townspeople five days a week from 1964 until well past his retirement in the late 1970s as a University physical education teacher. A tape with such lyrics as "Hush, little baby, don't you cry . . ." signaled the class would soon begin. Then Martincic's high-pitched "Good ole sit-ups . . . push-ups . . . bicycling . . . push-ups . . . curl-ups . . ." and the like kept the group moving. "The best tune on the tape is 'Sweet Gypsy Rose' because when those first notes begin, the exercisers know they are on the home stretch, but Martincic keeps an eagle eye on the group to make sure there are no slackers," Martha Evans wrote in the Tiger Rag. He died in 1991 at age seventy-six.

—Photo: AU Archives

◄ "I grew up hearing my daddy say he wanted a doctor in the family," Benjamin Franklin Thomas, Sr., once related, "so that's what I thought I was supposed to be." He had been a general practitioner in Auburn for fifty-seven years when he retired in 1977. Dr. Ben F. Thomas, Jr., shown with his wife Thelma, retired in 1987 after forty years as a GP in Auburn. Father and son practiced together in the remodeled old KA house on South Gay Street for more than three decades. Between them, they touched the lives of hundreds of families annually for several generations. Ben, Jr.'s sons, B. F., III, (he goes by Franklin) and John S., were surgeons at the Auburn-Opelika medical complex in the mid-1990s. Daughter Martha V. Thomas operated a veterinary clinic and daughter Ann Phillips was a partner in a CPA firm, both in Auburn. Another B. F. Thomas, Franklin's son, Ben, IV, became a high school senior in 1996 and hadn't decided whether to pursue a career in medicine.

—Photo: Opelika-Auburn News

Funderburk moved to Auburn as the University faced a major financial crisis during a nationwide economic recession. He was greeted with anything but enthusiasm by a faculty and student body disheartened by the politics involved in the presidential selection process, by criticism of higher education in general and Auburn in particular from Governor James, and by budget cuts necessary to get the school through a period of tight money. Another crisis for Funderburk and the trustees began on September 27, 1980, when Tennessee crushed Auburn 42-0 in a football game at Jordan-Hare Stadium attended by a record 75,942 fans. Alumni pressure for the resignation of Coach Doug Barfield increased each week during the fall, as Auburn lost all six of its SEC games. Barfield resigned December 1 at the request of the board. Two days later, Georgia Coach Vince Dooley announced he had turned down an offer to become head coach at Auburn, reportedly with a ten-year contract and base pay totaling $1.8 million. Pat Dye, a former All-American guard at Georgia, became Auburn's head football coach in January 1981. A few months later, after Lee Hayley had resigned and gone to the University of Georgia, Dye also became athletic director. Alumni looked to him to do for Auburn what Dooley, a former Auburn star, had done for Dye's alma mater—rebuild a football power.

State sales- and income-tax collections that failed to meet the Legislature's expectations meant the proration of funds for education in Alabama and serious cutbacks in library purchases and most services at Auburn. To meet the emergency, trustees approved tuition increases effective in the fall of 1981 of 37.5 percent for in-state and about 58 percent for out-of-state students. Fees became $330 for in-state and $760 for out-of-state students per quarter. The windfall from the tuition increase was partly offset by a reduction in funds for Auburn from the 1981-82 state appropriation for education.

The University celebrated its 125th birthday the week of Founder's Day in May 1981, five years before it would be able to share in the 150th anniversary of the founding of the community of Auburn.

Within a few months of his selection as AU president, Funderburk became the center of a dispute involving administration, faculty, students, alumni, and others. The controversy eventually reached the pages of the Chronicle of Higher Education, Time magazine, and USA Today. It kept editorial writers and letter writers busy in Alabama. From the beginning, Funderburk was handicapped because many faculty members believed his appointment had been based on politics rather than merit. Funderburk's arrival during a deep recession meant cost cutting, and he brought with him from Auburn University-Montgomery a reputation for wanting to control everything himself. In addition, he was accused of, in some instances, sacrificing quality instruction at AUM by leaning too heavily on temporary, part-time teachers to save money.

► *Nightspots come and go in Auburn, but the War Eagle Supper Club has been around since the 1950s, located 3.3 miles south of Toomer's Corner on Highway 29. After it became a private club in 1961, students flocked there for beer and pizza. Coeds weren't supposed to go there under pre-1970s University rules, "but gradually the guys would start bringing dates out," famous waitress Mildred Williams told the* Auburn Alumnews *writer Rosy Evans. In revisiting the club, a 1971 Auburn graduate said, "I stayed out here so much and wrote so many checks to the Supper Club that when my father came down for graduation he wanted to see the place. He walked in, glared at the bar, and exclaimed, 'Son, I thought this is where you had your meal plan.'" By 1996, the club had substituted for pizza the music of live rock 'n' roll bands. In the 1930s, the place reportedly was "a semi-legal drinking locale," with dice games and other dalliances, a later owner, Hank Gilmer, was told. In 1993, Chris Brandt (under eagle), a former Auburn High School basketball star and an ex-University starter, is shown checking IDs at his brother John's place.*
—*Photo: AU Archives;* Glomerata

In increasing numbers, faculty members at Auburn became convinced that the president was bypassing the well-developed system of "shared university governance" and depriving them of a voice in budget cuts and enrollment decisions. The University Senate eventually branded Funderburk's leadership "dogmatic, intimidating, manipulative" and "not highly principled" in connection with the resignation of vice presidents Grady Cox and Taylor Littleton. Some Funderburk supporters blamed the resignations "on a power struggle between those who had been in power and the new administration." History Professor Gordon Bond, chairman of the University Faculty and University Senate during Funderburk's last year at Auburn, later said the president "had no philosophical base or commitment to the basic standards of higher education." Some credited Funderburk with putting a bankrupt institution back on its feet financially and said he would be a good president if the faculty gave him half a chance. When he resigned in 1983, Funderburk charged that "in recent months mockery has been made of truth by some Auburn University faculty, and a propaganda campaign has been waged against the true facts." Funderburk's support seemed strongest in agriculture (he had taught botany and plant pathology) and his opposition the most determined in liberal arts, but allegiances crossed school boundaries.

Between February and November in 1982, the margin of no-confidence votes by members of the general faculty swung heavily against the president. In February, 455 voted no-confidence, 416 supported him, and 66 abstained; nine months later, 752 voted no-confidence and 253 supported him. In addition, the faculty asked that he resign or be fired. On December 4, 1982, thirteen of the University's top administrators—"in Funderburk's presence"—told the trustees that the president should resign. Not giving up, "the Alabama Farm Bureau circulate[d] pro-Funderburk petitions at its offices statewide," the *Birmingham News* reported. To save President Funderburk, the trustees considered appointing a chancellor to handle campus operations and limiting the president's responsibilities mainly to alumni and legislative matters. Alumni Association directors, who had supported Funderburk, opposed this plan, and it was dropped. The Student Senate, which had backed Funderburk a year earlier, voted 33-1 for him to resign. The end came after Funderburk lost the support of most of the trustees, and George Wallace replaced Fob James as governor and president of the Board of Trustees. Funderburk resigned February 26, 1983.

In parting, Funderburk said he had completed the tasks assigned him by the trustees: to "straighten out the financial affairs of the university, establish a goal and initiate a

▲ *Bo Jackson dived "over the top" in 1982, helping end nine lean football years against Alabama with a late-game touchdown. Auburn's 23-22 victory incited jubilation at Legion Field and Toomer's Corner. He went on to win the Heisman Trophy, to play major league football and baseball, and to become famous for his "Bo Knows" TV commercials. But a hip injury ended his football career and shortened his baseball days.*

—Photo: AU Archives

▶ *Dr. H. Hanly Funderburk became Auburn's twelfth president in April 1980 and immediately faced what the Glomerata termed an endless list of negatives: "proration, athletic probation, faculty discontent, aging campus buildings, accreditation problems, poor parking facilities, campus crime." He lost in two votes of confidence by the faculty, the second in November 1982 by an overwhelming tally of 752-253. Funderburk is shown answering questions by the news media after the January 7, 1983, meeting in which the trustees voted to keep him as president but to hire another person to handle the day-to-day affairs of the University. Funderburk resigned seven weeks later.*

—Photo: AU Archives

capital campaign fund, and correct fiscal and personnel problems in the athletic department." By 1996, he had served as the president of Eastern Kentucky University for eleven years.

The man who preceded him as Auburn president saw the faculty's role in Funderburk's downfall as evidence of its growing strength. President Emeritus Philpott, emphasizing that he did not intend to disparage Dr. Funderburk, said the Auburn faculty's escalating "influence in the decisions of the University" had been a "continuing gradual development" over thirty years. "Increasing the power of the faculty brought us into line with what the best institutions in the United States were doing at the time," Philpott said in an interview with AU archivist Dwayne Cox. "This was the accepted procedure on most campuses. We had been somewhat behind the times in effecting it."

Between 1980 and 1996, the city of Auburn continued to grow. It added 1,946 single-family houses, increasing the total number by nearly 44 percent to 6,395. The least expensive house built in 1995 was valued at $39,624, according to the building permit. The most expensive was probably greatly undervalued at $450,000 because the cost of the permit for larger houses is based on square footage rather than actual value, senior planner David Harris said. The average price for a new 2,000-square-foot house was $113,000. In addition, Auburn added 4,199 apartments, bringing the total to about 10,200. "Most residential growth since 1980 occurred on the south side of Auburn," said Wendy Hassett, assistant to City Manager Doug Watson.

As a village in 1900, Auburn had approximately 1,400 townspeople and about 400 students. In 1995, the estimated population was 38,959, which included 20,064 students. But bigger isn't always better.

When Auburn was smaller, crime wasn't as much a problem. "I don't remember ever locking my front door," a senior citizen recalled. The college didn't even have a separate security force other than student night watchmen until the mid-1940s, one source said, and for decades the city got along with a handful of police officers. More people and changing times, including the use and sale of illegal drugs, meant more crime and more police in Auburn. Reported in 1994 were 141 assaults, 391 burglaries, 14 robberies, 10 rapes (four fewer than the year before), 76 stolen vehicles, and 1,469 larceny thefts. To cope with more crime and heavier traffic, the city in 1996 had sixty-seven sworn police officers, including one woman and fourteen blacks. On campus, there were twenty-two police officers, including three blacks and two women. They helped make Auburn a much safer place to live than many other cities. So did the city's sixty firefighters, half of them Auburn University students. Eight firemen were blacks. Not all firefighters were satisfied during the 1980s, and several sued the city over personal grievances.

Long-time Mayor Jan Dempsey, twenty-five individual City Council members who served with her, and City Manager Doug Watson, department heads, and other city employees tackled many challenging problems. These ranged from eliminating inadequate housing and unpaved streets to guaranteeing local support for public schools and

Park and Sam Harris Park were built in northwest Auburn, and the city's largest, Kiesel Park, on 129 acres farther west. Grand National with 54 holes in Opelika and Auburn Links with 18 holes on Shel Toomer Parkway opened in the mid-nineties and gave Auburn golfers easy access to four public courses as well as Saugahatchee Country Club.

Fifteen plants operated in Auburn's industrial and technology parks in 1996. The first to open, Falk Corporation, began making couplings and gear drives in about 1976. One of the latest, Terry Farms, Inc., planned to begin producing 5,000 pounds of Morel mushrooms a week in 1996. Other manufactured items included laboratory furniture, computer software, treadmills, and door and window frames.

Auburn's largest employers in 1995, according to unaudited city hall estimates, included the University with 4,943 employees on the main campus; Auburn City Schools, 602; Master Lock, 424; the federal government, 401; Winn-Dixie, 366; Auburn University Hotel and Conference Center, 303; Gayfers, 203; Wal-Mart, 201; Foodmax, 201; and Kroger, 195. All except eight of Briggs & Stratton's first 300 employees were locally hired in 1995, a spokesman said. Hundreds more were to be employed there. The company makes small engines. It presented the University "the first gasoline engine produced entirely by AU student workers." The engine was for a garden tiller.

In an effort to eliminate substandard housing, mostly in northwest Auburn but also in other sections, the city rehabilitated 181 houses from 1984 to 1996 with federal grants at an average cost of $10,000 per house. In addition, a city/private loan program helped seventeen low-and-moderate income families become first-time home buyers. In 1996, the City Council made available a ten-lot subdivision in which Habitat for Humanity could build houses to help eliminate substandard housing.

These steps followed successful efforts by the Presbyterian Community Ministry (PCM) to help upgrade low-income housing, particularly in northwest Auburn.

attracting new industry and better paying jobs. Council members from 1980 through 1996, listed alphabetically, were: Mary Brooks, Kenneth Brown, Arthur Dowdell, Mary Fortenberry, Robert Gastaldo, Cheryl Gladden, Hal Goebel, Logan Gray, Frances Hale, Bill Ham, Jr., Samuel Harris, Kenny Howard, Trey Johnston, Denson Lipscomb, Gail McAlister, William Mixon, Alex Moore, Darrell Penrod, Jim Quillin, Lamar Sellers, Sam Teague, Joel Tremaine, Victor Vance, Charlotte Ward, and Dennis Wilson.

Probably the most important city improvements in the 1980s and nineties were the wastewater treatment plants because they made other improvements possible, Ms. Hassett said. Other major projects included completing East University Drive, widening Glenn Avenue, opening Technology Park, building Boykin Community Center Gymnasium, and building the municipal parking deck.

Improved recreational facilities just south of I-85 included the softball park, campgrounds, and the water park. Construction of a family entertainment center in that area with Go-Karts, batting cages, and mini-golf had been approved. In addition to Boykin Gym, Martin Luther King

Minister Wallace Alston, Jr., of the First Presbyterian Church had been alerted by Editor Neil Davis what to expect, but was still shocked in 1968 to find people living in shacks with leaky roofs in the Loveliest Village. Alston's congregation accepted his challenge to help provide decent housing. Members of Baptist, Methodist, Episcopal, and other Protestant churches, and Catholic and Jewish congregations also contributed. From about 1970 through 1995, PCM, with interest-free loans and grants, assisted more than one hundred families in building new houses and three hundred in adding inside plumbing and bathrooms. It also helped approximately 250 to repair or replace roofs, and kept hundreds more from being evicted or from having their electricity, gas, or water cut off.

In the mid-nineties, the East Alabama Food Bank in the old post office building at Tichenor Avenue and Gay Street collected and distributed more than 100,000 pounds of food a month. This fed the hungry without charge through churches, the Salvation Army, Hospice, and other organizations. Such food as cereal, pasta, canned vegetables, frozen meat and cheese were given, along with non-food items such as soap, diapers, and shampoo. By 1996, the Crisis Center had provided for twenty-five years "a telephone help line for people depressed or needing someone to talk to." Also that year, Head Start completed thirty-one years of service to children, and the Lee County Literacy Coalition helped 206 adults and twelve children learn to read. Another of many contributors, the East Alabama Medical Center, handled more than $8 million in charity cases in both 1994 and 1995.

EAMC's predecessor, the Lee County Hospital in Opelika, admitted its first patient on February 16, 1952. Four years later, William D. Lazenby, an Emory University medical student, interviewed for a surgery internship at University of Alabama-Birmingham Hospital. When Lazenby said he wanted to practice medicine at home in Lee County, he was told, "Not big enough to support a surgeon." In 1996, Lazenby had been a surgeon in Lee County for thirty-two years. Twenty-eight other surgeons also were practicing there, mostly serving patients from a five-county area. In 1964, the staff included twelve physicians and in 1996 about 110, ranging from obstetricians to neurosurgeons and from heart surgeons to psychiatrists. More than five hundred nurses worked there. Lazenby and a few other doctors began recruiting specialists and started the Medical Arts Center of East Alabama in 1968. The hospital's name in 1981 became East Alabama Medical Center. It had grown from eighty-eight beds in 1952 to 348 beds in 1996. The medical center admitted 14,538 patients in 1994-95.

After President Funderburk resigned, Dr. Wilford S. Bailey, a former Auburn vice president and department head in Veterinary Medicine, served as interim president in 1983-84. Bailey offered to reappoint three department heads who, in disagreement with Funderburk, had stepped down. One accepted; two had made other plans. Bailey became active in the self-study for reaccreditation, the $61.7 million Auburn Generations Fund drive, and the building program. During Bailey's presidency, work that began under Funderburk was completed on an electrical engineering building, and a site was prepared for a civil engineering building. Expansion was planned for Draughon Library and was in progress on the Scott-Ritchey Research Facility in Veterinary Medicine.

Later, during the Martin administration, Bailey persuaded the Alumni Association to keep Greater Auburn Foundation funds under the president's control and not place GAF money under control of the Athletic Department. Bailey, president of the National Collegiate Athletic Association at the time, warned that the proposed shift might put Auburn sports in jeopardy with the NCAA

▲ *The Reverend George "Jed" Smock, an itinerant member of Campus Ministry USA, preached on the lawn by Haley Center during this visit to Auburn in 1979. The minister and his wife, Sister Cindy, preached outdoors on dozens of* campuses *yearly and frequently engaged in heated arguments with dissenters in the audience. Students at Auburn looked forward to their appearances for nearly a decade. The* Plainsman *reported in 1986 that Brother Jed "attracted hundreds dur-* *ing two days of preaching near the Eagle's Cage" behind Haley Center. The couple was featured in an issue of* Rolling Stone *magazine that year.*

—Photo: AU Archives

again. The University already had served at least one year of probation for football recruiting violations during the 1950s, 1960s, 1970s, and 1980s under coaches Jordan and Barfield. Its men's basketball team had been on probation for two years, 1979-81, under coach Bob Davis.

Dr. James E. Martin, a six-foot, six-inch former API basketball player, became Auburn's fourteenth president at age fifty-one in 1984. With a background in agricultural administration, he had headed the five-campus University of Arkansas system before returning to his alma mater. As Auburn president, Martin became involved in two major controversies. One strengthened his position with many faculty members in 1988-89; the other weakened that relationship in 1990-91. He apparently hurt himself with one or more trustees in both instances. The first resulted in Jerry F. Smith stepping down as executive director of the Auburn Alumni Association. Faculty complaints of lavish spending had led Martin to initiate investigations by internal auditors and an Atlanta law firm. Alumni Association directors supported Smith, who denied any wrongdoing. But the Alabama Ethics Commission held there was "probable cause" to believe Smith had violated the state ethics law. "Mel Cooper, executive director of the Ethics Commission, said the commission found 'substantial evidence' that Smith 'used his position as a state employee for

his own financial gain,'" the *Birmingham News* reported. Despite the ethics findings, Cooper said Smith had "done a fine job" in his alumni work. Smith resigned less than two months later. The state attorney general's office then dropped its investigation of the allegations against him. Martin appeared caught between professors and trustees in the next big campus showdown, which resulted in his denying an eminent scholar's chair to a controversial Catholic priest, Father Charles E. Curran. The University Senate censured Martin on January 15, 1991, and about two months later, he announced that he would retire the next year. Martin said the Senate's action did not affect his decision to step down. Whatever his reasons, he left before a charge of rules violations was resolved that brought Auburn a national black eye and a fifth NCAA probation to its football team.

On Dr. Funderburk's watch, Pat Dye had succeeded Doug Barfield as head football coach in 1981. Before Dye arrived, Auburn had lost nine consecutive games to Alabama. The selection committee asked Dye, "How long will it take to beat Alabama?" Dye replied, "Sixty minutes," meaning Auburn would have to play a complete game to win. Approximately two seasons and one hour of football later, the Tigers won 23-22. In 1983, Auburn won its first of four Southeastern Conference championships under Dye, finishing third in the Associated Press national poll. It was in the top ten for five years in the 1980s. Through 1989, his teams went six-three against Alabama, and in 1990 the Tigers played in their ninth bowl game in nine seasons.

As the next football season approached, the NCAA was wrapping up investigations of the men's basketball and tennis programs. Both went on probation in November 1991 for two years, tennis for violating the extra-benefits rule and basketball for illegal recruiting. Auburn was barred from the SEC Basketball Tournament the next March.

The 1991 football season opened with three Auburn victories, including a 14-10 triumph over Texas in Austin. Then, in the words of one Dye assistant, "On Friday, September 27, the day before we played Tennessee in Knoxville, the Eric Ramsey story broke and everything came unglued." Ramsey, a former four-year letterman at cornerback from Homewood, told the *Montgomery Advertiser* he had received illegal payments from boosters and Auburn coaches. His attorney, Donald Watkins of Birmingham, released in October and November tapes secretly recorded by Ramsey during conversations with an Auburn booster and Auburn assistant coaches. In the tapes, Ramsey asked for money to help him support his wife and child. He also accused the football program of racism.

Developments made headlines almost weekly. Auburn lost six of eight games after the story broke and finished the season with six losses and five victories. The Tigers won five, lost five and tied one in 1992.

Thirteen months after Ramsey's accusations became public, the NCAA, on November 5, 1992, presented Auburn with nine allegations of rules violations. Dye, who had stepped down as athletic director in May, told his players in Birmingham the night before the Alabama-Auburn game that he was resigning as coach in the "best interests" of the University. He was not officially charged with any violations, but Auburn was cited for "an absence of institutional control." Dye received a settlement valued at about $1.1 million (called a "golden handshake" by one faculty leader) to compensate him for the remaining four years of his contract and for a loss of income from his television show and other outside sources.

Finally, in August 1993, after new Auburn coach Terry Bowden had started fall practice, word came the NCAA had found that illegal payments had been made; Auburn's football program had been placed on probation again. This meant no bowl games for two years, no television games for one year, and fewer scholarships. Another major violation within five years surely would put Auburn at risk of receiv-

▲ *These two students guided "Old Nancy," a steam-driven tractor owned by the College of Agriculture, up West Magnolia Avenue in this 1984 campus parade. The tractor was driven many a mile by J. W. Dupree family members on their farm near Beauregard. Dupree's grandchildren, Olieta Parker, Lilly Beulah Gowder, and J. Arthur Whatley, gave the antique to Auburn University in the 1970s.*

—Photo: AU Archives

▲ *Ethel and Olin L. Hill celebrated their seventieth wedding anniversary on July 25, 1996, by working at their men's clothing store. Olin, with Ethel at his side nearly all the way, had put in sixty-eight years as a merchant in downtown Auburn. Both were nineteen when they married. Olin decided early on that he was always going to have the last word at his house, which, he said, turned out to be "Yes Ma'am!" He also said their faith in God had made their marriage strong. "The man with the tape" started selling suits from a table in a barbershop in 1928 and opened his first men's clothing store in 1936. He recalled sixty years later that he had operated a store in eleven downtown locations and gave the address of each, ten on College Street and one around the corner on Magnolia Avenue.*

—*Photo: Celine Bufkin;* Opelika-Auburn News

ing "the death sentence," losing football altogether.

On the seventh anniversary of Martin's presidency, a listing of his administration's achievements included helping direct a $150 million construction program, which featured the $20.5 million addition to Draughon Library. A Martin detractor commented "construction totaling $150 million, yet not one brass farthing being set aside for maintenance." Student aid had been increased to one million dollars a year. Auburn had attracted ten National Merit Scholars in 1983-84 and boasted thirty-two in 1990-91. Martin's skill with the Legislature helped pass two acts benefitting the state's colleges and universities. One provided for state grants to match private gifts in attracting "world-class faculty" members, such as Curran, most of the University Senate voters apparently thought. The other act authorized the sale of vanity tags to pay for scholarships. Under Martin's leadership, University Relations said, "Such research centers as the Space Power Institute and the National Center for Asphalt Technology have taken their

place alongside such nationally prominent research facilities as the Alabama Agricultural Experiment Station and Veterinary Medicine's renowned Scott-Ritchey Center." Total campus research had increased in value from $30.1 million in 1984 to $64.4 million in 1991. The Extension Service had begun a satellite uplink system that enabled people state- and world-wide "to stay at home or work and take part in live teleconferences with AU faculty." Under Martin and Librarian William Highfill, the Draughon Library staff earned membership in the prestigious Association of Research Libraries in 1992. Martin pushed hard for creation of the Auburn University Hotel and Conference Center, built in 1989 across College Street from Draughon Library. But that project resulted in a lawsuit against the University and Martin in 1993 that remained in litigation three years later.

For about a decade ending in the early nineties, Auburn spent $12 million to $16 million removing small to large amounts of asbestos from nearly all the buildings on campus, said Dr. Charles Ray, director of Safety and Environmental Health. A major part of the renovation of the ten Hill Dorms was the removal of asbestos. Beard-Eaves-Memorial Coliseum and some other buildings were targeted for asbestos removal when renovated.

Auburn underwent a change in city government structure in 1986. Voters approved combining the separate offices of mayor and City Council president into one position, giving the mayor a vote and a leadership role on the council. Mayors would continue to be elected at large, and other council members would be chosen from wards. The first mayor under the new system was the last mayor under the old—Jan Dempsey, wife of surgeon Richard Dempsey. Their children, two boys and a girl, were ten, twelve and fourteen in 1980. That year Mrs. Dempsey was so close to a majority in her first race for mayor that her would-be run-off opponent conceded. In four subsequent elections, Mayor Dempsey won with 64, 81, 70, and 60 percent of the votes cast. Mayor Dempsey "has made some enemies along the way, but she has been and is good for Auburn," Publisher Paul Davis wrote in the *Lee County Eagle* in 1991. Mary Fortenberry, a council member since 1978, said in 1996 that the mayor favored spending city money conservatively, was compassionate, and was a strong leader. "When she makes up her mind, she digs in her heels," the councilwoman said. Mayor Dempsey's supporters credited her with bringing a new spirit of cooperation to City Hall, with achieving more respect for city government and its services, and with initiating the Committee of 2000 to help set city goals that later were largely achieved. Councilwoman Fortenberry recalled that for a number of years before Mrs. Dempsey became mayor there had often been dissension among city officials. But since then council members had been more likely to settle differences of opinion by working out compromises. Mrs. Fortenberry said one council

▲ *Chuck Person scored 27 points and pulled down 15 rebounds to lead Auburn to an 81-65 upset victory over St. John's in the 1986 NCAA West Regional Basketball Tournament at Long Beach, Calif. Shown clockwise with Person during the celebration are coach Sonny Smith and cheerleaders Beth Doverspike, Laura Gilmore, Kaye Myers, and Ron Anders. Auburn later beat University of Nevada Las Vegas 70-63 before being defeated in the West Regional finals— the Elite Eight—by Louisville 84-76.*

Person completed eligibility in 1985-86, but still held the Auburn career scoring record ten years later with 2,311 points in four seasons. John Mengelt, in 1996 the only one among the top nine scorers who played only three seasons, stood in fifth place with 1,920 career points, but he held the school's single-season record with an average of 28.4 points per game as a senior in 1970-71. His career scoring average of 24.8 points per game was tops and 4.4 points better than that of Mike Mitchell, who finished in 1977-78. Mitchell also was second in career points with 2,123 and 57 points more than Person's younger brother, Wesley, whose final season was 1993-94 and who scored on 262 of 594 three-point shots, a career average of .441.

Coach Smith compiled a 173-154 record in eleven seasons, 1979-89. Through 1995-96, he was the only coach to take Auburn to the NCAA Men's Basketball Tournament, and he did it five consecutive seasons. Joel Eaves had several teams with better records, but they missed the NCAA tournament one year because a football team probation also affected basketball and other years because fewer teams were invited than in the Smith era.

—Photo: AU Athletic Department

"might be accused of being pro-business and another anti-business," but she felt nearly all members were working toward the city's best interests. For some residents, a maverick councilman like Robert Gastaldo enlivened meetings with thought-provoking dissent. Like Mayor Dempsey, Mrs. Fortenberry rated hiring City Manager Doug Watson "one of the best things to happen" to the city. Mrs. Fortenberry said council members had "brains enough to know we needed a professional to manage a $20 million budget." In turn, the mayor and council set policy, made final decisions, and provided a climate in which Watson, his professional staff, and other city employees could do their jobs.

One of Mayor Dempsey's and the City Council's top priorities was to stabilize "local support for an outstanding public-school system." In an effort to do that, the council guaranteed from the general fund annually the equivalent of a 15-mill property tax levy. This was expected to amount to about $2.5 million in 1996-97. But unlike a voter-approved property tax, the school-tax ordinance could be rescinded by a future council. "Over my dead body," the mayor said in 1996.

Auburn's public-school enrollment had increased from 3,205 in 1981 to 4,067 in 1995. In 1995-96, some 60 percent of the students were white, 34 percent black, 5 percent Asian, one-half percent Hispanic, and one-half percent unidentified. There were 322 full-time teachers. Students moved into part of a new $3.6 million addition to Auburn High School in 1995. The latest new school, Auburn Early Education Center, was in its fourth year of operation in 1996. It housed kindergarten students, preschool handicapped students, and day care for employees' children. Plans had been approved for an addition to the Early Education Center and for construction of an elementary school and a middle school. Financing was to come from a voter-approved, 6-mill property tax expected to produce $900,000 or more annually to pay off a bond issue. Fewer than a dozen students graduated in 1915 in the first class at Lee County High School, today's Auburn High; eighty years later, 212 graduated.

Lee-Scott Academy planned to move during the 1996-97 school year from East Glenn Avenue to a nearly $6 million new facility on 75 acres at the end of Gatewood Drive in northeast Auburn. The school had 520 students, and the new buildings were designed for up to 600 pre-kindergarten-through-twelfth-grade students. Fifty to sixty teachers would be employed.

In 1996, the Village School on East Drake Avenue had three teachers and thirty-three students in kindergarten through the eighth grade.

Auburn University's fifteenth president, William V. Muse, fifty-two, an Arkansas Ph.D. and former University of Akron president, arrived in 1992. Within three years, he found the mid-nineties "not the best of times" for Auburn and other universities. "There is a growing distrust and even hostility toward higher education," Muse said. In 1995, Auburn suffered a 7.5 percent loss in state appropriations, costing the main campus approximately $9 million and all programs $13.5 million. Governor James proposed another $7.5 million cut for Auburn in 1996, but the Legislature provided level funding, plus $500,000 for serious needs in the College of Veterinary Medicine. In favoring reduced funding for Auburn, James said the number of administrators there was growing much faster than the growth in faculty members or students. Muse said the figures were misleading because they overlooked the

University's missions in outreach and research that are unrelated to instruction. Auburn continued to be rated a good buy for students in *U.S. News and World Report* and *Money* magazine. But observers wondered how long this would last if able teachers took early retirement or left for better salaries, if classes became larger and harder to get into, if aging equipment was not replaced, and if tuition continued its sharp increase.

Expecting less money in 1995, Auburn had begun a hiring freeze. To save on payroll, it offered a one-time retirement payout, and 220 accepted. This cost about $5.8 million, but saved $9 million per year in salaries. It also resulted in losing "senior faculty, administrators, and staff, many of whom were nationally recognized in their fields."

In facing the University's worst financial crisis since the early 1980s, Muse urged more state support for higher education. He also may have learned partly from the Funderburk administration's problems to get greater involvement of faculty and staff members in matters affecting them. "It is our desire," Muse said, "that we carefully, methodically, *and collegially* [italics his] determine how best to use what is available, in order to protect the instructional quality that has become characteristic of Auburn University." Each college and school was represented on a new budget advisory committee. Muse also asked administrators and faculty members campuswide to rank academic and administrative programs based on their importance to undergraduate instruction and other key elements of the University's mission. The rankings would be used in deciding how to spend available money. Although encouraged by Muse's openness and willingness to involve faculty and staff members in the budgeting quest for academic quality, some found his concern with numbers ominous. Muse said in his 1994-95 report: "I am troubled by the number of degree programs at Auburn that do not meet the viability standards established by the Alabama Commission on Higher Education as to the number of graduates per year. We need to consider those programs as candidates for elimination."

Muse's achievements in his first four years included conferring the 159,000th degree on campus, helping to secure Auburn's ten-year reaccreditation by the Southern Association of Colleges and Schools; receiving the "Academic Freedom" award from the University Chapter of the American Association of University Professors; instituting renovation of many campus facilities, including Plainsman Park, Thach Hall, Tichenor Hall and Samford Hall; assisting the Alumni Association in its six-year drive to raise $175 million to improve facilities and "enhance programs for people," promoting Paul Parks from vice president for research to provost and vice president for academic affairs, receiving trustee approval for placing an art museum at Samford Avenue and Wire Road; and, in University Relations' words, reordering "the University's intercollegiate athletics program" to ensure "that regulatory control goes hand-in-hand with competitiveness and good sport." He hired Mike Lude, former University of Washington athletic director, as athletic director to help restore Auburn's credibility with the NCAA and its winning performances on the football field. Thirty-seven-year-old Terry Bowden, coach at Samford University and son of one of the South's most successful college coaches, was a surprise choice as Dye's successor. Even greater surprises were his team's 11-0 record in 1993, a streak that ran 21 games without a loss, and a 2-1 showing against Alabama through 1995.

When "hired gun" Lude left, David Housel, AU's nationally respected sports information director, became athletic director in 1994. Housel, a widely known writer and speaker on Auburn University, found that he not only would have to be a leader in achieving sports victories, but also would have to police the program. He may have spared men's basketball the death penalty by his handling of an internal investigation. He first sidelined for the 1995-96

▶ *Three Auburn presidents and Dr. John Kuykendall, left, president of Davidson University and formerly head of Auburn's department of religion, wait for the festivities to start during the celebration of Auburn's 150th birthday in 1986. All four were program participants. The Auburn presidents, left to right: Dr. Harry M. Philpott (1965-80), Dr. Wilford S. Bailey (1983-84), and Dr. James E. Martin (1984-92).*

—*Photo:* Lee County Eagle

Through the years, AU student athletes have volunteered hundreds of times to participate in city school programs. Football players Tim Jessie, left, and Tommy Agee visited Wrights Mill Road School in 1986 to celebrate Spirit Day. They presented awards to winners of the school's safety contest, "Project Buckle Up." The winners, left to right: Katie Templeton, Anna Harris, Kelly Whitesides, Adam Hammett, Kevin Quindlen, and Daniel Thrasher. Agee, who received a B.S. in Youth Services in 1987, played nine years in the National Football League, six with the Dallas Cowboys. Jessie, an adult education major, played for the Washington Redskins in 1987.
—Photo: Auburn City Schools

season an assistant coach and two starting players. Later he announced self-imposed sanctions that included reducing scholarships by two for one year and forfeiting sixteen games coach Cliff Ellis' team had won in 1994-95. Men's basketball had already been in trouble within five years, and a collective sigh of relief came when the NCAA decided Auburn's "self-imposed penalties would be sufficient and no further action" was warranted.

It was the ninth citation against Auburn men's programs by the NCAA, with probations totaling seventeen and one-third years. Football had been on probation five times for a total of eleven and one-third years, basketball three times for four years, and tennis once for two years. Probation kept the Tigers out of football bowl games in 1956 (7-3), 1957 (10-0), 1958 (9-0-1), 1959 (7-3), 1960 (8-2), 1979 (8-3), 1993 (11-0), and 1994 (9-1-1). The teams went 69-12-2 during those eight years.

On a more pleasant note, Housel, archivist Dave Rosenblatt, and others opened a museum/hall of honor in the Athletic Center during 1996 that offered a memorable walk through Auburn sports history.

A fourteen-year-old college desegregation suit resulted in a court ruling in 1995 to combine Cooperative Extension programs at the state's two land-grant universities. Under the new Alabama Cooperative Extension System, predominantly white Auburn University would handle traditional rural programs, and predominantly black A&M University would have an urban focus. Auburn's president was to appoint the state extension director, to have headquarters in Auburn. A&M's extension salaries and benefits were to be raised to the level of those at Auburn. The Extension System's top teaching efforts were to continue to include making farming and forestry more profitable, improving

management of natural resources, and helping revitalize rural Alabama. Extension would rely heavily on research from Auburn's Agricultural Experiment Station. For instance, the station developed forest pest-management practices and systems in the 1970s, developed new plum, cantaloupe, and watermelon varieties in the 1980s, and developed genetically improved catfish in the 1990s.

A fight for a place on Auburn's Board of Trustees in 1996 became as rough as an Auburn-Alabama football game, the Associated Press reported. Colonial Bank Chairman Bobby Lowder, a controversial trustee whose term was up, sought another twelve years. But Governor James appointed Vice President Phil Richardson of Alfa Insurance to fill the slot. In the 1994 race for governor, the political action committee at Lowder's bank contributed $25,000 to Democratic incumbent Jim Folsom, while Alfa, one of James' earliest supporters, pumped $100,000 into his campaign. The competing interests "represented are agriculture and timber vs. business," wrote Auburn University-Montgomery professors Carl Grafton and Anne Permaloff. Lowder had been a key figure in hiring winning football coaches Pat Dye before becoming a trustee and Terry Bowden after becoming a trustee. He also was chairman of the search committee that resulted in Muse's appointment as president. Lowder's family had contributed several million dollars to Auburn, and the new School of Business building was named for his parents. The Farm Bureau Federation (now Alfa) had been a long-time contributor to Auburn agricultural programs and had maneuvered for a voice in Auburn policy—and had exercised power on the board—as far back as the 1920s. Lobbied heavily by Lowder supporters, the Senate refused to act on

▲ Harold D. Melton celebrated with supporters in 1987 after becoming the first black elected president of the Auburn University Student Government Association. Melton, a major in international business from Marietta, Georgia, also was the first independent elected president since George McMillan in 1965, the Glomerata said. He received 65 percent of the vote in the three-man race. He said his election shows "that Auburn students are . . . more interested in qualities that make good leadership—not in what fraternity you belong to or what color you are." Melton later received a law degree and joined the Georgia Attorney General's staff. Winston C. Tucker, a building science major from Elmore, became the second black SGA president in 1995.
—Photo: AU Archives

▲ Dr. John H. Jeffers came to Auburn in 1958 and served as pastor of the First Baptist Church for twenty-eight years. "'Brother John,' as he is affectionately called by some parishioners, has sent hundreds of newlyweds happily on their way and brought comfort to legions of others in times of sorrow," columnist Neil Davis wrote in 1983. Jeffers also was respected for his brave leadership on controversial issues of vital importance to his church, including racial desegregation. Davis said that Jeffers and his wife, modestly and humbly, did much for Auburn "through some very troublous times—times that would have brought passion out of control and hostile fracturing but for their wise, calm and courageous leadership." Jeffers and his wife Jeanette accepted preaching missions in the Philippines, Nigeria, Brazil and Spain in the 1980s and 1990, and served as hosts for eleven foreign tours.
—Photo: John H. Jeffers

James' appointee Richardson. The Legislature's regular 1996 session ended with Lowder still seated, but James used a state attorney general's ruling from a political ally to oust Lowder and another holdover trustee, Huntsville lawyer Jim Tatum. Lowder and Tatum filed suit. Coach Bowden, who had earlier taken Lowder's side, said he was "frightened" by James himself replacing Lowder as chairman of the trustees' athletic committee. "If the governor wanted to cut 4-6 percent from higher education, I'm not sure we can expect a different approach to the athletic department," Bowden told the Huntsville Times. James replied that, instead, Bowden should be concerned about playing Florida next season.

For the second time in slightly more than twenty years, Lee County became a federal disaster area in 1995. In September 1975, Hurricane Eloise had uprooted trees, downed power lines, and closed schools for several days in Auburn. In October 1995, Hurricane Opal pushed trees onto houses, cut off electric service except on campus where about 80 percent of the lines are underground, and caused postponement of the Auburn-Mississippi State football game. Billy Hall bought one of the first tree-removal licenses in Auburn in about 1954. He said Opal was "nearly twice as rough as Eloise," because it covered a wider territory. Hall's crew was still removing trees nine months after Opal hit on October 4. The only injuries he heard of

were to amateurs using chainsaws. Opal "caused well over $14 million worth of damage in Lee County," the *Lee County Eagle* reported. "The storm affected almost everybody, but miraculously nobody was killed. . . ." Footnote: The next June, a squirrel did what Opal couldn't do—knocked out the lights on most of the campus. The squirrel reportedly "stepped on a high-voltage power line." Then Professor Joseph Kicklighter led about 325 freshman history students from darkened Haley Center to sunny Jordan-Hare Stadium where they took their final exam.

More than 10,000 women students were enrolled at Auburn for the first time during the fall of 1995—10,351, in fact, or 46.8 percent of total enrollment. Large numbers of women were majoring in engineering, veterinary medicine, and other disciplines in which few female students would have been enrolled some decades ago. Male registration was 11,771, or 53.2 percent of the total. Of the 22,122 students, a record number—1,357, or 6.1 percent—were black. The University had its first black "Miss Auburn," Vania Clemons of Mobile, in 1993; and its first black vice president, David Wilson, in 1995. In an age of diversity, there were 91 American Indians or Alaskan natives, 269 Asians or Pacific Islanders, 19,570 Caucasians, and 194 Hispanics. Foreign students totaled 641. More than 35 percent of the students were from out-of-state in the fall of 1995, but fewer were expected to enroll after 1997. Effective that year, the State Legislature made it more difficult to gain in-state residency and to avoid the three times higher out-of-state tuition.

Tuition went up again in fall 1996, this time by $35 per quarter for in-state students and $105 for out-of-staters. The increase put in-state tuition at $785 a quarter, or $9,420 for four school years (12 quarters) and out-of-state tuition at $2,355 a quarter, or $28,260 for four years. The increase meant in-state students paid $200 more per quarter in fall 1996 than in fall 1992. One trustee said the board had no choice, adding, "We can either raise tuition or allow

▶ *The traditional Wreck Tech Pajama Parade came to an end in 1987 along with the annual Auburn-Georgia Tech football game. For decades, the band served as the vanguard for pajama-clad students and those bearing sorority and fraternity floats on a journey through the business district and across campus to a mass meeting at the stadium. Dogs have always been a part of any parade in Auburn, but the pup wearing a diaper in this scene from the late 1950s was a true crowd pleaser. Auburn and Tech had met ninety times on the gridiron starting in 1892. Auburn had won sixteen of the last nineteen games when the series ended, but earlier the Yellow Jackets won thirteen consecutive times. Tech officials said in terminating the series that the Jackets needed to concentrate on games with their Atlantic Coast Conference foes.*

—Photo: Lee County Eagle

classes to deteriorate." Per quarter in-state tuition was $220 in 1980-81, $441 in 1987-88, and $585 in 1992-93.

Enrollment for fall 1995 included 1,709 fraternity and 2,744 sorority members. There were twenty-seven social fraternities, one professional fraternity, and nineteen sororities. The fraternity system had received an overall Fraternal Excellence Award for at least five consecutive years from the Southeastern Interfraternity Conference. Many individual members also had helped tutor students at Dean Road Elementary School. Hazing was condemned. Kappa Alpha, one of Auburn's oldest fraternities, ceased to exist at Auburn in 1995 for hazing its pledges. KA national could apply after three years to place a chapter back on campus. The charter of Phi Delta Theta, another of AU's oldest fraternities, was withdrawn by its national organization in 1993

after what appeared to be the alcohol-related death of a junior-college student. In the mid-nineties, the sorority system had won the Southeastern Panhellenic Conference Risk Management Award for three consecutive years. The award is based on policies and programs preventing hazing and alcohol abuse. Auburn's Panhellenic Council in 1991 was named the nation's best for 1989-91, an honor held through 1993. The council also was honored in 1993-95 for "achieving the highest academic performance in the nation."

Toomer's Corner remained the place to celebrate other important events as well as athletic victories. Take the case of newlyweds Dennis and Kristi Barker. As they left the church en route to the conference center for the reception, a guest handed them a roll of the toilet paper left over from

▲ The AU Gospel Choir posed at the Capitol with Congressman Bill Nichols, far right, during its 1988 spring tour. The choir was formed in the 1970s by the Black Student Union, and Dr. Claude Gossett of the music department later served as its faculty adviser for more than eight years. Gossett and his wife Sylvia, also a member of the AU music department, are standing next to Nichols, an AU trustee for twenty years who died later that year. During the tour, the choir, under direction of Stephanie Banks of Birmingham, participated in the Black Music Caucus competition at Martin Luther King High School, New York City, and sang at a Baptist Church in Harlem, at schools in Philadelphia, and at the National Cathedral in Washington, D.C.

—Photo: Opelika-Auburn News

decorating their car, Kristi wrote *Auburn Magazine*. "We were told to use the roll 'wisely.' Of course we could think of no better way to use it than to roll Toomer's Corner and show all Auburn how happy we were on our big day."

In 1996, it had been 160 years since the Indians moved out, Georgia settlers moved in, and the Loveliest Village was begun. It had been 140 years since East Alabama Male College started laying the foundation for Auburn University. The ties that bind city and campus were expected to endure as "Sweet Auburn" moved into a new millenium. ‿

▶ *Gilda Campbell of Auburn was crowned Ms. Senior Alabama in 1987 and won the Ms. Senior America title in Atlantic City in 1988. She won with a crowd-pleasing song and dance routine, and, as writer Dru McGowen said, with "Inner beauty. Grace. Charm." "Adding years to our lives is great," according to Mrs. Campbell, "but it is more important to add life to our years." She was born in 1925. On one trip as Ms. Senior America, she visited St. Joseph's University, the Philadelphia school whose students voted to adopt the Auburn University football team. She led a "War Eagle" cheer there. "The St. Jo cheerleaders responded with a 'Beat Bama' cheer they had especially prepared for her," the* Lee County Eagle *reported. At seventy, Mrs. Campbell and her husband, John, had five children, sixteen grandchildren, and three great-grandchildren.*

—*Photo:* Opelika-Auburn News

◀ *Time was when only males ran in the Wilbur Hutsell-ODK Cake Race, and the winner received a kiss from Miss Auburn. Then men and women ran in the same race, but men being timed against men and women against women. The female winner in 1988, Sue Matschnel, is kissed by ODK President Dozier Smith T. after the sixtieth running of the race. Miss Auburn, Jennifer Wynn, kissed the male winner.*

—*Photo:* Glomerata

◄ Tracy Rocker won both the Outland Trophy and Lombardi Award in 1988 as the nation's outstanding lineman and was an All-American for the second straight season. The 278-pound defensive tackle was a dominant lineman for four years, during which coach Pat Dye's teams won two SEC championships and compiled a record of 37-9-2. Rocker made 354 tackles during his Auburn career, 48 of which were behind the line of scrimmage.

—Photo: AU Athletic Department

◄ Bob Sanders, WAUD's morning man, is an Auburn institution. He began his forty-second year of dispensing wit, news, and music at the station in the spring of 1996. Sanders started working there on April Fools' Day, 1955, "a coincidence," he has said, "that has not escaped the notice of some of my acquaintances." From the beginning he handled the early-morning shift on weekends, and he has been the Monday-through-Saturday morning man for many years (up at four o'clock and going on the air at five-thirty), continuing that role even after being named station manager. He noted that he was preceded in the morning "slot by two good men who became rather legendary in this area"—Marion Hyatt and Tony Carter. For a long time, Sanders also wrote an insightful newspaper column on topics as diverse as his growing-up years in Lamar County, jazz, the school situation, old movies, race relations, books, and World War II airplanes.

—Photo: Auburn Bulletin

▲ Four Auburn astronauts saw the Tigers defeat Mississippi State, 33-0, at Cliff Hare Stadium in 1988. They are, left to right, James S. Voss, AU class of '72; Kathryn Cordell Thornton, '74; Jan Davis, '77, and Henry W. "Hank" Hartsfield, '54. Hartsfield flew one mission as pilot and two as spacecraft commander. By 1996, Thornton had flown four shuttle missions and had become the second American woman astronaut to walk in space. Davis and her husband, Mark Lee, a fellow astronaut, "became the first married couple to fly in space together," Janet McCoy wrote in Auburn Magazine. Davis later was in the first American crew to be accompanied by a Russian cosmonaut. On his third flight, Voss became the first American to receive a promotion (to colonel) in space.

—Photo: Auburn Alumnews

▲ Jennifer Davis Michael, daughter of Carolyn and Nicholas Davis of Auburn and a graduate of Lee-Scott Academy in 1985, became a Rhodes Scholar in English literature four years later. She studied at Oxford University, England, in 1989-91 after graduating from the University of the South at Sewanee, Tenn. She was to receive her Ph.D. from Northwestern in 1996. She is an assistant professor of English at Sewanee.

—Photo: Carolyn and Nicholas Davis

▲ Cater Hall lawn had become a project in a campus-wide beautification program when this picture was taken in 1988. The area inside the curved driveway leading to the hall was transformed into a three-tiered island with flowers, shrubs, trees, and a pond. Hiram S. Cochran, an Auburn graduate from Atlanta, funded development of the comprehensive landscape plan, which an official said "will make Auburn one of the most beautiful campuses in the nation." The plan was approved in 1986, with implementation to be on a continuing basis into the twenty-first century.

—Photo: Lee County Eagle

▲ Frank Thomas, who lettered at Auburn as a six-foot-four freshman tight end in 1986, dropped football after batting .359, driving in 68 runs, hitting an Auburn record 21 homers, and being selected the All-SEC first baseman as a freshman. He also made all-conference the next two seasons and became Auburn's first consensus All-American baseball player at the end of his junior season, then signed a pro contract with the Chicago White Sox after being selected seventh overall in the 1989 draft. Seven years later, he remained Auburn's career leader in home runs with 49, single-season home runs with 21, RBI leader with 205, and single-season RBI leader with 83. He was selected Most Valuable Player in the American League in both 1993 and 1994.

—Photo: AU Athletic Department

▲ These 1988 Auburn High School seniors were named National Merit Scholars and were among more than six thousand receiving Merit Scholarships worth more than $23 million for college undergraduate study. In the decade ending in 1996, Auburn High had averaged eight scholars a year. Left to right: Kaoru Hinata, daughter of Satoshi and Yoshiko Hinata; Wade Killingsworth, son of Roger and Mary Killingsworth; Lyle Johnson, son of LaVaughn and Peggy Johnson; Jim Born, son of Charles and Cheryl Born; and Sree Krishnagopalan, son of Gopal and Jaya Krishnagopalan. A sixth winner, not pictured, was William Chen, son of An-Ban and Mayurase Chen.

—Photo: Auburn City Schools

▲ These twenty-one 1968 graduates of Drake High School returned for a reunion twenty years later. The group met August 19, 1988, at Boykin School and the next night, shown here, at Drake for a banquet. Both were public schools for blacks until becoming part of the integrated city system in the late 1960s. The reunion drew graduates from Washington, D.C., and ten states, including those as far away as Colorado and Texas.

Attendees, left to right, seated: Dora Walker Moss, Rosie Milner Small, Diana Drake Walker, Geraldine Floyd Taylor, Carolyn Hill Hart, Elaine Gillam, Geraldine Lockhart Philpot, Brenda Walker Haygood, Dorothy Yancey Lee, and Linda Woods Ford. Standing, Horace Milner, Robert Sexton, Doretha Gentry Sturdivant, Theotis Callaway, Geraldine Pitts, Norman Brown, Richard Hall, Joseph Tensely, Johnny Frank Hudson, Willie Mae Hodo Brown, Ella Lampkin Weymon.

—Photo: Opelika-Auburn News

◀ Groundbreaking came in spring 1988 for the mammoth $20.5 million addition to Ralph Brown Draughon Library. With formal dedication in November 1991, the size of the library had been more than doubled, to a total of 380,000 square feet. Its capacity was increased to 2.5 million volumes and to 2,000 readers at a time.

—Photo: Auburn Alumnews

▲ These students were among 18,000 who received free inoculations at Drake Infirmary in 1989 after several cases of measles were reported on campus during A-Day weekend. The federal government provided the vaccine. The University announced in 1996 plans to discontinue providing medical services for students and in May called for bids from firms wishing to take over the program.

—Photo: AU Archives

▲ Sissy Costner was the NCAA women's indoor champion in the high jump in 1990, after finishing fourth in both indoor and outdoor competition in 1989. Her leaps of six feet, two inches indoor and six feet, one- and one-half inches outdoor were Auburn records.

—Photo: AU Athletic Department

▲ "Squeal Day," the culmination of sorority rush week for more than half a century at Auburn University, was that Friday in September just before school started when freshmen-to-be became pledges. Girls received an envelope that morning containing the name of the sorority selecting them, then squealed with delight before making the traditional run to the respective sorority's dorm to accept. This 1989 shot indicates that for many the traditional run had turned into a walk by the time the coeds were halfway up the slope between the stadium and the Hill Dorms. More than eight hundred pledged that year. By the mid-1990s, nineteen sororities were on campus and Squeal Day had been changed to Bid Day, but the squealing and traditional run—or at least fast walk—continued.

—Photo: Lee County Eagle

▲ Cindy Holland finished second among four candidates in the spring of 1988, then polled 54 percent of the votes in a runoff to become the first female elected president of the AU Student Government Association. She was a public relations journalism major from Dothan and conducted an aerobics class at 7:30 a.m. three times a week for Kaz Fitness Center. Cindy later received a law degree and joined the firm of Balch & Bingham in Montgomery.

—Photo: AU University Relations

▲ Pictured is the largest crowd ever to attend a football game in the state. The scene is Jordan-Hare Stadium December 2, 1989, and the first meeting ever between Auburn and Alabama on the Auburn campus. Auburn won 30-20. Attendance was announced as 85,319, but probably was at least a thousand or more higher. Auburn Stadium had 7,500 permanent seats when dedicated in 1939. Ten years later, when capacity was increased to 21,500, it was renamed Cliff Hare Stadium after the retired dean of the School of Chemistry and API Athletic Committee chairman. Major expansions in 1955, 1960, and 1970 made the stadium a complete bowl, seating 61,261. It was renamed Jordan-Hare Stadium in 1973 in recognition of Coach

Ralph "Shug" Jordan. After two more additions in the 1980s, twelve "capacity" crowds of 85,214 were recorded during the next eight seasons.

—Photo: AU Archives

▲ A way of life for Auburn University students: waiting in line each September for football season tickets. The bronze War Eagle looks down on students in front of Beard-Eaves-Memorial Coliseum. Students were allocated 14,200 tickets per home game in 1995. The eagle, almost twice the size of a real golden eagle, was dedicated December 2, 1989, the day of the first Auburn-Alabama game at Jordan-Hare Stadium. It weighs a ton, has a twelve-foot wingspan, and soars atop a twenty-six-foot column. Engraved at the base: "War Eagle, fly down the field, ever to conquer, never to yield. War Eagle, fearless and true, fight on, you, orange and blue . . ." Jack Hucks of Huntsville sculpted the eagle, and alumni financed it. John E. Davis designed the base.

—Photo: AU Archives

◀ The Auburn band marched near the nation's Capitol in the inaugural parade for President George Bush in January 1989. "It was a painfully cold day; the poor majorettes nearly froze," recalled Johnnie Vinson, then director of the 315-member band. It was the band's first inaugural parade since Harry Truman's inauguration in 1949. The musicians played the "Hosts of Freedom" and "Footlifter" marches as they, representing the State of Alabama, passed the Bush reviewing stand at the White House. When the band members posed for a photograph on the steps of the House of Representatives, then in session, Vinson had them strike up "War Eagle," to the dismay of a disapproving security guard.

—Photo: Auburn Alumnews

▲ *James E. Martin, third from left at front, posed with his administrative team in front of Samford Hall in 1989, five years after he became the fourteenth president of Auburn University. Others are, left to right, front row: Paul F. Parks, vice president, Research; Pat Barnes, vice president, Student Affairs; George H. Emert, executive vice president; Ronald J. W. Henry, vice president, Academic Affairs; Ann Thompson, vice president, Extension; Rhett Riley, vice president, Business and Finance. Second row: Jack E. Blackburn, acting vice president, Academic Affairs; J. Boyd Scebra, act-ing dean, College of Education; James E. Marion, dean, College of Agriculture; Ray K. Parker, dean, School of Architecture; Mary P. Richards, dean, College of Liberal Arts; Winifred Worman, acting dean, School of Nursing. Third row: William C. Highfill, University librarian; June M. Henton, dean, School of Human Sciences; William H. Campbell, dean, School of Pharmacy; Emmett F. Thompson, dean, School of Forestry; Ben Fitzpatrick, chairman of the Faculty. Fourth Row: Gerald S. Leischuck, director, Planning and Analysis; Darwin Liverance, director, Personnel Services; William F. Walker, dean, College of Engineering; Lowell T. Frobish, director, Agricultural Experiment Station; J. Thomas Vaughan, dean, College of Veterinary Medicine. Fifth row: Theodore Hemingway, fellow, American Council on Education; J. Herbert White, director, University Relations; Emily Leischuck, assistant to the president and Board of Trustees; J. Ivan Legg, dean, College of Sciences and Mathematics; K. Stanley Drake, assistant vice president, Facilities.*

—Photo: AU Archives

▲ More than 130 planes landed at the Auburn-Opelika Robert G. Pitts Airport for the 1989 Auburn-Alabama game. Most are shown in this aerial view. As of 1996, the record fly-in was for the 1984 Tennessee game, when 186 planes arrived, University aviation Director Jim Hendrick said. Many years earlier, more than ninety military aircraft, including about thirty two-engine bombers, had been parked at the small airfield, according to General Robert Knapp. As director of flight training at an air base, he brought all his graduating class to Auburn on a mission to recruit pilots.
—Photo: AU University Relations

▶ Rosalind Pendergraft-Council became the first women's NCAA track champion from Auburn when she won the indoor 55-meter hurdles in 1986. She became a double winner by finishing first in the outdoor 100-meter hurdles the same year. She is shown winning the 100 in a meet at Auburn's Wilbur Hutsell Track. Her husband Daron Council was an NCAA qualifier for four years in the 200-meter dash. A decade later, Rosalind still held the school record for the fastest time in her two events and Daron the record for the 200-meter outdoor event. After graduation, the couple operated a physical fitness center in New Orleans.
—Photo: AU Athletic Department

▲ The Reverend Charles R. Britt became pastor of Auburn United Methodist Church in 1968 and served nearly twelve years, the longest period of any minister. "An exciting preacher, he, in Christ, could inspire people, make them laugh and move them deeply," a Methodist said. Britt remained an influence in the community for many additional years, contributing time to numerous church, University, and civic organizations and events while serving on the faculty in the AU Department of Family and Child Welfare in 1979-1990. His "greatest joy [in service] is to have been part of the founding group of Auburn City Schools Dental Clinic." Britt and his wife, Blanche, were educational and evangelistic missionaries in Africa, except for one year, during 1947-54. They served in the leprosy-control effort there. Britt continued to teach part-time into the nineties and was a member of the Curriculum Committee on Health and Sex Education of the Auburn City Schools in 1995-96.

—Photo: Charles R. Britt

▲ Ninety-two-year-old Alma Stoves of Auburn had attended every varsity football game played in Jordan-Hare Stadium for forty-five years when this picture was taken in 1990. "I cut my teeth on Auburn football," she said at the time. "I've been going to games since I was a child, and there's nothing I like better." She had attended 212 consecutive games in Auburn, including 46 homecoming games, before her death in 1992. Mrs. Stoves received a degree in American history from API in 1919 and a master's in education in 1927. She taught history at Auburn High School from the late 1940s to the mid-1960s. Her mother, Emma Smith, operated the town's telephone switchboard in the early 1900s in her home over what became Lipscomb's Drugstore. Shown with Mrs. Stoves are a granddaughter, J. J. Fagen, who graduated from Auburn in 1993, and daughter, Emaleen Stoves Fagen, a 1950 graduate. Emaleen was an Auburn cheerleader in 1948 and 1949 and married classmate Arnold Fagen, a three-year football letterman at tackle.

—Photo: Auburn Alumnews

▶ These Lee County High School graduates are shown at their fiftieth class reunion in July 1989. Twenty of the thirty-three attendees started together at Auburn Grammar School on Tichenor Avenue at Gay Street in 1927. The class, front row, left to right: Doris Oxendine Bice, Mel Atkins Gibbons, Doris Mitchell Budd, Georgene Hawkins Purdy, Henrietta Reeves Long, Minnie Tippins Fries, Jim Flanagan, Mrs. Mary Combs Hitchcock (teacher). Middle row: Polly Rogers Cutts, Evelyn Knapp Rogers, Ruby Thigpen Bethune, Harold Smyer, Madrid Davis Bailey, Millard Dawson, Eugene Vann, Jack Moore, Harold Pittman, Gwen Hunter Plant, Wallace Hannum, Homer "Jug" Wright, Pete Almquist, John C. Ball. Back row: Rene Bidez, Jack Earnest, John Bruce Martin, Arthur Wood, William Ham, Fuhrman Hunter, Ed Sahag, and Jack Bright. Attending the reunion, but not in the picture: Lily Bradley, Dorothy Floyd, Marilyn Meagher Perry, Virginia Riley Noa. The Post Office was built on the site of the high school in the 1930s and remained in operation until a new Post Office was opened on Opelika Road in the 1990s.

—Photo: Opelika-Auburn News

▶ Writer Paul Hemphill published The Heart of the Game, *his eleventh book, in 1996. The* New York Times Book Review, *in a complimentary article, wrote that Hemphill finds "a baseball playing Huck Finn to write about, Marty Malloy from the piney woods along the Suwanee River." His first book was* Nashville Sound, *started in 1968-69 while he was a Nieman Fellow at Harvard. Others include* Long Gone, *a baseball novel, and* Leaving Birmingham: Notes of a Native Son. *Hemphill, a Plainsman sports editor and 1959 Auburn graduate, worked for the* Birmingham News *and was a columnist at the* Atlanta Journal *before devoting his efforts full time to writing books and magazine articles. He has written for* Esquire, Atlantic Monthly, Playboy, Sport *and* Cosmopolitan. *He lives in Atlanta with his wife Susan Percy, a free-lance writer, and daughter, Molly, seventeen.*

—Photo: AU Archives

◀ Tommy Goff directed Auburn High School bands for thirty-two years. His symphonic, concert, and jazz/lab bands always were among the best in the state. Goff's "Superior-Excellent-Good-Fair-Poor record in competitions would read 220-4-0-0-0," the Bulletin/Eagle reported when he retired in 1989. A group of band parents later commended Goff as follows: "Not only have you pushed, pulled, threatened, cajoled, teased, kidded, and nagged these students to become excellent musicians, but you have given them an example of fair play, good humor, responsibility, and energy that will serve them well for years to come." Goff, a former member of the Auburn Knights Orchestra, is seen playing "Tall Cotton" at a lab band concert. His favorite trumpet piece is "Do You Know What It Means to Miss New Orleans." In retirement, he has arranged religious music such as "In the Garden," "How Great Thou Art," and "Amazing Grace," and has published a few arrangements.

—Photo: Tommy and Jane Goff

◀ *The foul odor and awful taste of Auburn's drinking water became front-page news several times over almost two decades. "Y'all oughta bottle and sell it as liquid barnyard fertilizer," a visitor told several Auburn Grille regulars at lunch one day in the 1980s. "Smells like it, and sure tastes like it!" But it was no laughing matter to the Alabama Department of Environmental Management or the Whatleys of Beauregard. Charles Whatley and a holstein are pictured at Chewacla Creek on the family farm in late 1988 during the height of a running legal battle.*

It started when ADEM accused the Whatleys of letting their cows contaminate the creek before it empties into Lake Ogletree, Auburn's main source of water. The Whatleys, maintaining that ADEM was picking on them, were particularly displeased by an ADEM order that limited animal access to the stream on their property and another requiring that they devise a plan for managing the animal waste. The Whatleys finally gave up the fight, selling at auction nine hundred holsteins and much of the equipment from the state's largest dairy farm.

It may have been the city's installation in 1991 of a $300,000 carbon contact basin to get rid of nutrients and algae from Lake Ogletree, or maybe it was removal of the cows in late 1991, but for whatever reason, the unpleasant odor and taste finally disappeared from Auburn drinking water.

—*Photo: Carmel Thomaston; Lee County Eagle*

▶ *Doug Watson earned the reputation of problem solver after becoming Auburn's city manager in 1982. Working with Mayor Jan Dempsey and City Council members, Watson solved a major sewage-disposal problem. Under his guidance, the city privatized wastewater treatment with new treatment plants. Watson became a nationally recognized authority on privatization and other municipal government matters, publishing three books and twenty-two articles in scholarly and professional journals. In about a decade, the city won nine awards tied to projects helpful to citizens; the latest, Alabama's Best Recycling Program in 1994. Watson has supported career-development programs for city employees ranging from literacy training to tuition reimbursement for university courses. He credited the nearly three hundred regular city employees and twenty-seven Auburn Water Board employees with improving city services. Watson received a Ph.D. from Auburn University in 1992 in public administration and public policy.*

—*Photo: Lee County Eagle*

▲ "Pops for Lunch" was a popular event at Graves Amphitheatre on spring days in the 1970s and eighties. The AU Concert Orchestra provided music, and school children were bused with their lunches to the performances. Faculty members and students also attended in considerable numbers. During the summers, choirs and groups of musicians frequently performed at the amphitheatre or at Pebble Hill in a similar program, opened to the public.

—Photo: Opelika-Auburn News

▲ Dr. Bessie Mae Holloway, a Mobile County educator, is Auburn University's first black trustee. She was named by Governor George Wallace in 1985 to fill an unexpired term. She was reappointed to a full twelve-year term in 1987. Dr. Holloway is shown greeting Auburn graduates at commencement. She earned a doctorate in education from Auburn, a master's from Xavier University in Louisiana, and a bachelor's from Alabama State. Dr. Holloway became the second woman to serve on the Board of Trustees. The first, Sue Fincher, served from 1975 through 1979.

—Photo: AU University Relations

▲ This 158,000-square-foot structure, shown under construction in 1991 on Magnolia Avenue west of Noble Hall, was one of the last major projects of the James E. Martin administration. It became the School of Business home in fall 1992. The six-story $15 million facility later was named Edward L. and Catherine K. Lowder Business Building for the Montgomery couple whose family gave the school $1.2 million to endow two eminent scholar chairs. Thach and Tichenor halls underwent extensive remodeling after Business moved out. The history and psychology departments then moved into Thach, and communications, journalism, and geography moved from Haley Center into Tichenor.

—Photo: Opelika-Auburn News

▶ AU music faculty members were all smiles as they participated in the 1988 dedication of a new grand piano. Seated, left to right, are Julia Morgan and Sylvia Gossett. Standing are Bob Richardson, Billy Tamblyn, Harold Kafer, Joseph Stephenson, Roy Wylie, and Bill Summerville. Tamblyn's bachelor's degree in 1948 was one of the first in music from API. His master's and Ph.D. came from the Eastman School of Music, University of Rochester. Tamblyn had been a member of the first Auburn High School Band in 1936 and first played the organ at church services when he was thirteen. When retiring in 1990, he had been on the AU music faculty for more than forty-two years and also had served as choir director and organist at Auburn First Presbyterian Church. The church and Music Department established an endowed scholarship in his name.

—Photo: AU Archives

▲ Dedication of city-owned Martin Luther King Park at the end of West Glenn Avenue and Byrd Street took place January 15, 1989. This was the site of Lee County Training School, a twelve-year school for blacks, from 1929 into the late 1950s. A memorial pavilion bearing the school's name became part of the park in 1993. Those pictured include, left to right, former City Councilwoman Mary E. Brooks; Bertha Willis; Bernice Rutledge; Mayor Pro Tem Sam Teague; Mayor Jan Dempsey; the Reverend W. L. Muse, Ebenezer Baptist Church; City Councilman Samuel Harris; Ernestine H. Robinson; Melanie Echols, daughter of George and Patricia Echols; Councilwoman Mary Fortenberry; Mary Lynn Porter; and Councilwoman Frances Hale.

—Photo: Opelika-Auburn News

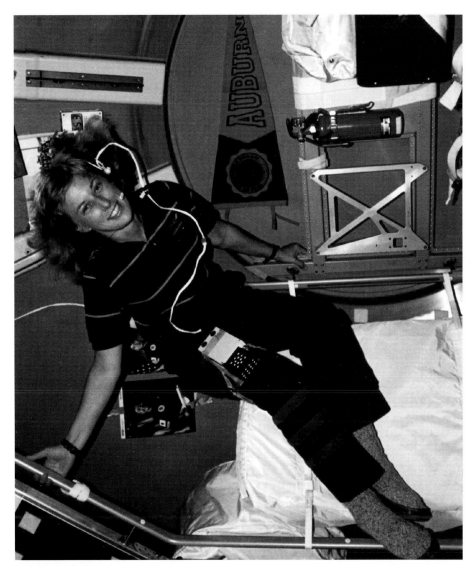

▲ The Auburn "License to Learn" program, started in the late 1980s, had attracted more than 75,000 participants and generated $3,685,301 in endowment funds for scholarships by 1996. Specialty AU car tags cost $50 a year more than the regular tag, and the scholarship fund gets $48.75 from each specialty tag purchased. President James E. Martin obtained approval of the Legislature to start the program, and the first two recipients of scholarships, Jeff Baumbach of Huntsville and Meredith Bell of Montgomery, are seen at graduation in June 1993. Baumbaugh was a cheerleader and biomedical sciences major, and Bell, an international business major.
—Photo: Auburn Alumnews

▲ Astronaut "Jan Davis carries a piece of Auburn into space, as do all of the Auburnauts," Auburn Magazine said. These items have included "a section of the Alumni Center's marble wall, a centennial football coin, an AU vanity tag, a print from the centennial of women celebration, a recording of AU's marching band, and a first-edition copy of Oliver Goldsmith's poem 'The Deserted Village,'" Janet McCoy reported.
—Photo: AU University Relations and the National Aeronautics and Space Administration

▶ Sol of Auburn, a solar-powered car, drew a crowd between the eagle's cage and the stadium in 1991. Students built the nearly 20-foot long, 768-pound, electric vehicle at a cost of about $150,000 in donated parts, and more than 40,000 student hours, said faculty adviser Dr. Sushil Bhavnani of mechanical engineering. Sol has a maximum speed of 63 m.p.h. and a cruising speed of 30 to 35, but it averaged 44.29 in finishing fourth among sixteen cars in a 50-mile race at Indianapolis in 1993. It operated on "less energy than most hand-held dryers use." It finished third in a 760-mile Sacramento-to-Los Angeles race, "ahead of all of the California teams, and was judged the safest vehicle in the competition." Sol's body was rebuilt for the second time in 1995-96.

—Photo: AU Archives

► It seemed fitting that Charles E. Curran, a controversial Roman Catholic priest and theologian, pose in 1990 with Samford Hall in the background. Samford's chief occupant at the time, President James E. Martin, was censured by the Faculty Senate, 48-39, after withholding an advertised permanent teaching/research position from Father Curran. The Board of Trustees supported Martin's action. Curran had accepted a conditional offer to become the tenured Goodwin-Philpott Eminent Scholar in Religion, but Martin reduced the offer to a nine-month appointment after two or more trustees reportedly "raised strong objections" to tenuring Curran. Martin had approved the original offer, said Academe, bulletin of the American Association of University Professors, but Martin never acknowledged giving the go-ahead to offer tenure.

Curran, a top scholar in his field, had published about thirty books and 150 to 200 articles, but he had been suspended from teaching moral theology at Catholic University after twenty-three years on the faculty. Curran had clashed often with the Vatican. He had spoken out in 1968 against the "papal encyclical condemning contraception" and had later supported "limited exceptions to the church's rejection of premarital sex, homosexual acts, abortion and euthanasia," the New York Times reported. The AAUP censured Catholic University for its treatment of Curran, but he lost a lawsuit to the University.

According to Academe, Martin had met with Promotion and Tenure Committee members, and "reportedly (1) expressed the [incorrect] belief that Professor Curran had 'closed down' Catholic University, an alleged action he intended to keep from being repeated at Auburn University, (2) expressed the belief that Professor Curran would continue his dispute with Catholic University using Auburn University as his platform, and (3) expressed a 'gut feeling about these things.'" Martin reportedly told the committee "there were other reasons which he chose not to reveal, saying that 'if you knew what I know, you would probably feel the way I do.'" Martin also said his denying tenure "had nothing to do with moral turpitude, or ethical reputation or scholarship." Curran said he was never told the real reason he didn't receive tenure.

The Tenure and Promotion Committee, which approved tenuring Curran, said Martin had not violated Curran's academic freedom. The group said the president "met the letter of the policy on promotion and tenure concerning his decision in the case." The University Senate disagreed. Senate committees accused Martin of violating the University's tenure guidelines by deciding to deny tenure before considering a recommendation of the Tenure and Promotion Committee, of giving in to pressure from several trustees outside the tenure process (including, others said, the lone Catholic among the trustees), of disseminating "biased or misleading information" about Curran and the Department of Religion, and of seriously damaging Auburn's national reputation. The board of directors of the Auburn Alumni Association defended Martin and rebutted the Senate accusations. The Board of Trustees backed Martin publicly, denying that it had intruded on tenure decisions. Martin said he alone decided not to tenure Curran.

Yet, Academic Vice President Ronald Henry told faculty representatives, as stated in past Senate Chairman Miller Solomon's report from the Senate's Rules and Executive committees, "that the president had decided not to grant tenure to Curran because of pressure from the board; and that the board had threatened to take away his authority to grant tenure if the president did not

comply." Henry, a University senator, sat in silence when Solomon read the statement to the Senate. It voted on January 15, 1991, to censure Martin.

That April, Martin announced he would retire effective a year later. He said the Curran controversy had nothing to do with his decision. In 1991-92, Curran became a tenured professor at Southern Methodist University. In 1994, the Religion Department, begun under the Philpott administration, was downgraded to a program in religious studies.

—Photo: AU Journalism Department

▲ Fired-up marchers—mostly students—headed toward Toomer's Corner in support of American troops during "Operation Desert Storm" in late January 1991. "Marchers chanted, 'We're behind Bush!'" (President George Bush). Joining the march was a group whose leader said they supported the soldiers, but opposed the war. Three yellow ribbons were displayed at the city police station, honoring two officers serving in the Gulf War and another called to active military duty.

—Photo: AU Archives

▲ Kaye Lovvorn interned at the Auburn Alumnews in 1964 while a senior in journalism and returned a few months later to start twenty-five years of chronicling the activities of the alumni and their alma mater. She served as Alumnews editor in 1968-1990 before becoming director of advancement services. She died of cancer in 1994, a few months after Auburn Magazine had replaced the Alumnews as the major alumni publication. The Alumnews had been born in 1946 as a successor to the Auburn Alumnus, published from 1913 through 1939.

—Photo: Auburn Magazine

▲ As part of the University's football centennial observance, fans were asked to vote by mail for an Auburn Team of the Century. Fullback Tucker Frederickson, a consensus All-American in 1964, was selected Player of the Century and Ralph Jordan, 1951-75, Coach of the Century. Seventeen members of the team on hand and honored A-Day 1992 were, kneeling, left to right: Lewis Colbert '86, Terry Beasley '72, Jimmy "Red" Phillips '58, Zeke Smith '60. Kevin Porter '88. Standing: Jackie Burkett '60, Ken Rice '61, Ben Tamburello '87, Steve Wallace '86, Joe Cribbs '80, Al Del Greco '84, James Brooks '81, coach Pat Dye (not selected to the team but who coached nine of the players), Tracy Rocker '89, Aundray Bruce '88, Donnie Humphrey '83, Gregg Carr '84, Mike Kolen '70. Others selected were Lawyer Tillman '89, Ed King '91, Pat Sullivan '72, Bo Jackson '86, Mike Fuller '75, Walter Gilbert '37.

—Photo: Auburn Alumnews

Mel Rosen, left, after twenty-eight seasons as Auburn's head track coach, turned over the reins in 1991 to his most illustrious pupil, Harvey Glance, shown wearing the Olympic Gold Medal he won at Montreal in 1976. Rosen retired from Auburn to become head coach of the 1992 U.S. Men's Olympic Track Team, which won twenty medals, including five golds, at Barcelona for its best showing since 1956. After the Olympics, Rosen returned to assist Coach Glance, with the title of consultant.

Glance burst upon the American track scene as an Auburn freshman in 1976 by winning the NCAA 60-meter indoor and the 100- and 200-meter outdoor championships. He won the NCAA 100-meter outdoor again the next year. Glance dominated the SEC championships for four years, winning nine dash events, the long jump three times and running on four winning relay teams. He was a world-class sprinter for twelve years and won gold medals for relays in both the Pan Am Games and World Championships when he was twenty-eight. During Glance's first four seasons as head coach, Auburn records were rewritten for eighteen women's events and seven men's events.

Rosen's Auburn teams won four SEC indoor and one outdoor team championships, and his charges won sixteen NCAA and sixty-three SEC titles. Rosen was NCAA Coach of the Year in both indoor and outdoor competition in 1978 and repeated as indoor Coach of the Year in 1980.

—Photo: AU Photographic Services

▶ Five of Auburn University's First Ladies paused for this picture at the President's Home in spring 1992. Left to right: Ann Freeman Martin '57, wife of James E. Martin '54 (president 1984-92); Caroline Draughon, wife of Ralph Brown Draughon '22 (1947-65); Marlene Muse, whose husband, William V. Muse, had taken office March 1; Kate Bailey, wife of Wilford S. Bailey '42 (1983-84); and Polly Philpott, wife of Harry M. Philpott (1965-80).

—Photo: Auburn Alumnews

▶ *Auburn voters turned out in record numbers for the 1992 general election, creating long lines and delays in voting of more than two hours. This mid-afternoon scene shows the line outside City Hall. Ruth Speake, chief election official at that location, recalled later, "When the polls were supposed to close at 7 p.m., we had a long line of voters outside the door and down the sidewalk. We herded them inside and locked the doors, then let them line up in the halls while waiting to vote. It took about an hour and a half." Hundreds of Auburn students voting for the first time stood in line for hours, only to discover they were at the wrong precinct. The Auburn vote total was 16,118 in the November 1992 George Bush-Bill Clinton-Ross Perot presidential race, 4,213 more than in the presidential race four years earlier.*
—*Photo:* Lee County Eagle

◀ *Jeanne Swanner Robertson, left, called six males from the audience up front during her presentation at the Auburn Alumni Reunions of 1992 and proceeded with a beauty contest. The six-foot-two Auburn graduate of 1967 was Miss Congeniality as a Miss America contestant and later became a tremendously popular after-dinner speaker. The contestants in the alumni beauty contest were supposed to show their legs and let the audience pick the winner by its applause. Left to right, Charles Whatley, '67, Walter W. Dean, '47, Walter J. Weatherly, '52, William M. Beasley, '62, Batey M. Grisham, '57, and Joel G. Raines, '72. Four years later, every contestant claimed to have been the winner.*
—*Photo:* Auburn Alumnews

▶ *Mrs. Evelyn Jordan of Auburn presented this Betsy Ross flag to Wrights Mill Road School in 1992. At the time, she was president of the Light Horse Harry Lee Chapter of the Daughters of the American Revolution. Four years later, the local chapter celebrated its one-hundredth birthday. Mrs. Jordan's husband had been Auburn football coach Ralph Jordan. Students shown were, kneeling left to right: Taylor Keeton and Latoya Harvey. Standing: Jemall Vinson, Forrest Ham, Andrew Phelps, and Joshua Woods.*
—*Photo:* Auburn City Schools

▲ Pat Dye held his final news conference as Auburn's football coach on November 26, 1992, at Legion Field after Alabama beat the Tigers 17-0. Flanked by his players, he called his wife Sue, next to Dye at microphones, and his children, front, left to right, Missy, Pat, Jr., and Wanda, to his side. Players, back row, are Mickey Sutton, Jason Davis, and James Willis. "Their tears before the cameras started his," the Birmingham News reported. Dye told one daughter and then the other to stop crying, but he was crying, too. "Hell, we ought to be celebrating," he said to his family. "We've been in this seven days a week for thirty years." During the twelve seasons ending that day, Dye's Auburn teams won four SEC championships, went to nine bowl games, and compiled a record of 99-38-4.

Dye's resignation had been announced the previous night, coming more than a year after former player Eric Ramsey accused assistant coaches and boosters of improperly giving him money, gifts, and favors. Ramsey had secretly recorded conversations with coaches and at least one booster. Dye told his players and assistants he was resigning, and President William V. Muse told the public during a news conference in a Birmingham hotel at 10 p.m., fourteen hours before kickoff of the Auburn-Alabama game.

Dye had maintained for more than a year that he had no knowledge of NCAA rules violations committed by members of his staff or boosters. But three weeks before his resignation, the NCAA alleged in an official letter of inquiry that Dye knew of violations and failed to report them. Dye has repeatedly stated, "I may have made management mistakes and mistakes in judgment, but I did not willfully or intentionally violate any rules."

President Muse said the University had been "generous" in its settlement of Dye's contract, which had four years remaining at $146,500 per year. Dye, fifty-three, was to receive that in full, spread over a seven-year period, and also receive partial compensation for outside income he would have received from television and radio appearances, shoe contracts, and other endorsements. The package totaled about $1.1 million, an Auburn official said.

On August 18, 1993, almost nine months after Dye resigned, the NCAA placed Auburn on probation for violations that surfaced during the Eric Ramsey case inquiry: No bowl games for two seasons; no television appearances for one; loss of two football scholarships a year for three years. The estimated cost to Auburn: three million to five million dollars.

—Photo: AU Photographic Services

▲ Anne Rivers Siddons, a former Plainsman *columnist feature editor, by 1993 had published these novels that made the* New York Times *bestsellers list:* Peachtree Road, Outer Banks, Colony, *and* Hill Towns. *Her first novel,* Heartbreak Hotel, *was set at a fictional Alabama college, a place much like the Auburn she attended in the 1950s. "With that partially autobiographical work she molded the themes used in many of her novels—the nature of being Southern, the effect on people and place of the dawning of the civil rights movement, and the specific journeys of her female characters," Mary Ellen Hendrix wrote in the* Auburn Alumnews. *As a* Plainsman *writer Mrs. Siddons published a column "anticipating and welcoming integration. . . . [It] ran with a disclaimer that [API] didn't approve of it," Mrs. Hendrix said.*

—Photo:
AU Center for the Arts and Humanities

▶ *Five of the nine Alabama Supreme Court justices in 1992 were Auburn graduates. They were Mark Kennedy, '73; Gorman Houston, Jr., '55; Chief Justice Sonny Hornsby, '59; former Auburn trustee Henry Steagall, II, '47; and Kenneth Ingram, '51. The five had been preceded on the high court by Chief Justice C. C. "Bo" Torbert, who graduated from Auburn in 1951.*

—Photo: Auburn Magazine

▲ *Amid a huge chorus of jeers and catcalls from angry Auburn classmates, former football player Eric Ramsey and his wife, Twilitta, shown in caps and gowns, each received a bachelor's degree at fall graduation on December 16, 1992. Eric majored in criminal justice and Twilitta in mass communications. Three weeks earlier, head football coach Pat Dye had resigned, as Auburn faced charges of serious violations of NCAA rules. The saga began when Ramsey told the* Montgomery Advertiser *in September 1991 he had received money and other benefits illegally from Auburn coaches and boosters and had tape recordings to prove the allegations. Ramsey's attorney made several of*

the tapes public in October and November, and the CBS program "Sixty Minutes" aired some in December. In August 1993, almost twenty-three months after the first story appeared, Auburn received penalties described by an NCAA representative as "slightly over the minimum" allowed. The University was barred from playing in postseason bowl games and the SEC Championship for two years and from appearing on television for one year. SEC Commissioner Roy Kramer estimated the TV ban could cost Auburn $2.5-$3 million. In addition, Auburn had $750,000 in legal fees stemming from the Ramsey case.

—Photo: Mickey Welsh;
Montgomery Advertiser

◄ Luckie Meagher's kindergarten class learned about newly hatched chicks during the Easter season in 1972 from Dr. Claude Moore, head of Auburn's Poultry Science Department. Mrs. Meagher ran her kindergarten from 1942 to 1977 in a little red schoolhouse on Glenn Avenue. When each group graduated from high school twelve years later, she gave them a party. Starting at lower left, moving clockwise, are two unidentified children, Emil Berger, Rebecca Whitten, Troy Eddy, Ginger Moore, Lesley Powell (ribbon in hair), Randy Mountcastle, Steven Channell (in front of Mrs. Meagher), Moore, Chris Snow, others unidentified except for Craig Connally (wearing Auburn jacket).
—Photo: AU University Relations

▲ The Auburn post office in 1939 finally surpassed the $44,500 in receipts required for a first-class rating. In 1996, the post office produced $5.3 million in over-the-counter revenue, new postmaster Jerry Chrietzberg said. Average weekly delivery was about 236,000 letters, 106,000 magazines, and other flat-size envelopes, and more than 5,000 packages. Postal services moved to 300 Opelika Road in 1992 after fifty-nine years at Gay Street and Tichenor Avenue. The post office had thirteen employees in 1933 and seventy-nine in 1996. Dan McLaughlin, postmaster for nearly twelve years, said the post office was handling up to five times as much mail when he retired in 1996 as when he began working in 1964. The new building had more than four times as much usuable space as the old one. In 1996, the service could sort 30,000 letters an hour electronically, more than twenty-seven times the number that could be done by hand.

▶ *Vice President Dan Quayle and his wife, Marilyn, waved at thousands of supporters at a Bush-Quayle rally at Plainsman Park before the 1992 presidential election. The Quayles flew in by helicopter. Volunteers from the Auburn band and sign-waving Republicans generated a pep-rally atmosphere. Outnumbered Democrats responded with Clinton-Gore signs. Auburn President William V. Muse, who helped welcome the Quayles, and basketball coach Tommy Joe Eagles are at Mrs. Quayle's left. Quayle also had campaigned on campus in 1988, and he returned to Auburn in 1995 for a family values conference.*

—*Photo:* Lee County Eagle

▲ *Black students and some whites protested the Old South parade in 1992. Most blacks considered the Kappa Alpha event a racist reminder of their ancestors in slavery. To the fraternity, the parade celebrated positive Old South values and did not condone slavery. Many white students, standing across the street from the blacks, expressed support for the parade by waving Confederate battle flags. Angry words and gestures were exchanged. The parade was forced to detour around protesters on South College Street on the way back to the fraternity house. The apparent near-violence in 1992 helped persuade Kappa Alpha to voluntarily discontinue the parade in 1993. SGA President Pat Sefton praised the KAs for taking an important step toward improving race relations on campus.*

—*Photo: AU Archives and* Auburn Plainsman

▼ *Four-star generals Carl E. Mundy, Jr., left, and Jimmie V. Adams, 1957 Auburn graduates, shared a handshake in Adams' office at Hickam AFB, Hawaii, in the early 1990s. Mundy was commandant of the Marine Corps and a member of the Joint Chiefs of Staff. Adams was commander-in-chief of the Pacific Air Forces, extending over Alaska, Guam, Hawaii, Japan, Republic of Korea, and the Philippines. "There was a spirit at Auburn that said much to me about loyalty to an institution, which is very much a part of being a Marine," Mundy later told Mary Ellen Hendrix in an* Auburn Magazine *interview.*

—*Photo:* Auburn Magazine

▲ *President L. N. Duncan and Jim*
    —Photo: AU Archives

Auburn University presidents have found ways to relax from a stressful job. "I have always loved baseball," said William Muse (1992-), former second baseman, who played the game from Little League through high school and college and into the semipro ranks. "Probably the most relaxing thing to me is to go out to the ball park and just get fully absorbed in the game and forget about everything else." Like other Auburn presidents, Muse also likes football, basketball, and reading. His wife Marlene became a

▼ *President James E. Martin*
    —Photo: AU University Relations

driving force in Habitat for Humanity almost from the day of arrival in Auburn.

Muse's predecessor, James Martin (1984-92), a pianist, plays jazz by ear. He enjoys three 1956 Ford Thunderbirds, flying, reading John Grisham novels, remembering Robert W. Service poems, and walking with his wife Ann, a former Auburn cheerleader. As guest co-pilot of an F-5 Air Force jet while president, Martin made three passes over Samford Hall. The six-foot-six former Auburn basketball player's knees were wedged under the plane's instrument panel. Martin said he would have been "in deep trouble," had he needed to eject.

Wilford Bailey (1983-84) has taken pictures for about fifty-five years. He used cameras in his career in pathology and parasitology. Photography became his hobby. He has collected thousands of slides on research-related trips to about forty countries, including China, Poland, Egypt, Greece, and Australia. He particularly enjoys photographing flowers. His most beautiful flower slides were made in Victoria, Canada.

Hanly Funderburk (1980-83) walked two miles a day on campus, about five days a week. He continued this exercise as president at Eastern Kentucky University, walking in sunshine or snow there. Having grown up on a farm, he enjoys the weather channel on television. He likes to do yard work when visiting his children in Montgomery. Grandchildren also have a high priority with him and his wife Helen as is the case with other presidential families.

Harry Philpott (1965-80) is an accomplished chef. Several of his recipes appeared in cookbooks and in the October 1966 Southern Living magazine. But he kept a secret his recipe for mint pie with chocolate crust. His dishes range from Virginia cheese pie to lamb

▲ *President Ralph B. Draughon*
    —Photo: AU Photo Services

curry. Since retiring, he has prepared dinner, except for salads, done by his wife, Polly. Philpott used to play golf with Tom Russell of Alexander City and a few others, but in 1996 he hadn't played in four or five years because "all my partners are dead." His reading includes six daily newspapers a day. Philpott has been in all the states except North and South Dakota, and has traveled to all the continents. He jokingly said he has "been everywhere except the North Pole."

Ralph Draughon (1947-65) perfected his fly-fishing at Lake Auburn while his wife, Caroline, taught the children how to swim. "George Core, a wonderful old black man, paddled the boat and kept the right distance between the boat and shore for catching bream and bass," Mrs. Draughon said. Draughon also read books ranging from westerns to biographies of Andrew Jackson. He enjoyed watching "Gunsmoke." In retirement, he grew roses.

Draughon's predecessor, L. N. Duncan (1935-47), loved to hunt quail with his dog, Jim. He also enjoyed fishing and taught his young granddaughter, Ann Pearson, how to fish. She still believed at fifty-five in his axiom that a fish will bite if a dragonfly lands on the end of the pole. Duncan once rubbed blisters on his hand pitching horseshoes and had his chauffeur buy him gloves so he could continue the game. He also liked farm chores, including shelling peas.

▲ Leah Rawls Atkins, whose three degrees from Auburn included the school's first history doctorate, returned to her alma mater in 1985 to serve ten years as the first director of the University Center for the Arts and Humanities. Under her direction, the center received $865,514 in grants from the National Endowment for the Humanities for four reading and discussion programs led by NEH scholars at public libraries throughout the state. The programs focused on Alabama authors or those with an Alabama connection, the Civil War as a crossroads for the South, World War II from both a war-front and home-front perspective, and Southern autobiographies. Dr. Rawls published in nineteenth-century American, Southern, and Alabama history. Recent works included Carolyn Marshall Draughon (Auburn University Campus Club, 1996), author; Alabama: History of a Deep South State (University of Alabama Press, 1995), co-author; and A Century of Women at Auburn: Blossoms Amid the Deep Verdure (1992), author. Dr. Atkins and her husband George A. Atkins, an associate director of the Auburn Office of Alumni and Development, both retired in 1995.
—Photo: Leah Rawls Atkins

▶ Dr. Wayne Flynt arrived at Auburn as head of the history department in 1977 and quickly became one of the University's most visible faculty members. His ten books from 1971 into 1996 included Poor But Proud: Alabama's Poor Whites (University of Alabama Press, 1989), for which he received the Lillian Smith Award for Non-Fiction, the oldest regional book award in the South. He stepped down as department head in 1985 while serving as Hollifield Professor of Southern History, and became a Distinguished University Professor in 1990. He was named "Alabamian of the Year" in 1992 by the Mobile Register for his writing and lectures on the state's social problems. Flynt's series "Alabama at the Crossroads" identified education, taxes, health care and the Alabama Constitution as urgently needing reform.

—Photo: AU Archives

▲ Bob Sanders snapped this picture March 13, 1993, shortly before 4:30 a.m. at Gay Street and Magnolia Avenue, looking west toward Toomer's Corner. He was on his way to put Radio Station WAUD on the air when greeted by the start of a paralyzing blizzard. Lee County received four to six inches of snow, then freezing rain and sleet, all accompanied by frigid winds of up to 45 miles per hour. Limbs from ice-laden trees broke and fell on power lines, leaving more than 382,000 customers in the state without heat or lights. Meteorologist Roger Getz noted that a storm in February 1973 dumped more than eight inches of snow on Auburn, but said the 1993 storm produced the most ice and snow in Alabama in fifty years.
—Photo: Bob Sanders

► *Former Auburn Knights Orchestra members started an annual three-day reunion in the early 1970s and soon were drawing standing-room-only crowds for their Friday and Saturday night concerts at the Conference Center down Highway 29 South. Don Culley '52 of Pelham, Alabama, Terry "Doc" Mosley '37 of Asheville, North Carolina, and Ed Wadsworth '41 of Metairie, Louisiana, are shown fiddling around during the 1991 reunion. The program featured alumni from each decade starting with the 1930s on stage as an orchestra for a one-hour concert. But for many the impromptu jam sessions into the wee hours were even more fun. By the 1990s the Knights had locked in the last weekend in July for their reunions.*
—*Photo:* Auburn Alumnews

▼ *Toomer's Corner, 4:25 p.m., November 20, 1993—Auburn 22, Alabama 14*
—Photo: Todd Van Emst;
Auburn Plainsman

▲ *Coach Joe Ciampi arrived in Auburn in 1979, determined to make solid defensive play the key to victory, and his women's basketball teams became a national power in the 1980s. They won 96 games and lost 7, best in the nation over one three-year period. Auburn teams played in the NCAA Tournament championship game in 1988, 1989, and 1990 and were among the final eight tournament teams twice and the final sixteen twice from 1986 through 1993. Ciampi's teams won 410 games and lost 120 in his seventeen seasons through 1996 for a .774 winning percentage. During 1986-1991, the Lady Tigers won sixty-eight consecutive home games, an NCAA record at the time. Ciampi is shown during a 1990 game in his trademark "palms up" stance, questioning an official's call. At right is Auburn assistant Joanie O'Brien, who two years later became head coach at University of Massachusetts. By 1996, former Ciampi assistants also were head women's coaches at Florida, Maine, Butler and St. John's.*

—Photo: Opelika-Auburn News

◄ *Resurfacing of College Street from Samford Avenue to the railroad track, a distance of eight-tenths of a mile, became a rush project in September 1993. Work couldn't start until September 9—the Monday after the Auburn-Samford football game—but needed to be finished before students returned to campus September 23. One block at a time, East Alabama Paving Company "milled" two inches of old asphalt off the street and into dump trucks with the machine shown here, then put down new asphalt and repainted the traffic lines and parking places. It took going into overtime, but workers met the deadline.*

—Photo: Alan Davis;
Lee County Eagle

► *The Drake Middle School Parent-Teacher Organization sponsored a fashion show and luncheon as a 1993-94 fundraiser. Special entertainment came from an all-star cast including, left to right: Auburn Board of Education member Carol Pittard, Superintendent Ed Richardson, Board member Carolyn Mathews, Assistant Superintendent Jim Douglas, and Board members Clifford Jones and Fred Hoerr. Auburn school superintendents have done well in state politics. Richardson became Alabama superintendent of education in 1995, succeeding Wayne Teague, who served almost two decades as state superintendent after moving up from superintendent at Auburn.*

—Photo: Lee County Eagle

◄ *These members of the Auburn Heritage Association posed in 1994 before participating in a program on their remembrances of school days in the community. Pictured left to right, front row: Mary Green, Corrie Boyd, Suzelle McGehee. Back row: Chris Danner, George Echols, Babe McGehee. The association was instrumental in restoring in 1979-80 the antebellum Scott-Yarbrough Home, where the program was held. In 1993 members cleaned up, surveyed, and turned over to the city for maintenance Baptist Hill, Auburn's historic black cemetery off Dean Road. Among association projects in the mid-1990s was an effort to find funds for perpetual care of the city cemeteries.*

—Photo: Opelika-Auburn News

▲ A fire apparently started by a torch being used to remove old paint caused $200,000 or more in damage to the Auburn University President's Mansion in May 1994. In addition to wooden portions of the building, the heating, ventilating, and air-conditioning systems on the second floor and considerable wiring had to be replaced. President and Mrs. Muse moved to a motel for seven and a half months. The five-bedroom, 6,750-square-foot structure had by the time of the fire been home to five other Auburn presidents and their families—the Duncans, Draughons, Philpotts, Funderburks, and Martins. The Baileys used it for social events, but didn't live there. Built in 1938 at a cost of $38,412, it was the first building on campus financed with Public Works Administration funds. The mansion, which fronts on Mell Street, is located where the old Duggar Home stood until it burned in about 1937.

—Photo: AU Report

◀ After almost three decades at Auburn as student, administrative assistant, instructor of journalism, and sports information director, David Housel became the University's director of athletics in March 1994. He brought to the position pride in and love for Auburn and a keen sense of history of the University, nurtured by untold hours of research and by personal friendships with hundreds, ranging from trustees, Samford Hall administrators, and community leaders to clerks and laborers. He counted as friends over the years scores of students, many of whom he advised and helped. He wrote two books on Auburn athletics, Saturdays to Remember and From the Desk of David Housel—A Collection of Auburn Stories. His wife, the former Susan McIntosh, graduated from AU in 1973 and later became a teacher at Wrights Mill Elementary School. Housel described his personal philosophy by quoting Cliff Hare, whose name the stadium bears, "'Athletics makes men strong, study makes men wise, and character makes men great . . .' The Auburn athletic program has to stand for all three qualities."

—Photo: AU Athletic Department

◄ All-American end Frank Sanders made several "sensational" pass catches during four years at Auburn, but is remembered best for a reception against Alabama in 1993 and against Florida in 1994. Auburn trailed Bama 14-5 at Jordan-Hare with 6:09 left in the third quarter. It was fourth and fifteen at the Alabama thirty-five. Substitute quarterback Patrick Nix, who had just replaced the injured Stan White, lofted the ball deep—almost fifty yards. At the goal line, Sanders fought off and outleaped defender Tommy Johnson to score, providing the Tigers with the momentum for a 22-14 victory and coach Terry Bowden with an 11-0 record in his first season at Auburn. The next year against No. 1 Florida in Gainesville, Sanders caught an eight-yard lob from Nix with thirty seconds remaining to bring Auburn from behind for a 36-33 victory and extend its winning streak to eighteen games over two seasons. He is shown (81) muscling the ball away from Alabama defender Antonio Langham (43) for one of his five catches in the 1993 game as Johnson (10) looks on. Sanders caught 121 passes for 1,998 yards and 15 touchdowns in four seasons at Auburn. He trailed only Terry Beasley in receptions and total yardage and was tied for second in touchdown receptions.

—Photo: AU Athletic Department;
Copyright 1994 by Mike Cortez

▲ Tiger, Auburn's golden eagle mascot, seems to be getting a pat and congratulations from President William V. Muse after an announcement in late 1994 that a warm, dry shelter for the bird would be built in the aviary behind Haley Center. An Alpha Phi Omega service fraternity campaign brought in $49,000 to finance the shelter. With Muse are, left to right, student handler Rodney Cox, holding Tiger, APhiO faculty adviser Jim Mitchell, and Vice President of Student Affairs Pat Barnes.

—Photo: AU Report

◄ NBA basketball star Charles Barkley gives mascot Aubie a hug during a visit to Auburn. Even though Barkley passed up his senior college season to join the Philadelphia 76ers, he remained in 1996 the school's top career shot blocker with 145 and field-goal percentage shooter at .626. Barkley was honored as the Southeastern Conference Player of the Decade for the 1980s by the Birmingham Post-Herald. In 1984, he became the first Auburn player chosen SEC Player of the Year, selected by both the Associated Press and United Press International. Barkley was named the NBA's Most Valuable Player in leading the Phoenix Suns to second place in the championship playoff in 1992-93. Through 1995, he played in nine consecutive NBA All-Star Games. He was a USA basketball "dream team" member and won Olympic gold medals in both 1992 and 1996. By the mid-1990s, Barkley had contributed more than $100,000 to establish a scholarship for minority students at Auburn, his financial adviser said.

—Photo: AU University Relations

◄ *William James Samford*

▶ *Thomas D. Samford*

A Samford thread has run through Auburn University's history, beginning with William James Samford who in 1860-61 became the first family member to attend Auburn, then named East Alabama Male College. He became governor of Alabama, and Samford Hall is named after him. For eighty-four of the first ninety-six years in the twentieth century, Samford's descendants have been on Auburn's Board of Trustees. The governor's son, Thomas D. Samford, was a member of the board in 1902-1906 and in 1914-1947. The governor's grandson, Frank P. Samford, served in 1947-73, the governor's great-grandson, Frank P. Samford, Jr., in 1973-84, and another great-grandson, William James Samford, Jr., began a twelve-year term in 1987. Governor Samford's grandson William J. Samford was the University's general counsel in 1948-65, and the governor's great-grandson Thomas D. Samford, III, served as general counsel in 1965-95.

—Photos: AU Archives

◄ *Thomas D. Samford, III*

▶ *Frank P. Samford*

◀ All-Americans Vickie Orr, left, and Carolyn Jones were basketball teammates when Auburn won 33 of 35 games in 1988-89 and finished as runnerup to Tennessee for the national championship. Orr led the Lady Tigers to a 32-3 record in 1987-88, and the third loss was to Louisiana Tech, 56-54, in the NCAA championship game. Jones sparked the 1989-90 team to a 28-7 season and its third straight appearance in the NCAA championship game. The two are shown as members of the U.S. Olympic team after winning bronze medals at Barcelona in 1992. Gold medal winners in the 1996 Olympic Games included former Auburn basketball players Ruthie Bolton-Holifield and Charles Barkley and two juniors from the 1996 Auburn men's swimming team, Scott Tucker and John Hargis. Former Tiger track star Sam Matete won a silver medal for his second-place finish in the 400-meter hurdles.

—Photo: AU Athletic Department

▶ Terry Bowden, sopping wet from perspiration, celebrates Auburn's 36-33 come-from-behind football victory over Florida at Gainesville in 1994. The Gators, No. 1 nationally, had won seventeen straight at home and were a sixteen-point favorite. Auburn trailed by four points with thirty-six seconds remaining when Patrick Nix lobbed a pass from the Florida eight between two defenders to Frank Sanders, who leaped and caught it for a touchdown. Thirty seconds later, unbeaten Auburn had won eighteen games since Bowden became head coach and all since being placed on NCAA probation before the start of the 1993 season.

The Tigers won two more before being tied by Georgia, 23-23, and ending the season with a 21-14 loss to third-ranked Alabama. Auburn, off probation in 1995, went 8-3 in the regular season, including a 31-27 triumph over Alabama that made the Tigers 3-0 against Bama in games played at Jordan-Hare Stadium. Then came an embarrassing 43-14 loss to Penn State in Tampa's Outback Bowl January 1, 1996.

—Photo: AU Athletic Department

◀ *Coach David Marsh, at left of diving board, raises his right hand in celebration moments after Yoav Bruck finished first in the 400-yard freestyle relay and gave Auburn the 1994 championship in Southeastern Conference men's swimming. Yoav, in the water, indicates, "We're Number One!" Auburn played host for the meet at its new $10.5 million James E. Martin Acquatic Center. The Tigers finished fourth that year in the NCAA championship and third the next after repeating as SEC champs. In 1996, the men finished second in both the conference and national meets. Marsh was selected as an assistant Olympic coach in 1996 and three Auburn swimmers qualified for the Games.*

—Photo: AU Athletic Department

◀ *Ernest Justice got several men from the Auburn Methodist Church choir together as a singing group in the early 1970s. When it was time for an introduction at its first performance, Justice recalled, the group didn't have a name. Caine Campbell, master of ceremonies on that occasion, suggested, "How about 'The Oliver Goldsmith Singers'?" Years later the group still had that name, given to honor the Irish author whose opening line of a 1770 poem was "Sweet Auburn! loveliest village of the plain . . ." The Singers worked with a wide range of music—patriotic, religious, country-western, spirituals, Broadway, Christmas—and they "performed for various groups anywhere within easy driving distance of Auburn for any occasion that provided a free meal or small honorarium or both," Justice said. Participants when this 1994 picture was taken included, left to right, seated: Ove Jensen, Ernest Justice, Ed Kern, Verne Irvine. Standing: John Ball, Jerry Koellsted, Cal Reber, Earl DeBrunner, John Manning, Dee Glueck, Sonny Dawsey, Jim Maloy, Mack Williams, Drew Brown, Jim Worthington, Marshall Baker, Foster Owen.*

—Photo: Opelika-Auburn News

▶ *James Echols began making lemonades at Toomer Drug Store in 1958, and he was still making them in 1996. He squeezed about two hundred lemons a day during hot weather. Lemonades became more popular than the limeades that students had favored in the 1930s and 1940s. Echols is shown pouring syrup to sweeten a lemonade in 1975. His more famous customers included former Auburn President Harry Philpott, Football Coach Terry Bowden, and Athletic Director David Housel.*

—Photo: Auburn Alumnews

◀ *These Auburn University Singers were outside the NBC Today Show studios in June 1995 after singing two songs when show host Katie Couric, seated center, joined them. The Singers, founded in 1972, have performed during summer tours in Los Angeles, Denver, San Francisco, Lincoln Center in New York City, the President's Park in Washington, D.C., and Opryland, U.S.A. Members of the Singers and AU Concert Choir toured Eastern Europe in 1996, with appearances in Austria, the Czech Republic, Poland, The Slovak Republic, and Hungary. A 1993 tour included performances in Switzerland, France, Holland, Germany, and Great Britain. Dr. Thomas R. Smith, AU choral activities director, is second from right in the second row.*

—Photo: AU Department of Music

▶ *Frances Vowell of Auburn posed in 1987 while president of the Lee County Humane Society with Sammy, left, a Samford Avenue stray, and Polly, from the Glyde Memorial Shelter on U. S. 280. The shelter handles five-thousand to six-thousand dogs and cats a year, plus a few pigs, ferrets, and goats. The Humane Society works for pet adoptions, a neutering program, animal pickups, and improved shelter care, said Ann Pearson, a longtime volunteer. Dot Millican of Opelika, veterinarian Ralph Womer, wildlife artist Barbara Keel, and Howard Woodley helped found the organization in 1974. Dru Reagan was its first president. Despite the shelter's continuing efforts, most stray animals are not adopted and have to be put to sleep.*

—Photo: Opelika-Auburn News

▶ *Habitat for Humanity volunteers raised a wall for a new home on Bedell Avenue in Auburn in 1994 aimed at helping eliminate poverty housing. Identifiable are, left to right, Sam Coker, David Hamilton, Ronald Tucker (in bandanna), and Jason Wingfield (in shorts). Habitat's Lee County and Auburn University student chapters built twelve houses from 1989 through 1995. Auburn's was the first student chapter to build a house and raise the money for the project. Habitat International's founder was Millard Fuller, a 1957 Auburn graduate in economics. "Using volunteer labor and tax-deductible donations of money and materials, Habitat builds homes with the help ['sweat equity'] of future homeowners [called 'partners'],"* the county Habitat office said. *"Houses are sold to partner families for no profit. The average house in Lee County is 1,000 square feet and costs $27,000, including cost of land."*

—Photo: Nancy Michael

The city began development in 1991 of Kiesel Park, a 129-acre tract west of Auburn off Lee County Road 51. It had been willed to Auburn by Dr. George K. Kiesel, a professor of veterinary medicine at the University. He stipulated that it was to be a "passive park," with no organized recreational facilities such as ball diamonds, fields, or courts. Shown is the pavilion which seats one hundred but can accommodate up to two hundred for a picnic and is available to organizations and groups in the community. Other projects completed in the first phase of development included a two-and-a-quarter mile walking trail, a nature trail, improved parking facilities, sidewalks, restrooms, and an environmental lab for school children. Plans included moving the antebellum Neva Winston house from South Gay Street to Kiesel Park in late 1996 or 1997.

◄ They honored Earnest Dowdell with a fish fry when he retired in 1994, and no wonder. He had worked forty-seven years in the Department of Fisheries and Allied Aquacultures. "When I started working, we used mules and flip scrapes to build ponds, and the professors worked only on bream and bass, the most common fish in Alabama," Dowdell told the AU Report. "Now there's all kinds of science involved, and the professors work with fish from all over the world: catfish, tilapia, carps, even crawfish."
—Photo: AU Archives

▲ In a few hours during the night of October 4, 1995, Hurricane Opal destroyed 7,500 trees in Auburn and changed the face of many streets and subdivisions in the community. City Manager Doug Watson said damage estimates to 477 homes totaled five million dollars, but said the destruction of large oaks, pecans, and pines throughout the city would take decades to replace. Pictured are stumps from sixty-year-old pecans uprooted in the yard of a home in Willow Creek.
—Photo: Lassie Jo Simms

Jan Clifford, editor of the Auburn Plainsman in 1994-95, is shown with Dr. Jerry E. Brown after her newspaper was awarded a National Pacemaker for excellence, the collegiate equivalent of the Pulitzer Prize. It was the tenth National Pacemaker for the Plainsman. The first was awarded to the 1966-67 Plainsman, edited by Brown, who returned to Auburn as a faculty member in 1979 and who became journalism department head in 1992. Through 1995, the Plainsman also had received a Regional Pacemaker five times and a Pacemaker Finalist award once.

—Photo: Mobile Press Register

▲ State Representative Pete Turnham of Auburn, left, received from President William V. Muse in 1994 the 130th honorary degree conferred by Auburn University. Turnham had served thirty-eight years as a House member from Lee County in 1996, the longest tenure of any member of the Legislature. He sponsored legislation requiring kindergarten programs in all of the state's public school systems and also sponsored legislation establishing community health centers throughout Alabama. His wife, Kay, operated a nursery school for sixteen years.

—Photo: Auburn Alumnews

▲ Mrs. Annie Lee Drake Foster, seated, at 104 was Auburn's oldest resident when this picture was taken in 1995. Two years earlier, Mrs. Foster and her daughter, Elsie Foster Mitchell, right, visited Baptist Hill Cemetery and the grave of Mrs. Foster's grandfather, Ephraim Drake, an ex-slave, servant, and bodyguard of the college physician, Dr. John Hodges Drake III. Ephraim accompanied John Hodges when the latter joined the Conferedate Army as a drummer boy in 1861. Also pictured with Mrs. Foster are a grandson, Danny Mitchell, and a granddaughter, Judy M. Battiste. Many buried in Baptist Hill were born slaves but later succeeded in teaching or business. A white man gave in the early 1870s most of the four acres for Auburn's first separate black community cemetery. The oldest grave is dated 1879.

—Photo: Opelika-Auburn News

▲ These retirees supported a property tax increase in 1995 to provide $900,000 to one million dollars a year for thirty years to finance construction of additional public schools in Auburn. This picture appeared in a newspaper advertisement stating, "We know quality schools are essential to the quality community where we've retired." The ad urged support of a referendum, which was approved by an 825-vote margin on 3,739 votes cast. Top to bottom, starting at left: Marshall Baker, Evelyn Jordan, Jane Baker, Marshlea Dawsey, Carol Bramlett, Marleah Hobbs, Joyce Newland, Ken Cadenhead, Lucy Hagler, Royce Beckett, Sara Kenan, Ben Hagler, Wilford Bailey, Sara Sabot, Suzelle McGehee, Billie Ruth Wood, Jean Henderson, Alice Fick, John Fries, Jim Warman, Keith McPheeters, George Foster, Babe McGehee, Henry Henderson, Cayce Scarborough, Joe Hood, Joel Copeland, Ken Sanderson, Jean Goodwin, Ed Russell, Tom Cope, Morris Gillespie, Ed Hobbs, Margaret Latimer, Caroline Persons, Fran French, George Goodwin, Margaret Scarborough, Sara Hudson, Mary Green, Fred Adams, Ralph Harris, Art Fourier, Gene Bramlett, Rob Wiley, Gen Worley, Ruth Williamson, Platt Boyd, Frank Young, Kenneth Picha, Ed Williamson, Dick Amacher, Clint Baker, Sam Coker, H. C. Morgan, Foster Owen, Bobbye Owen, Larry Jones, Tex Williams, Shirley Beckett, Reuel Fick, Bill Weidner.

—Photo: Lynda Ranier;
Auburn City Schools

◄ Joe Wilson found himself head coach of the Lee-Scott Academy football, basketball, and golf teams during the 1994-95 school year. His team won the state championship for independent schools in all three sports that year. He is shown on the sidelines consoling an opposing coach after a Lee-Scott football victory. Wilson retired in 1996 after coaching in high schools for thirty-six years.

—Photo: Opelika-Auburn News

▲ Graduates from as far away as California and New York attended the Lee County Training School reunion in July 1995. Chairman J. C. Woodall said the 125 attendees represented virtually every graduating class of the school, which opened in 1929 and closed in 1958.

The three-day event included a "getting reacquainted" social and banquet, both at the Auburn Conference Center; the LCTS Reunion Golf Tournament at Auburn Links; a visit to the Lee County Training School Memorial Pavilion in Martin Luther King Park; and a picnic at Kiesel Park.

Shown at the pavilion, site of the old training school, were, left to right, kneel-ing: Isaac Dowdell, Ella Payne Marshall, Mable H. Robinson, Ernestine H. Robinson, J. C. Woodall. Standing: Ollis Bryant, Julia Ann Deathridge, John Zellars, A. C. Wright, Fannie B. Stephens, Lou Clifford Pitts, Susie D. Bryant, Beauford Thomas, Willie L. Tolbert, Glennie A. Williams, Cozetta A. Trimble, Claudia A. Duncan, Harrison Kendall, Sarah Slaughter Danner, Julia H. Marshall, Ethel Scott Washington, Barbara S. Debrow, Hilda Pitts, Grace Melton Wright, Wylene Welch, Katie Crawford Tucker, Curtis Harper, Jessie R. Williams, Merian Smith, John A. Aldridge.

▲ Ben Hagler, retired head of Horti-culture for the Cooperative Extension Service, is seen in 1995 at eighty-two in his vegetable garden, one of the best in east Alabama, a showplace on North Dean Road a block from the railroad tracks. His extension work began when he came to Auburn in 1942 with his wife Lucy to train teachers in vocational agri-culture. He made an impact almost immediately by operating a canning plant at Lee County High School on Samford Avenue (later to become Auburn Junior High) that provided food for local families during World War II. But he is proudest of his volunteer work through fifty-two years in the Kiwanis Club of Auburn. "A lot of things wouldn't get done without volunteers," he noted. Kiwanis is one of more than 160 clubs and organizations listed by the Auburn and Opelika Chambers of Commerce that provide manpower for community ser-vice work in Lee County.

—Photo: William White; Opelika-Auburn News

▶ Dr. Cecil Yarbrough, Jr., is shown mak-ing a few remarks in May 1995 at the site for the Margaret M. Yarbrough Middle School, named after his late wife. The retired veterinarian gave the city 21.2 acres on North Donahue Drive, eight-tenths of a mile past Shug Jordan Parkway. The school was expected to open in 1997 for sixth-, seventh-, and eighth-graders. Yarbrough lived as a child in the Scott-Yarbrough House at the end of East Magnolia Avenue. His father was a physician, mayor of Auburn for fif-teen years, and a state legislator.

—Photo: Auburn City Schools

▶ *Dr. Wayne McLaughlin is seen at a party about to present a patient of his with a set of fake false teeth that chatter. The popular dentist announced in 1996 plans to retire at year's end from a practice in Auburn that began almost forty years earlier. McLaughlin said he saw fluoridation "virtually end tooth decay as we knew it. When I started here in March 1957, most Auburn children had a mouthful of cavities or fillings or both. Now, you seldom see tooth decay." Old-timers remembered the outcry in the early-1950s that accompanied a proposal to fluoridate the city's drinking water. Officials pretended to drop the idea, but secretly sneaked in fluoridation. Almost two years went by before the public was told. The late Gil Brownfield, a dentist and City Council member who campaigned for fluoridation, deserves much of the credit, McLaughlin and his wife, Joanne, said. Mrs. McLaughlin, a medical technician graduate from Birmingham Southern, served twelve years as receptionist for her husband "after the children were out of the way." McLaughlin, '52, and all four children—Carol, '77; Thomas, '80; Laura, '83; and Lianne, '85—are AU graduates.*
—Photo: Jane S. Love

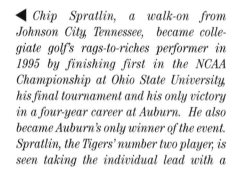

◀ *Chip Spratlin, a walk-on from Johnson City, Tennessee, became collegiate golf's rags-to-riches performer in 1995 by finishing first in the NCAA Championship at Ohio State University, his final tournament and his only victory in a four-year career at Auburn. He also became Auburn's only winner of the event. Spratlin, the Tigers' number two player, is seen taking the individual lead with a first round five-under par 67, a lead that he never relinquished. Other Auburn players went home after the second round when the team failed to survive the cut. Spratlin finished the 72-hole tournament with a five-under 283, one stroke better than runners-up from Arizona and Oklahoma State.*
—Photo: AU Athletic Department

▶ *Barry Mask, Auburn's first Aubie, became National Mascot Champion in 1980. And during the 1980s and 1990s, Aubie became as much a symbol of The Auburn Spirit as did Toomer's Corner during a victory celebration. Aubie was selected No. 1 collegiate mascot in 1991, 1995, and 1996 after championship finals of the Universal Cheerleaders Association at Walt Disney World in Orlando, Florida. Three students share Aubie duties each school year. Aubie is pictured during a 1986 parade.*
—Photo: Glomerata; AU Archives

▲ Plans in 1996 called for this main north-south runway to be lengthened to 5,260 feet at the Robert G. Pitts Auburn-Opelika Airport. The additional 1,260 feet will provide safer conditions for takeoffs and landings, but the same size corporate jets and other planes are expected to continue using the runway, airport Manager Jim Hendrick said. More planes may use the longer runway, however. The extension would be part of an estimated $13- million development of the airport, which is owned by Auburn University. Lee-Scott Academy was to receive $2.6 million for its 16.5-acre campus (at right of runway). The private school was moving to 75 acres at the end of Gatewood Drive in Auburn in the 1996-97 school year. East Glenn Avenue would be rerouted about 1.7 miles to pass south of the extended runway, tentatively by early 1998. A city landfill would be closed to make room for the extension. Airfield improvements would be funded 90 percent by the Federal Aviation Administration and 10 percent by the University, the cities of Auburn and Opelika, and Lee County. AU and the local governments would pay the full cost of a new terminal building and hangars. The state would fund rerouting East Glenn. The overall project was expected to be completed between the years 2001 and 2004 if funding arrived promptly.

—Photo: AU Photographic Services

◄ In April 1946, when Lamar was twenty-one and Libby Ware nineteen, they opened a jewelry store just south of Toomer's Corner on $5,000 in borrowed money. Fifty years later, Wares was among the oldest downtown businesses operating in the same location and the oldest operated by the same family. During those fifty years, Lamar said, the downtown store had been expanded several times, and Wares also operated stores at Village Mall and at Parkway in Opelika. Sales climbed from $34,000 the first year to more than $5 million in 1995. A son, Ronnie, had taken over day-to-day operations by the mid-1990s. Lamar is shown with a Diamondscope, used to determine the relative quality of precious stones.

Other long-time downtown landmarks included Toomer Drugstore, The Auburn Grille, The Bootery, Johnston & Malone Bookstore, and Hill's Jewelry. Although the marquee was still there, Tiger Theatre closed its doors in the 1980s. Lipscomb Drugstore went out of business in 1995. Tiger Recreation Center on North College Street closed in 1996. It was the last of a number of pool halls in that location that followed Reed's Billiard Parlor, opened in the 1930s.

—Photo: Libby and Lamar Ware

▲ *The five men in this undated photograph were leaders of the Lee County justice system in 1996. With the year each took office, they are, left to right, Circuit Judge James Gullage, 1977; District Attorney Ronald Myers, 1973; Circuit Judge Robert Harper, 1986; District Judge Michael Nix, 1987; and Sheriff Herman Chapman, 1980. District Judge Richard Lane, 1985, is not shown. Gullage, Harper, Lane, and Nix are Auburn University graduates. "Probably the most significant change" during Gullage's nearly twenty years on the bench has been* "a greater workload in controlled-substance cases," *he said. Many other criminal cases are drug-related, Harper said, noting that crack cocaine is* "very frequently tied in with other crimes." *Domestic-relations cases have increased substantially. In about 1993 or 1994, Gullage found there were more new divorces than marriage licenses issued in the county. The Circuit Court ranks at or near the top of the forty circuits in the state in timely disposition of criminal cases.*

—*Photo:* Lee County Eagle

▲ *The coldest day of 1996 was February 5 when the temperature dipped to 9 degrees, creating this winter wonderland effect on the fountain in front of the city library on Ross Street at mid-morning.*

—*Photo:* Brian Ekberg;
Lee County Eagle

▶ *The Auburn Beautification Council was established in 1972 on a $500 grant from Auburn Rotarians, and it almost immediately created the Tidy Tiger Award to recognize individuals and businesses for efforts to make their property more attractive. Grace Jones is shown presenting a certificate to Gene Young of Young's Plant Farm in 1988. Other committee members, left to right, are Gaynell Parks, Jo Ann Huffman, Jane Dunkelberger, Ruth Parker, Jean Reeves, and Ed Thrash. In addition to sponsoring several annual projects, the Council financed construction of "Welcome to Auburn" signs on major roads into the city and provided manpower to plant the more than 11,000 shrubs and trees donated to landscape the Interchange at U.S. Highway 29 and Interstate 85. The Council in 1996 was working on a restoration and preservation plan for Auburn cemeteries.*

—*Photo: AU Archives*

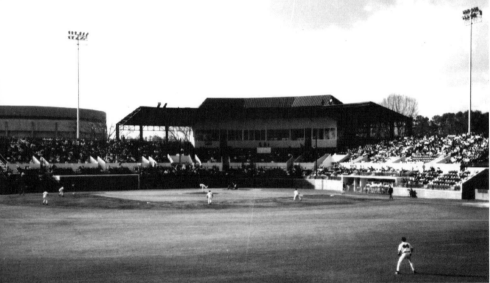

◀ These Auburn City School Teachers of the Year were local winners or local and district winners from Congressional District 2 and one was a state winner during 1985-95. From left, front row: Sharon Trimble, Wrights Mill Road, l990; Glenda Havens, Cary Woods, l987; Doyle Keasel, Wrights Mill Road, l993 Alabama Elementary Teacher of the Year; and Clara Clothiaux, Auburn High, l987 Congressional District 2 Secondary Teacher of the Year.

Back row: Terry Kirchler, Drake, l992; Mahlon Richburg, Auburn High, l994; Mary Richburg, Dean Road, l985; Carole Rogers, Drake, l988; Mary Ann Rygiel, Auburn High, l988 Congressional District 2 Secondary Teacher of the Year; Ismenia DeSouza, Auburn Junior High, l995 Congressional District 2 Secondary Teacher of the Year; Susan Housel, Wrights Mill Road, l991 Congressional District 2 Elementary Teacher of the Year; Effie Cannon, Auburn High, l989; Cathy Long, Auburn High, l993; Betty Burgess, Auburn High, l990; and Bernella Knight, Dean Road, l986.

—Photo: Auburn City Schools

▲ This picture recorded the first pitch of the first baseball game in Auburn's refurbished $4.2 million Plainsman Park. It was February 9, 1996, and All-American Ryan Halla allowed one hit in seven innings as Auburn beat Virginia Commonwealth 10-1 in the Tigers' season opener. Capacity of the stadium was increased from 1,500 to 3,000, and renovation included replacing bleachers with chairback seats. Restrooms were added as well as new concession areas and a new pressbox. M. W. Donaldson, who had been attending Auburn baseball games for more than forty years, commented, "I have been to every other place in the Southeastern Conference, and none compares to this."

◀ Ten years after receiving the Heisman Trophy as America's most outstanding football player, Vincent "Bo" Jackson donned cap and gown in December 1995 to receive a bachelor's degree from Auburn. Bo left school to pursue a career in professional football and baseball. He said he promised his mother shortly before she died that he would someday graduate. He credited his wife Linda and their three children with pushing him to complete the required correspondence courses. Bo and Linda met during his junior year and after she had received a B.S. from Tuskegee and a master's in education from Auburn. She received a doctorate in education from Auburn in 1992.

—Photo: William Martin;
Opelika-Auburn News

◀ *Kristi Orellana, class of '94, and Dennis Barker, '92, married in June 1994 and were headed for a reception at the AU Conference Center when someone handed them a roll of toilet paper left over from decorating their car, counseling, "Use it wisely." So they took time to roll a tree at the Main Gate on Toomer's Corner, Kristi said, "and show all Auburn how happy we were on our big day."*

—Photo: Auburn Magazine

▼ *Thousands celebrated into the night in the vicinity of Toomer's Corner after Auburn's dramatic 31-27 football victory over Alabama at Jordan-Hare Stadium on November 18, 1995. This is a morning-after shot of the Main Gate, with the sun and wind playing through the myriad of white paper streamers on the oaks. Toomer Drugstore and The Auburn Grille across the intersection provided the backdrop.*

Eight men worked from 4 a.m. until noon on Sunday to clean up most of the debris at Toomer's Corner, and two men spent eight hours working in that area Monday and again Tuesday, Wendy Hassett, assistant to the city manager, said. The person regularly assigned to policing up downtown found paper and other debris the rest of the week that had been blown to other areas from The Corner.

—Photo: Lassie Jo Simms

◀ *Lucy Hagler, a retired public-school teacher, asks a tough question of the speaker at a session of the Dynamic Seniors in 1992. The group's purpose was to get senior citizens together each month "to discuss educational topics that would be of interest to them in a social environment." It was short-lived, but the Auburn University Academy of Lifelong Learners, a continuing education program established in 1990 with thirty-nine members, seemed to fill the bill for some. More than two hundred, including the Haglers, were members by 1995. University alumni and military personnel returned to Auburn in substantial numbers from the mid-1980s through 1996, boosting the ranks of retirees beyond expectations. Chamber of Commerce and city officials believed the retiree rate of growth would continue to accelerate.*

—Photo: Opelika-Auburn News

◀ *These children found front-row seats on Gay Street for a parade in downtown Auburn, but by the mid-1990s the only ones to be seen each year were the high school Homecoming Parade and the community Christmas Parade. The Burn the Bulldog parade was still part of the festivities every other year when the Georgia football game was played in Auburn.*
—Photo: AU Archives

BIBLIOGRAPHY and SOURCES

Academe

A History of First Baptist Church of Auburn, Alabama, Leland Cooper

A History of Noble Hall, Allen M. Pearson and Ann B. Pearson

A History of the Alabama Agricultural Experiment Station, 1883-1983, Norwood Allen Kerr

A History of the Auburn University Band, 1897-1972

A History of the Church of Holy Innocents and Its Predecessor, Trinity Church, in Auburn, Alabama, Helen H. Peet

A History of the Methodist Church, Auburn, Alabama, 1836-1944, Letitia D. Ross

"Alabama Polytechnic Institute," an address by Ralph B. Draughon

Alabama's Tapestry of Historic Places: an Inventory, Alabama Historical Commission

Art News Magazine

Associated Press

AU, API, A&M, Board of Trustees minutes

AU, API, A&M, East Alabama Male College bulletins

AU Archives

AU Athletic Department

AU Department of Institutional Analysis

AU Photographic Services

AU President's Report

AU Report

AU Special Collections

AU University Relations

Auburn Baseball Media Guide, AU Sports Information

Auburn Basketball Media Guide, AU Sports Information

Auburn City Council minutes

Auburn City School Board minutes

Auburn First Baptist Church, 1838-1888, John H. Jeffers

Auburn Football Media Guide, AU Sports Information

Auburn Football, The Complete History, 1892-1987, Dan W. Hollis

Auburn Knights Collection

Auburn Loveliest Village of the Plain, Mollie Hollifield

Auburn-Opelika, South Central Bell

Auburn Magazine

Auburn Presbyterian Church, 100 years, Malcolm C. McMillan

Auburn Starts a Second Century, Charles W. Edwards

Auburn Swimming and Diving Media Guide, AU Sports Information

Auburn Track and Field Media Guide, AU Sports Information

Auburn United Methodist Church, 1837-1887: a History of a Great Church and the People Who Made It That Way, Carolyn Ellis Lipscomb

Auburn Women's Basketball Guide, AU Sports Information

Between the Hedges: A Story of Georgia Football, Jesse Outlar

Birmingham Post-Herald

Blossoms Amid the Deep Verdure: A Century of Women at Auburn, Leah Rawls Atkins

Class of 1917: "World War I Class," Alabama Polytechnic Institute, now Auburn University: a History, 1913-1982, William K. Askew

Creating the Big Game: John W. Heisman and the Invention of American Football, Wiley L. Umphlett

CVM Quarterly

"Early History of Auburn," *Auburn Alumnus*, Alicia Melton

Early History of Auburn, Mrs. W. B. Frazer

"East Alabama Male College," *Alabama School Journal*, Charles W. Edwards

Football's Greatest Coaches, Edwin Pope

From the Desk of David Housel: A Collection of Auburn Stories, David Housel

George Petrie—the Early Years, 1866-1892, Brenda H. Mattson

Glimpes into the Past from My Grandfather's Trunk, John Peavy Wright

Harry M. Philpott Oral Transcripts, Dwayne Cox

History at Auburn, Robert R. Rea

History of Auburn, Alabama, Mary E. Reese

History of the East Alabama Male College Located at Auburn, Alabama, Earle Russell Smith

Houston Daily Telegraph

In the Arena, Pat Dye, with John Logue

Isaac Taylor Tichenor and the Administration of the Alabama Agricultural and Mechanical College, 1872-1882, Joel Colley Watson

Lee County and Her Forebears, edited by Alexander Nunn

Lee County deed books

Lee County: How It Began, H. Ray Black, David M. Hall

Lengthening Shadows, Auburn University

Life magazine

Macon County Tractbook

Memoirs of the Abbots of Old Bellevue, James P. C. Southall

Opelika-Auburn City Directory

Photoplay magazine

Recollections of a Cavalryman of the Civil War, Colonel W. D. Hamilton

"Recollections of the Early History of Nu Chapter of Kappa Alpha Fraternity at the Alabama Polytechnic Institute," Leroy Stafford Boyd

Redskins, Ruffleskirts and Rednecks; Indian Allotments in Alabama and Misssissippi, 1830-1860, Mary Elizabeth Young

Robert Wilton Burton: A Biographical Sketch Including a Selection of His Writings, Gladys S. Stewart

Saturdays to Remember, David Housel

Slavery in Auburn, Meriwether Harvey

"Some Auburn History," *Auburn Alumnus*, Charles W. Edwards

Southern Living

Swimming World magazine

The *Alabama Confederate Reader*, Malcolm C. McMillan

The *Alabama Journal*

The *Atlanta Journal*

The *Auburn Alumnews*

The *Auburn Bulletin*, particularly Ann Pearson's articles

The *Auburn Gazette*

The Auburn Heritage Association

The *Auburn Plainsman*

The *Auburn University Walking Tour*, R. G. Millman

The *Birmingham News*

The *Centreville Enquirer*

"The Early History of Auburn," The *Auburn Bulletin*, Leland Cooper

The *General: Robert L. Bullard and Officership in the United States Army 1881-1925*, Allan R. Millett

The *Glomerata*

The *Huntsville Times*

The *Lee County Bulletin*

The *Lee County Eagle*

The Lee County Historical Society

The *Life and Times of William J. Samford*, George Hudson Scott

The *Montgomery Advertiser*

The *New York Times*

The *Opelika-Auburn News*

The *Orange & Blue*

The *Tiger Rag*

The *Road to Disappearance*, Angie Debo

The *Way We Were from Civil War to Depression, Engineering's Tale*, Jimmy Johnson

Through the Years, Malcolm C. McMillan and Allen W. Jones

Trails in History

U.S. Census Report

Yesterdays in Loachapoka and Communities Nearby: Roxana, Rocky Mount, Macon's Mill, Beehive, Pine Knot, Armstrong, Crossroads, Concord, Alexander Nunn

War Eagle: A Story of Auburn Football, Clyde Bolton

Zelda: A Biography, Nancy Milford

INDEX

Daniels, Tom 56
Danner, Chris 296
Danner, Sarah Slaughter 307
Dantzler, George William 54
Darby, John M. 25, 32
Davis, Bob 232, 258
Davis, Carolyn 270
Davis, Donald E. 32
Davis, Frank B. 193
Davis, Harry "Happy" 129
Davis, Henrietta W. 158, 246
Davis, Jan (Lee) 270, 283
Davis, Jason 288
Davis, Jefferson 26
Davis, Jennifer (Michael) 270
Davis, John E. 275
Davis, Lamar 173
Davis, Neil O. 61, 98, 132, 148, 204, 215, 246, 257, 265
Davis, Nicholas 236, 270
Davis, Owen 96, 128, 246
Davis, P. O. 166, 202
Davis, Mrs. P. O. 177
Davis, Paul 246, 248, 260
Dawsey, Marshlea 306
Dawsey, Sonny 302
Dawson, Millard Edwin 181, 231, 279
Dean, Walter W. 287
Dearing, Harry 156
Deathridge, Julia Ann 307
Debardeleben, Henry T. 54
Debrow, Barbara 307
DeBrunner, Earl 302
Del Greco, Al 285
Dempsey, Jan 171, 248, 255, 260, 262, 280, 282
Dempsey, Richard 260
Deramus, John 106
DeSouza, Ismenia 311
Devance, Joe 224
Dick, Darby 144
Dickey, James 225
Dill, Mrs. Kate 35
Dillard, Mrs. A. L. 95
Dillard, Fran Pick 249
Dillion, Jim 115, 199
DiOrio, Dorothy 248
Dixon, Frank M. 155, 158
Dixon, Mrs. Frank M. 155
Dixon, G. W. 49
Dixon, Solon 135
Dobbs, Zoe 217
Donahue, Bill 78
Donahue, Eileen 79
Donahue, Michael J. "Mike" 67, 75, 76, 80, 82, 86, 89, 92, 97
Donaldson, M. W. 311
Dooley, Vince 207, 252
Doran, Patrick J. 75
Dorsey, Rufus Thomas "Dutch" 54, 56, 57
Doster, Billy 144
Doster, Howard 81
Douglas, D. S. T. 19
Douglas, James B. 144
Douglas, Jim 296
Doverspike, Beth 261
Dowdell, Arthur 256
Dowdell, Betty 93
Dowdell, Charlie 202
Dowdell, Earnest 304
Dowdell, James F. 23, 24
Dowdell, Isaac 307
Dowdell, Lizzie 40
Dowdell, Madie 82
Dowdell, Sudie 79
Dowell, Camille 106
Dowell, Spright 95, 97, 98, 104, 106, 115
Doyle, Danny 44
Drake, Amy 130, 159
Drake, Brittain 103, 130
Drake, Caroline "Bessie" 79

Drake, Caroline Elizabeth (Samford) 29, 134
Drake, "Dude" 111
Drake, Ephraim 24, 305
Drake, Herbert 138
Drake, Hodge Freeman 114, 148, 203
Drake, James "Po'k Chops" 83
Drake, John Hodges III 24, 42, 61, 64, 80, 104, 219, 305
Drake, Mrs. John Hodges II 29
Drake, J. W. W. 21
Drake, Joseph Fanning 148
Drake, K. Stanley 276
Drake, Velma (Bedell) 103, 130
Draper, Zilpha Ann 180
Draughon, Ann 145
Draughon, Caroline Marshall 128, 210, 217, 286, 292, 293, 297
Draughon, Ralph B. 40, 61, 101, 128, 162, 167, 170, 174, 192, 193, 204, 206, 209, 210, 211, 212, 214, 217, 218, 219, 226, 286, 292, 297
DuBose, Caroline Drake 79
Dubose, Frank 119
Dudley, Virginia 130
Duggar, Frances 144
Duggar, Frank 143
Duggar, John Frederick 25, 57, 80, 143
Duggar, Paul 143
Duke, Herschel C. 180
Duke, Mrs. Herschel C. 180
Dunaway, Jim 227
Duncan, Claudia A. 307
Duncan, Fanny 92
Duncan, George W. 52, 78, 97
Duncan, Libba 130
Duncan, Luther Noble 97, 120, 127, 134, 155, 158, 159, 164, 167, 179, 191, 193, 226, 292, 297
Duncan, Mrs. L. N. 130, 297
Duncan, Robert 79
Duncan, Thomas 78
Dunham, Jule 56
Dunkelberger, Jane 310
Dunlop, Elizabeth "Lib" Harwell 139
Dunlop, Jack 139, 232
Dunn, Berta 217
Dunn, John 224
Dunstan, Arthur St. Charles 40, 58, 80, 107, 138
Dunstan, Lula 65
Dupree, J. W. 259
Durant, Mary Matherly 212
Dye, Missy 288
Dye, Pat 252, 258, 259, 263, 264, 270, 285, 288, 289
Dye, Pat, Jr. 288
Dye, Sue 288
Dye, Wanda 288

E
Eagar, Mary Belle Thomas 44, 49
Eagar, William H. 44
Eagles, Tommy Joe 291
Earle, Melanie 52
Earle, Ruth 52
Earnest, Jack 279
Earnest, Milligan 204
Eaves, Joel 206, 207, 211, 212, 261
Echols, George 282, 296
Echols, James 302
Echols, Melanie 282
Echols, Patricia 282
Eddins, Joe 171
Eddy, Troy 290
Edgar, S. Allen 170
Edwards, "Beaut" 56

Edwards, Charles W. 16, 20, 95, 101, 102, 120, 128, 156
Edwards, Dave 227
Edwards, J. R. 121
Edwards, James Hudson 144
Edwards, Tommy 204
Ellis, Buck 119
Ellis, Carolyn (Lipscomb) 144, 145
Ellis, Cliff 264
Ellis Clyde B. 181
Ellis, Gay 145
Ellis, Lamar 145
Ellis, Mike 4
Elizur, 20
Elman, Ziggy 163
Emert, George 276
Emrick, Verl R. 22, 202
Esslinger, M. S. 82
Evans, Ben E. 80
Evans, Jesse 227
Evans, Martha 252
Evans, Rosy 253

F
Fagen, Arnold 278
Fagen, Emaleen Stoves 278
Fagen, J. J. 278
Farr, Scott 227
Feaster, Bill 107
Ferguson, Charles W. 80
Fesperman, Rowe 237
Fibbe, Jimmy 211
Fick, Alice 306
Fick, Reuel 306
Fincher, Buster 238
Fincher, Jay 238
Fincher, Stanley 144
Fincher, Sue 215, 238, 281
Finn, Huck 78, 279
Fitzgerald, F. Scott 105
Fitzgerald, Ben 276
Fitzpatrick, Spillman 152
Flanagan, C. C. 16
Flanagan, Elizabeth Taylor Harper 12, 14, 15, 16
Flanagan, Jim 152, 279
Flint, Tom 202
Floyd, Ewell 78
Floyd, Dorothy 279
Floyd, Kate 106
Floyd, Stanley 241
Flynt, Wayne 293
Folsom, James E. "Jim" 166, 167, 171, 193, 201, 215, 264
Ford, Henry 166
Ford, Linda Woods 272
Fortenberry, Mary 256, 260, 262, 282
Foster, Annie Lee Drake 305
Foster, George 306
Foster, James D. 97
Foster, Mrs. Leda 29
Foster, Lewis Allen 29
Foster, Mary 79
Foster, Oelia 103
Foster, Robert "Bob" 103
Fourier, Art 306
Foy, Emmalu 210
Foy, Erle 210
Foy, James E. 210
Franklin, Anna Jean 187
Franklin, Byron 201
Franklin, Harold L. 209, 211, 216
Frazer, Addison 24, 35
Frazer, Mrs. W. B. 14
Frazier, Bob "Sponsor" 54, 84
Frazier, Joe 103
Frazier, Johnny Gus 103
Frederick, Rex 212
Frederickson, Tucker 218, 219, 285
Freeman, Bobby 199
Freeman, W. M. 20

French, Fran 306
Fretwell, Anna Louise 145
Fricks, Roland 82
Fries, John 306
Fries, Minnie Tippins 279
Frisbie, Mr. 121
Frobish, Lowell T. 276
Fucci, Linda 237
Fulghum, Kate Conway Broun 162
Fullan, Lysbeth 106
Fullan, M. Thomas 61, 64, 65, 80
Fuller, J. P. III 99
Fuller, Melton 143
Fuller, Mike 285
Fuller, Millard 303
Fuller, Sidney 145
Funchess, Helen 130
Funchess, Marion J. 80
Funderburk, H. Hanly 220, 237, 241, 251, 252, 253, 255, 257, 258, 263, 292, 297
Funderburk, Helen 292, 297

G
Gafford, Monk 162, 168, 171
Gaines, Rowdy 242
Gamble, Bob 257
Gammage, David 168
Gandy, Joe 168
Gantt, Greg 229
Gardiner, Helen 130
Gastaldo, Robert 256
Gatchell, Lillian 82
Gatty, Harold 133
Gay, Ray 238
Gay, Toni 238
Gazes, Emmanuel 193
Gazes, John 193
Gazes, Lucas 193
Gentry, Andy 234, 246, 249
Getz, Roger 293
Gibbons, Mel Atkins 279
Gibbons, Olive 112
Gibbs, Elsie 79
Gibson, Alice Cary Pick 23, 58, 201, 249
Gibson, Daniel DeKalb 92
Gibson, Danny Sue (Conner) 92, 180, 249
Gibson, Dee 76
Giddens, John H. Darnell 74, 133
Giddens, Susie Hughes 74, 133, 165
Gilbert, Porter 211
Gilbert, Walter 148, 285
Gillam, Elaine 272
Gillespie, Morris 306
Gilmer, Ben S. 107, 266
Gilmer, Hank 253
Gilmore, Laura 261
Gissendanner, A. R. 80
Gladden, Cheryl 256
Glance, Harvey 211, 241, 242, 286
Glenn, M. A. "Allie" 16, 40, 80, 129, 177
Glenn, Charles 180
Glenn, Emory Thomas 16, 40
Glenn, John Bowles 16, 21
Glenn, W. F. 31
Glueck, Dee 302
Goebel, Hal 256
Goff, Tommy 279
Going, Richard Billup 54
Gomillion, C. G. 210
Goode, Betty Ware (Armor) 173
Goode, Edwin R., Jr. 173
Goodwin, George 306
Goodwin, James W. 239, 243
Goodwin, Jean 306
Goodwin, Virginia 239
Gossett, Claude 268